LOUVRE ABU DHABI

STORY OF AN ARCHITECTURAL PROJECT

Jean Nouvel

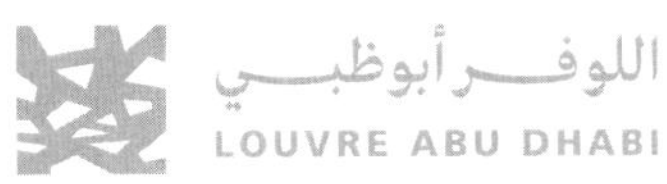

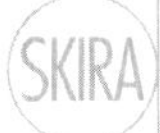

Constructing a museum is much more than constructing a building. A museum is a place for people of all ages and all nationalities to gather, a place to share experiences and ideas. Its architecture must engage visitors and prompt them to play an active part in the discovery. The building is there to arouse curiosity, to encourage visitors to go in search of new ideas and new people. A museum seeks to be a place of stories, of works of art and of the people who give birth to them.

Within the framework of the cultural ambitions of Abu Dhabi, Saadiyat Island is the site of three places of this nature: the Louvre Abu Dhabi, the Zayed National Museum and the Guggenheim Abu Dhabi, still under construction.

The French architect Jean Nouvel based the architectural principles of the Louvre Abu Dhabi on its immediate environment: a place where the land meets the sea and the sky, an age-old balance that alludes to the travels of the people of Abu Dhabi.

The Louvre Abu Dhabi is surrounded by water. The museum looks onto the Arabian Gulf, the sea that opened up our vast territories to trade and exchange. The museum seems to float just above the water, whereas in fact its foundations are deeply embedded in the earth, the land of our ancestors, who learned that in order to survive here it is important to live in harmony with nature.

The vast dome of the museum dominates the view for visitors, who, on entering, marvel at the gleaming pattern of light and shadow aptly described as a "rain of light". Beneath the dome, the Louvre Abu Dhabi also evokes a medina. Like the museum, the traditional villages of the area consist of densely clustered groups of buildings whose gleaming white walls reflect the sunlight that sparkles on the water.

Walk the quiet streets of the museum and let yourself be filled with wonder at the superb works of art. Take time to contemplate the ways in which we are all connected. We have always been and will always be neighbours. The Louvre Abu Dhabi is a village where everyone is welcome and where we hope to greet you today.

MOHAMED KHALIFA AL MUBARAK
Chairman of the Department of Culture and Tourism – Abu Dhabi

Jean Nouvel's design for the Louvre Abu Dhabi is marked by tranquil simplicity. An ethereal dome floats above what looks like an Arab village with its white-walled buildings. It protects the village from the heat of the sun, while also flooding it with gleaming fragments of light. Water surrounds the buildings. The entire structure seems to float on the sea: a magnificent illusion.

In fact, the dome rests on huge foundations skilfully dissimulated by the museum buildings. Nouvel's style is often thus: apparently simple but actually the result of extraordinary human ingenuity and technology. The museum is made up of hundreds of thousands of elements, each created with great precision and then meticulously assembled on site in Abu Dhabi.

As an architectural creation, the Louvre Abu Dhabi reflects both the place where it was built and the mission for which it was designed. The shafts of refracted light call to mind palm trees and courtyards. They also evoke the region's traditional carved windows that provide shelter and shade. In the Louvre Abu Dhabi, the fresh water that brings life to the desert nourishes the mind as much as the body. Spaces for contemplation, rest and reflection are also to be found beneath the dome.

Today, with the opening of the Louvre Abu Dhabi to the public, the building is transformed into a museum. Outside, the works of contemporary art commissioned from the Italian Giuseppe Penone and the American Jenny Holzer bring life to the architectural design. These unique collaborations confirm the commitment of the Louvre Abu Dhabi not only to the masterpieces of the past but also to those of the future.

Inside, a journey unfolds that turns conventions upside-down. The complex interplay of natural light and shadows accompanies our experience of the collection. The architecture of the galleries harmonises with the essentially chronological and thematic approach adopted by the curators. Intimate spaces foster the sense of discovery. Walking through the galleries means being open to surprises, and visitors are prompted to ask questions and seek the answers themselves. Above all, these spaces shed light on the countless stories to be discovered in the Louvre Abu Dhabi, not only of the works of art but also of all those who come to visit the museum.

MANUEL RABATÉ

Director of Louvre Abu Dhabi

THE MUSEUM AND THE SEA

All climates like exceptions. Warmer when it is cold. Cooler in the tropics. People do not resist thermal shock well. Nor do works of art. Such elementary observations have influenced the Louvre Abu Dhabi. It wishes to create a welcoming world, serenely combining light and shadow, reflection and calm. It wishes to belong to a country, to its history, to its geography, without becoming a flat translation, the pleonasm that results in boredom and convention. It also aims at emphasising the fascination generated by rare encounters.

It is rather unusual to find a built archipelago in the sea. It is even more uncommon to see that it is protected by a parasol creating a rain of light. The possibility of accessing the museum by boat or finding a pontoon to reach it by foot from the shore is equally extraordinary, before being welcomed like a much-awaited visitor willing to see unique collections, linger in tempting bookstores, or taste local teas, coffees and delicacies.

It is both a calm and complex place. A contrast among a series of museums that cultivate their differences and their authenticities.

It is a project founded on a major symbol of Arab architecture: the dome. But here, with its evident shift from tradition, the dome is a modern proposal. A double dome 180 metres in diameter, offering horizontal, perfectly radiating geometry, a randomly perforated woven material, providing shade punctuated by bursts of sun. The dome gleams in the Abu Dhabi sunshine. At night, this protected landscape is an oasis of light under a starry dome.

The Louvre Abu Dhabi becomes the final destination of an urban promenade, a garden on the coast, a cool haven, a shelter of light during the day and evening, its aesthetic consistent with its role as a sanctuary for the most precious works of art.

JEAN NOUVEL

I have always considered a great museum as a neighbourhood, as a natural destination in a city, as a mark of its character. Ideally, the thrill of discovering masterpieces should be crowned by a landscaped composition – street, architecture, and light all contributing to the aura of cities.

Thus, at the Louvre Abu Dhabi, the shadow that the white dome places on the buildings of the museum is traversed by a strange light made of rays, of lines. Often in the souks, loose boards or holes in the walls create lines of sun in the dust in the air, illuminating the goods and customers in the shadows. At the Louvre Abu Dhabi, the dome displays a complex geometry, and random gaps of differing shapes and sizes emerge; a kinetic game varies the form and slow movement of the flashes of light on the white walls of the museum. We are talking about spaces that are not completely inside, not totally outside. They aim to awaken the artistic emotions in the visitor aroused by the collections. Closed, protected, the galleries of the museum take on a palatial character.

As much as the exterior light of the built volumes evokes the Arab city through simple geometric forms assembled in a hidden order, the geometry of the sequence of large exhibition spaces is strictly orthogonal: the height of their ceilings organising exceptional spaces for the ordered presentation of contrasting works from different civilisations. Their natural illumination by large open windows, mainly on the underside of the dome, and the large windows framing the sea or the exterior spaces under the dome create a constant awareness of being in Abu Dhabi, on the Gulf, in 21st-century architecture.

JEAN NOUVEL

This is the first sketch of the project, drawn by Jean Nouvel in 2006, on a train that was taking us to London to visit a building under construction. The question of context, dear to Jean Nouvel, which had determined the architectural concept for the project in this historical neighbourhood of London, was to be reconsidered in a new way for a site much further away, on the desert shores of Saadiyat Island in Abu Dhabi.

Pencil in hand, Jean Nouvel tells me about his recent meeting with the director of the Guggenheim, who had spoken to him about the ambitious project of the Emiratis to create a series of cultural institutions for their capital, including a "classical art museum" that would be entrusted to him. We would learn six months later that the museum was to become the Louvre Abu Dhabi.

Beyond the sketch, primitive as it was in every sense, there are the very precise words employed by Jean Nouvel. They go straight to the essential, and these first pencil marks that accompany the discourse already contain the entire project in its essence as well as the formulation of its concept:

The island on the island / The neighbourhood-museum / The dome and its microclimate
Its belonging to a place, to its geography and its history, to its culture.

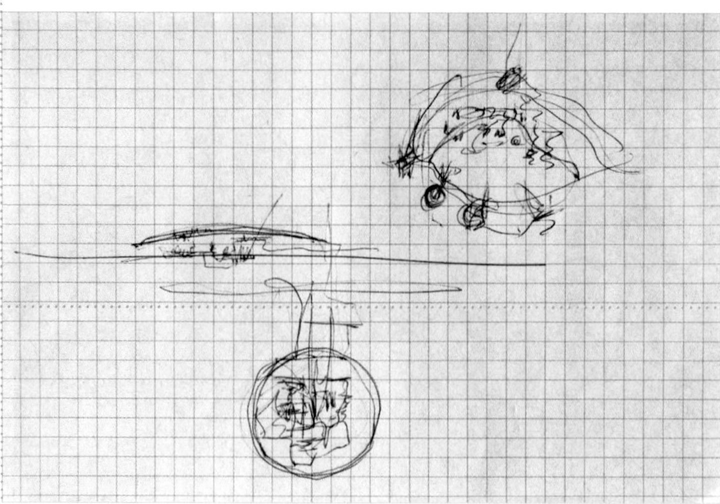

All is said and yet everything remains to be done. To be designed and to be set to music. With two key words: "Geometry and Light".

A vast task of interpretation, orchestration and implementation.

How to invent a "reversed archaeology"?

How to create a "rain of light"?

How to get closest to the idea

Interpret, transcribe, translate

Possess the subject, be possessed by it

How to find the right vocabulary

The writing, the drawing,

The measure, the rhythm,

The breath, the respiration,

The emotion...

How to integrate the culture of the place

Be immersed, understand, reinterpret...

And then,

How to assemble all the parameters of production

The team, the individual and multiple talents

The experts, specialists of all kinds

The tools, empirical and digital

How to implement

Research materials of today

Develop prototypes

Identify the best firms

Know how to build

More than ten years of gestation, creation and savoir-faire to finally give birth to the Louvre of the desert, which cries just as well its rain of sun.

HALA WARDÉ

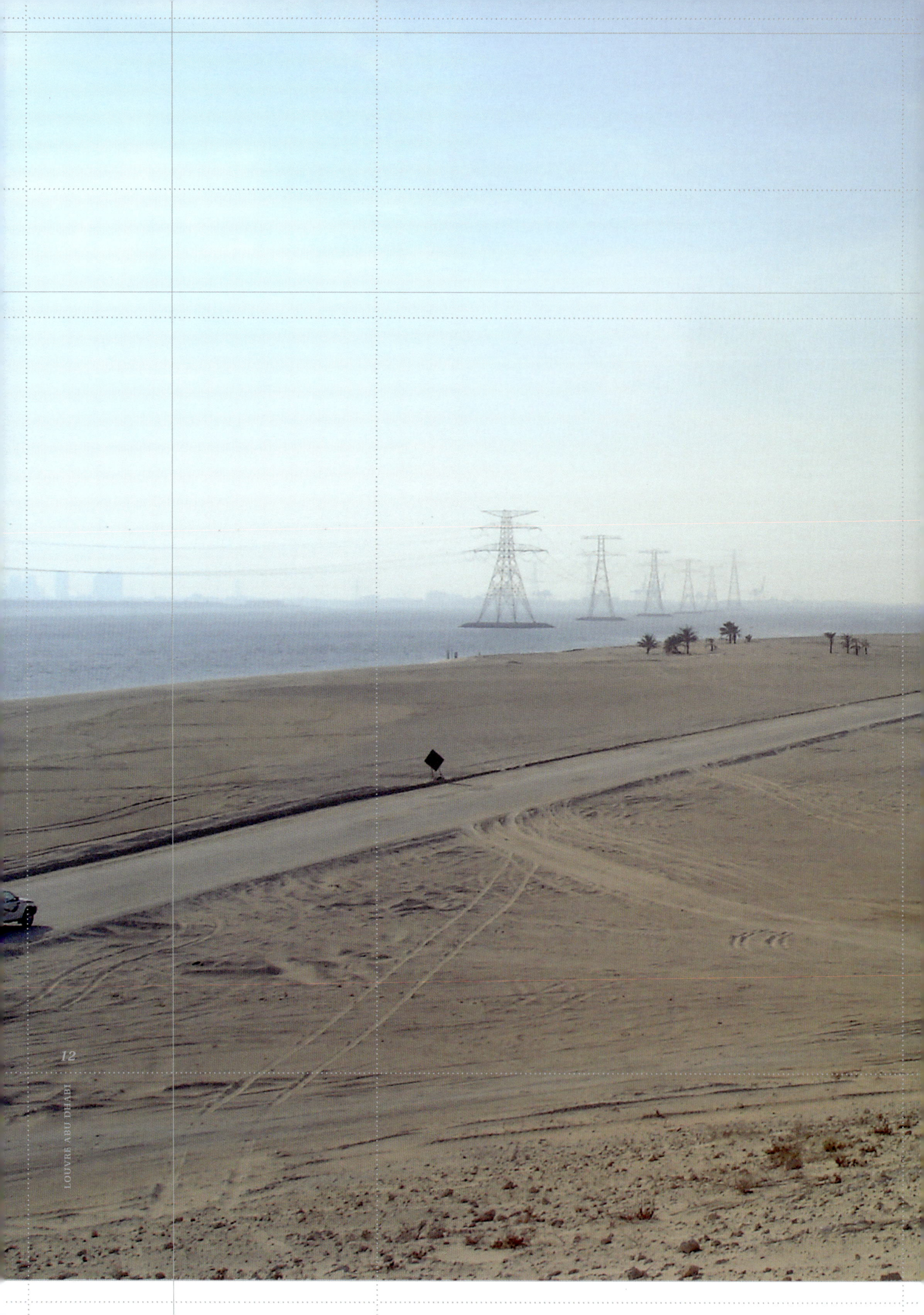

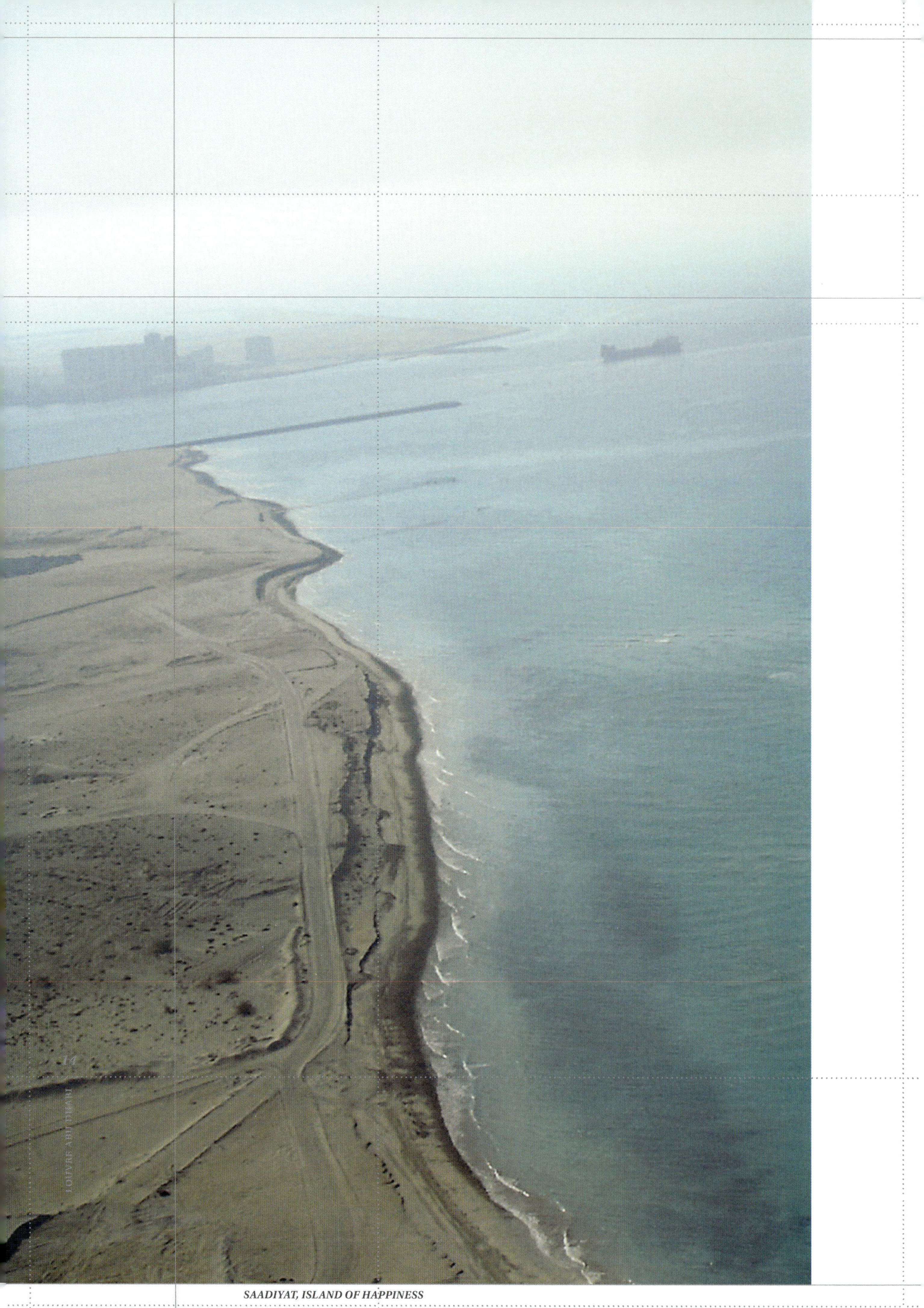

SAADIYAT, ISLAND OF HAPPINESS

In the beginning there was the desert with its long strips of sand coming to merge with the waters of the Arabian Gulf and form a coastline scattered with islands. From the mouths of the Tigris and Euphrates to the Strait of Hormuz, the populations lived for many years according to the rhythm of fishing and their age-old trade with the Indian subcontinent, Africa and the Levant. After the discovery of black gold, it took just a few short decades for these territories to enter fully into modernity and join the concert of nations at the forefront of the world economy.

TERRITORY

It was the thinker and poet Édouard Glissant who suggested replacing the notion of globalisation with the more subtle concept of a world made up of archipelagos where each little island possesses its autonomy while being connected to the world in real time via the internet. An eloquent and literal example of this image of the archipelago is provided by Abu Dhabi and its coastal islands Al Maryah, Al Reem and Saadiyat, the Island of Happiness. Under the guidance of the late Sheikh Zayed Bin Sultan Al Nahyan, the founding father of the union and an enlightened statesman, the United Arab Emirates quickly diversified their activities in various sectors of the economy. The combination of tourism and culture constitutes one of the most visible facets of this progress. The large triangle of Saadiyat Island and its long stretch of beach have underdone ambitious development in terms of real estate, with residences and hotels of great prestige, a golf course, a marina and a cultural district, of which the Louvre Abu Dhabi is one of its first and most illustrious landmarks.

After the intergovernmental agreement was signed between the United Arab Emirates and France in 2007, the appointment of Jean Nouvel as architect of the future Louvre Abu Dhabi came as no surprise. The most famous French architect of his time, he enjoys a sterling reputation in the Gulf due to his long-standing familiarity with the Arab world. His Arab World Institute in Paris was awarded the Aga Khan Prize in 1987. The author of several projects in Morocco, Rabat, Tangiers and Qatar, he was also involved in the studies for the Sheikh Zayed Grand Mosque in Abu Dhabi. Everything in the architect's past made him the obvious choice for this bold undertaking.

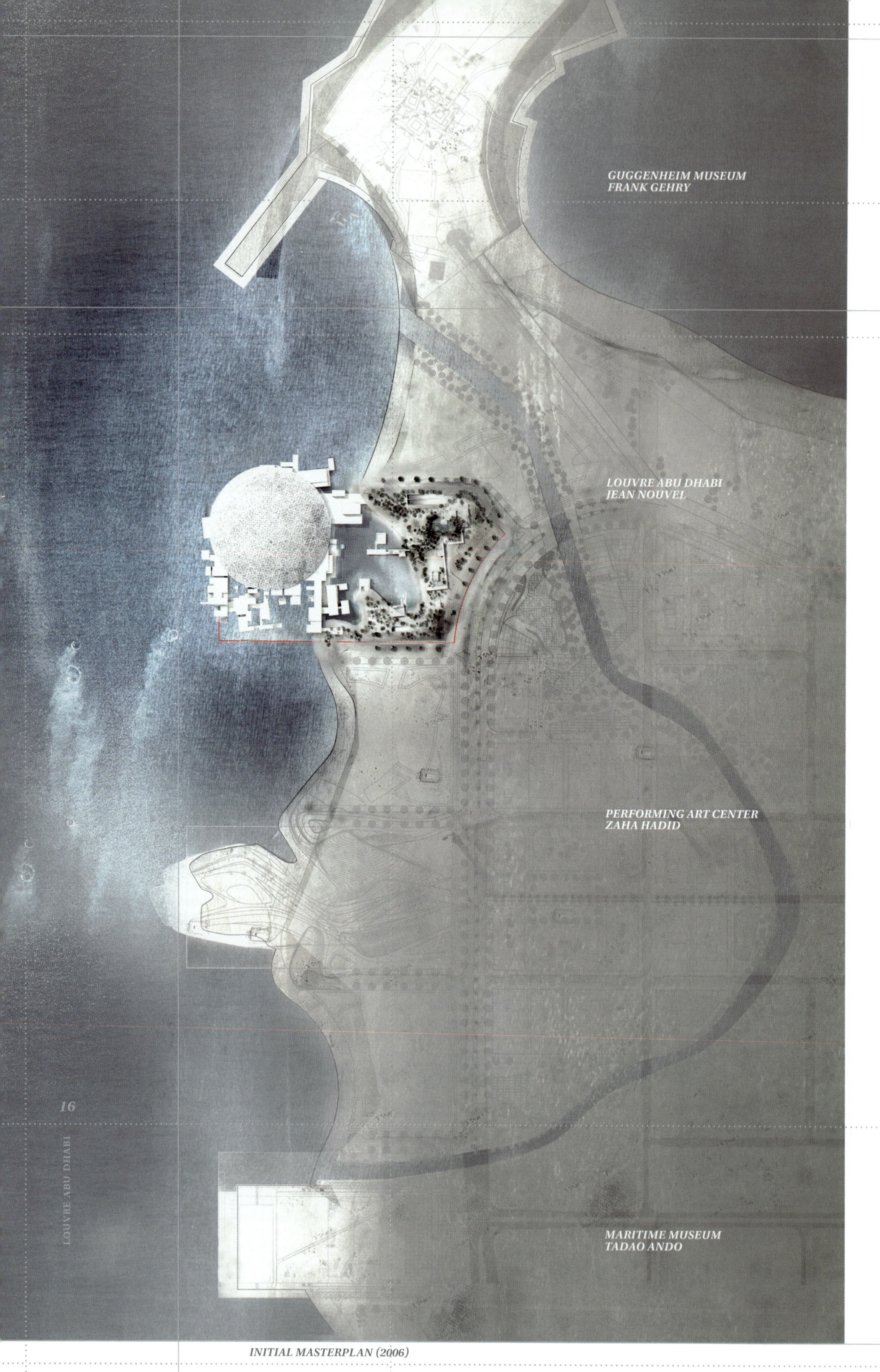

INITIAL MASTERPLAN (2006)

The name of Jean Nouvel for a museum of classical art was suggested to the authorities of Abu Dhabi by Thomas Krens, then director of the Solomon Guggenheim Foundation and adviser for the development of museum projects on Saadiyat Island. Jean Nouvel's museum was given pride of place in the line of buildings stretching along the branch of the Gulf known as the Khor Laffan, together with the Guggenheim Museum of contemporary art designed by Frank Gehry, the Sheikh Zayed National Museum, devoted to the history of the young nation, the project for a centre of performing arts by the late Zaha Hadid, and, slightly further along the coast, a maritime museum designed by Tadao Ando (all architects of international renown and winners of the famous Pritzker Prize, the architectural equivalent of the Nobel Prize).

The edifices that will eventually make up the cultural district on Saadiyat Island will occupy the western edge of a long strip of land bordering the Khor Laffan, and be bound to the east by the Sheikh Khalifa Bin Zayed highway leading to the airport and then to the nearby emirate of Dubai.

The strip of shore connecting the Louvre Abu Dhabi and the future Guggenheim is laid out as a garden of local and exotic species, thus helping to mitigate the harmful effects of traffic and provide a breathing space that offsets the daring architecture of the museums. Children's playgrounds and areas for relaxation and picnics are laid out along the promenades. The garden ends before the east façade of the museum in a sort of sinuous, tiered amphitheatre of ultra-high-performance fibre concrete panels above the water level that isolates and presents the Louvre Abu Dhabi on its offshore platform.

As a basis for consideration, Jean Nouvel was provided with a flexible general programme and a few indications. While Frank Gehry was considering a vertical monument for his site at the north-west tip of the island, Zaha Hadid had in mind a huge and spectacular wave close to the Khalifa Bin Zayed bridge across the Khor Laffan.

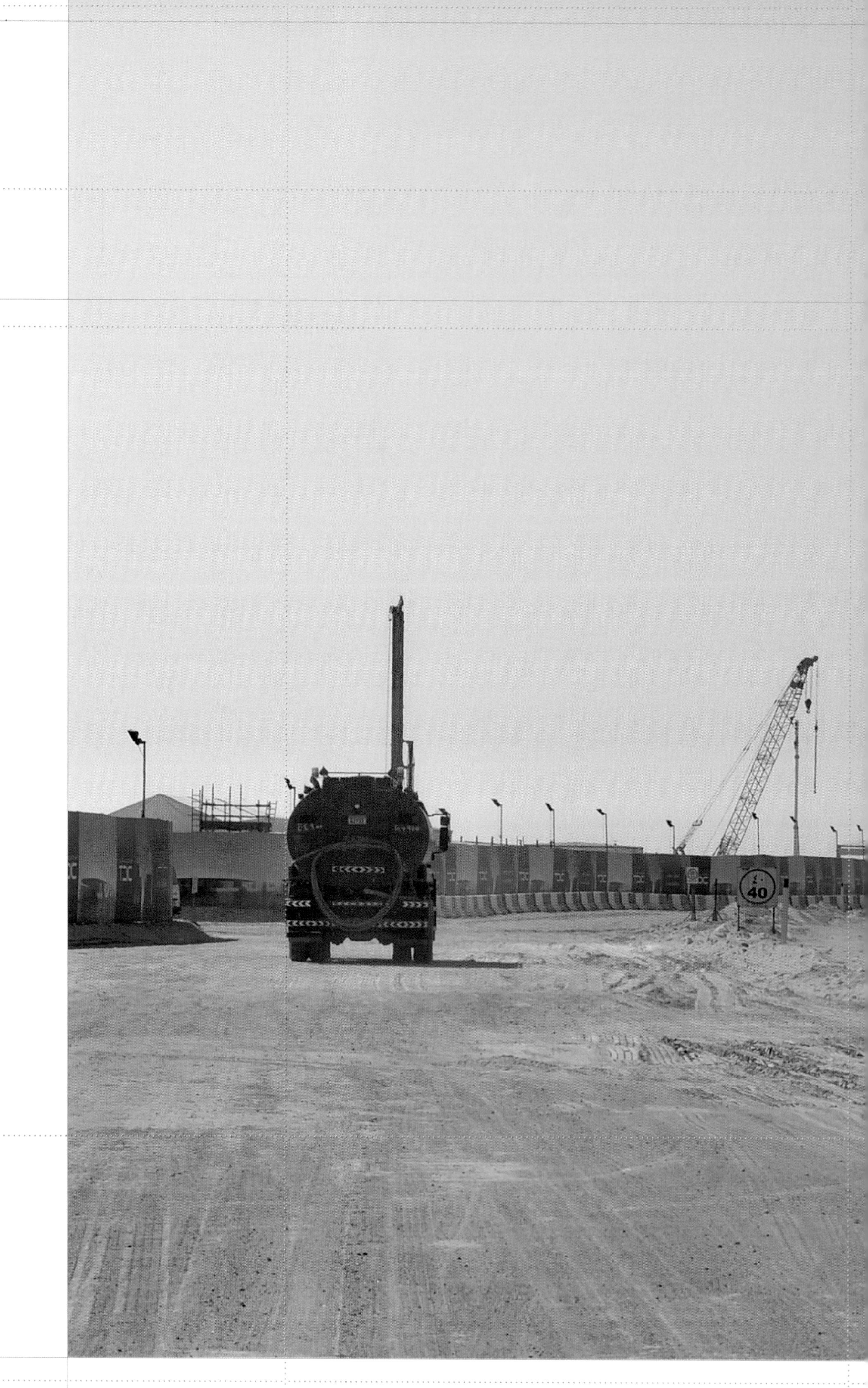

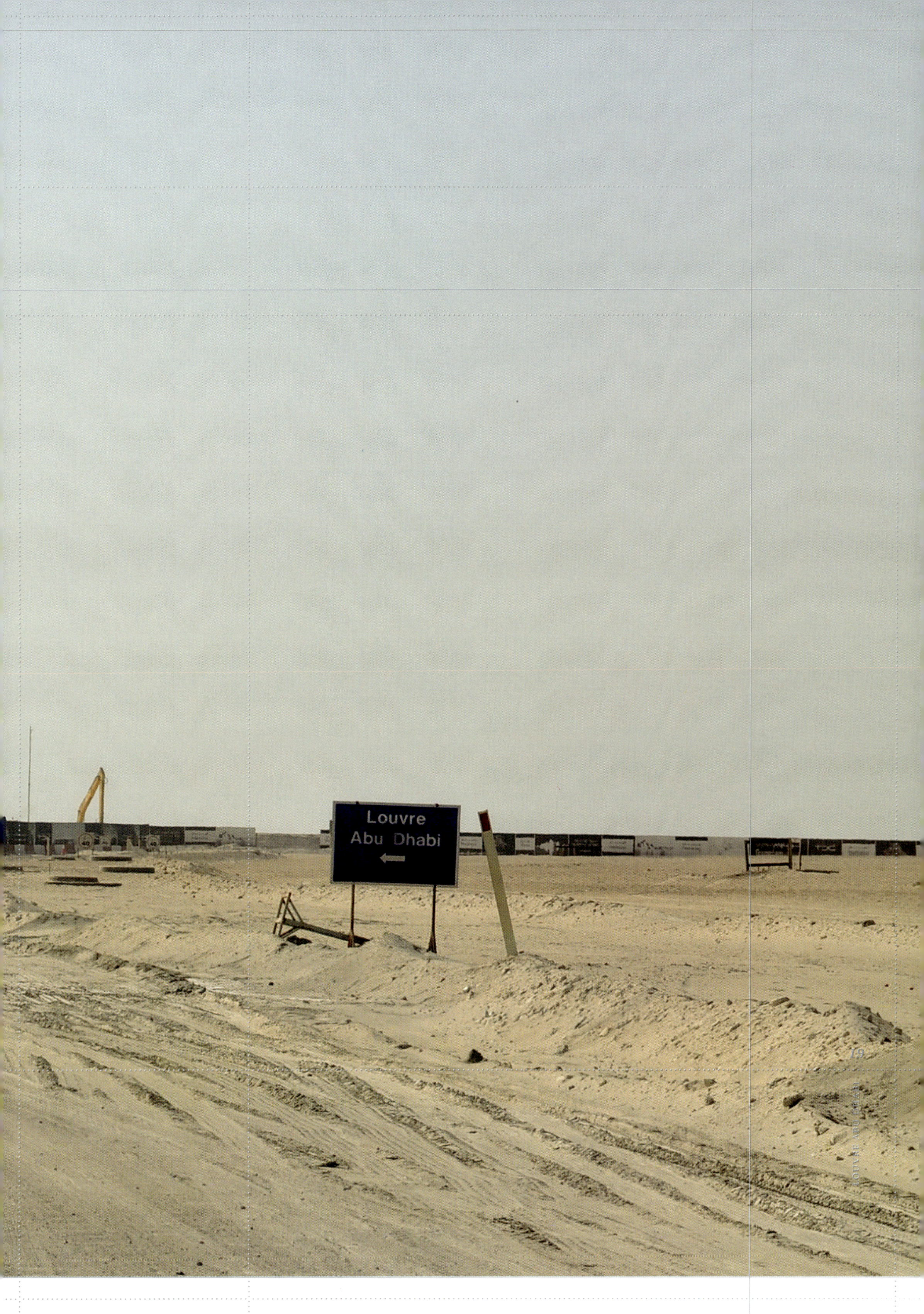
Louvre
Abu Dhabi

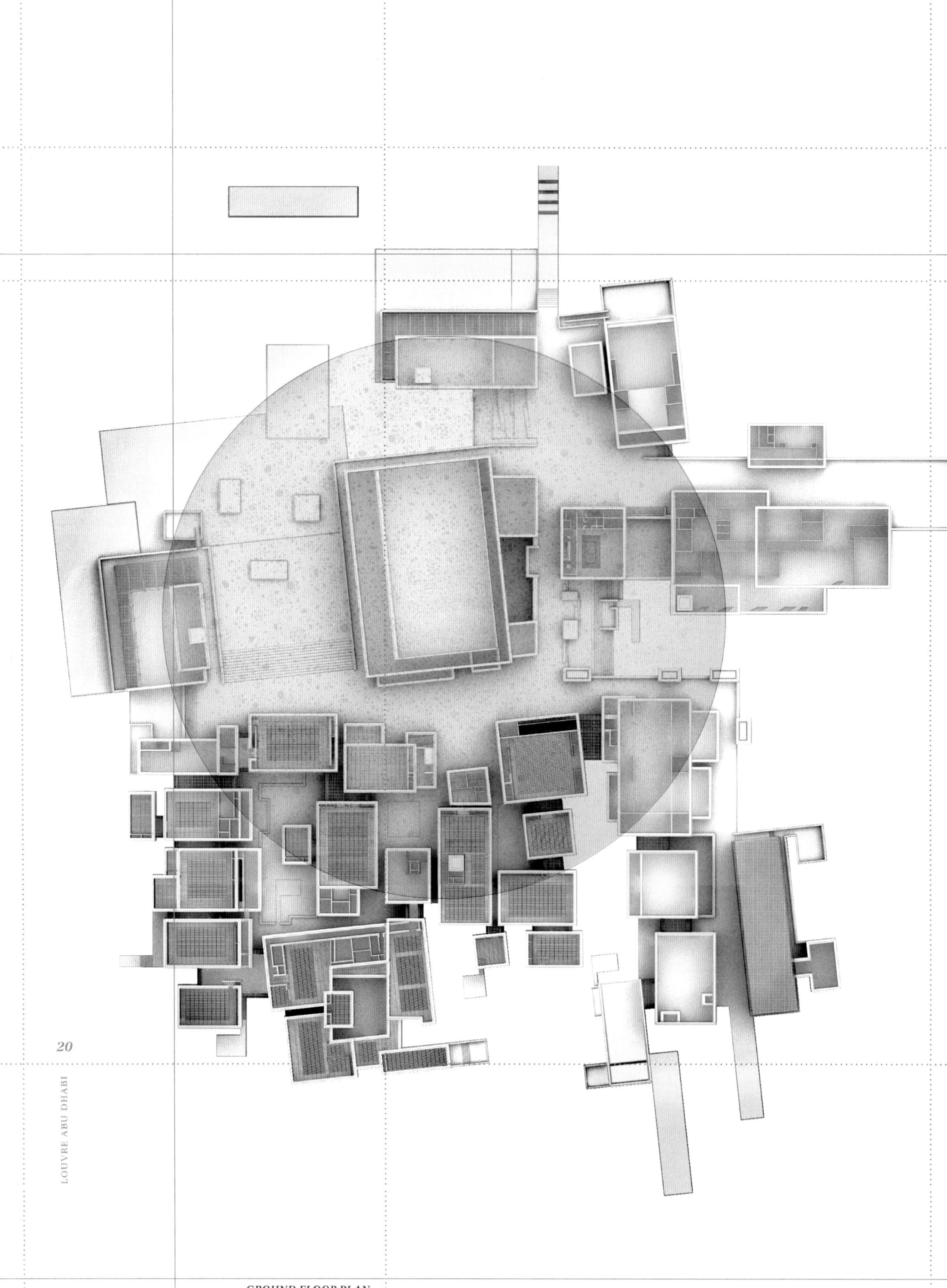

GROUND FLOOR PLAN

Jean Nouvel had concerns unlike those of his colleagues and friends. His familiarity with the region soon led him to realise that the paramount consideration was a tropical desert climate with summer temperatures very close to 50°C. As he observed, people are poorly equipped to withstand thermal shock and so are works of art. These "elementary observations" led him to devise a direct means to moderate these excesses and the heat of the sun, namely a huge parasol to shelter the various buildings of the museum, a radical idea that also recalls Frei Otto and Buckminster Fuller with their earlier utopian dreams of covering entire cities.

But how could Nouvel resist playing with light, his favourite material and the element that enshrouds all Arab architecture in its glow? Thus it was that the parasol turned into a vast, horizontal *mashrabiya*, circular and domed, perforated to admit a "rain of light", an expression that already seems refreshing in itself.

Another factor serving to mitigate the excessive heat is the site of the Louvre Abu Dhabi on the banks of the Khor Laffan. Jean Nouvel laid out the buildings of the museum on a sort of peninsula, literally an offshore platform whose base is just above the water at high tide, when the level of the Gulf rises by about one metre. Access to this platform is provided to the south by a footbridge for visitors and to the north-east by a bridge for deliveries and services. Jetties also provide access by boat from the Gulf and from the Khor Laffan, a kind of Grand Canal recalling the old dream of turning Saadiyat into an eastern Venice with small picturesque canals and arched bridges. The museum and its medina are surrounded by water, whose proximity and gentle lapping in the slightest breeze contribute to a feeling of beneficial coolness.

Jean Nouvel sees a museum not as a building closed in upon itself but first of all as a district, an integral part of the city. Entrusted with the memory of a civilisation, it enhances the dignity, prestige and aura of the city, participating in its day-to-day life and urban dynamics. It must offer simple and familiar access, and facilitate regular visits. Hence the need to integrate the duality of its slightly contradictory nature as a "people's palace", noble and domestic at the same time.

PALACE

The palatial scale of museums is bound up with their origins. Before becoming museums, the Louvre in Paris, the Castle in Prague and the Hermitage in St Petersburg were royal or imperial residences filled with works of art. The first museums built early in the 19th century drew directly on these models. The architect Klenze designed the Alte Pinakothek in Munich after building the extension of the Hermitage. Some of their features became standard, like ceilings about eight metres in height, serving the purely functional purpose of accommodating three rows of paintings, and the use of skylights for overhead lighting, electricity not yet existing at the start of the 19th century.

In the Louvre Abu Dhabi, Jean Nouvel divided a large museum into functional units for his own "*petit palais*" or little palace while confessing his inability to say whether it is actually "*petit ou grand*", small or large. There was one indication, however. The walls were to be *cyclopean*, an allusion to the remote pre-Hellenic civilisation of Mycenae with its city walls and Lion Gate, made of such enormous stone slabs as to suggest that only beings of extraordinary strength like the giant Cyclops could have built them.

URBS

With their simple and rigorous geometry and the uniform whiteness of their walls of ultra-high-performance fibre concrete, the buildings laid out on the platform are evidently members of the same family. Despite this apparent unity, however, they display distinguishing qualities and a certain degree of specificity in their different configurations and dimensions. This urban district on Saadiyat thus recalls the prototypes of the Arab city, comparable in appearance in places as distant from one another as Fez, Cairo and Bukhara. It presents the same compact disorder as their medina quarters, where houses, marketplaces and caravanserais are closely interwoven in a maze of streets, lanes and squares, large and small, haphazard places full of surprises.

The "boxes" or "houses" making up the medina beneath the dome of the Louvre Abu Dhabi are laid out apparently at random, like dice rolled out over the platform by some carefree titan. A long plaza stretches between the southern part occupied by the conglomerate of buildings for the permanent collection, the northern section with the children's museum, the gallery for temporary exhibitions and the café, and the restaurant and the auditorium still further north. This opens towards the west onto a panoramic view of the Khor Laffan, the bustle of the Zayed harbour with its container ships, its black and red freighters, its cranes and silos on the opposite bank, as well as the first skyscrapers erected on the islands of Al Maryah and Al Reem. The skyline of the city in the distance stands out in the evening against the crimson sunset. Autonomous buildings, the galleries are connected with one another by glazed passageways forming a complex of lanes, dead ends and small squares with an expanse of water every so often, and the shimmering reflection of the "celestial vault" of the dome. Large picture windows offer glimpses of the interior of the galleries from the plaza.

External artworks acquired by the museum or commissioned from artists stand out against the urban landscape of the buildings dispersed over the platform, including a Mamluk pavement, a Rodin sculpture perched on a column, artworks by the American artist Jenny Holzer and by the Italian artist Giuseppe Penone. Others will be added through the acquisition of ancient works or contemporary commissions to make the museum city an open-air exhibition space.

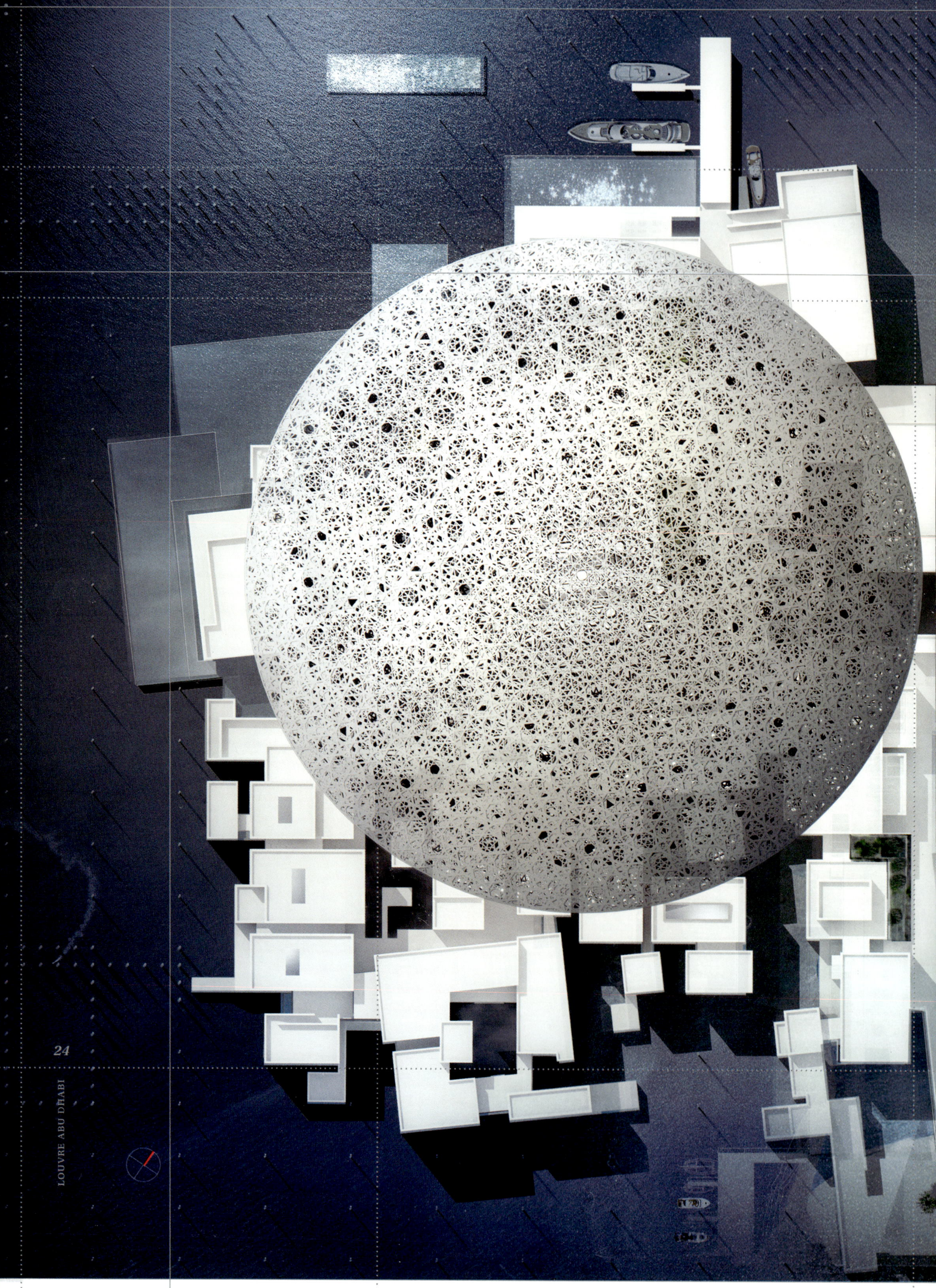

LOUVRE ABU DHABI

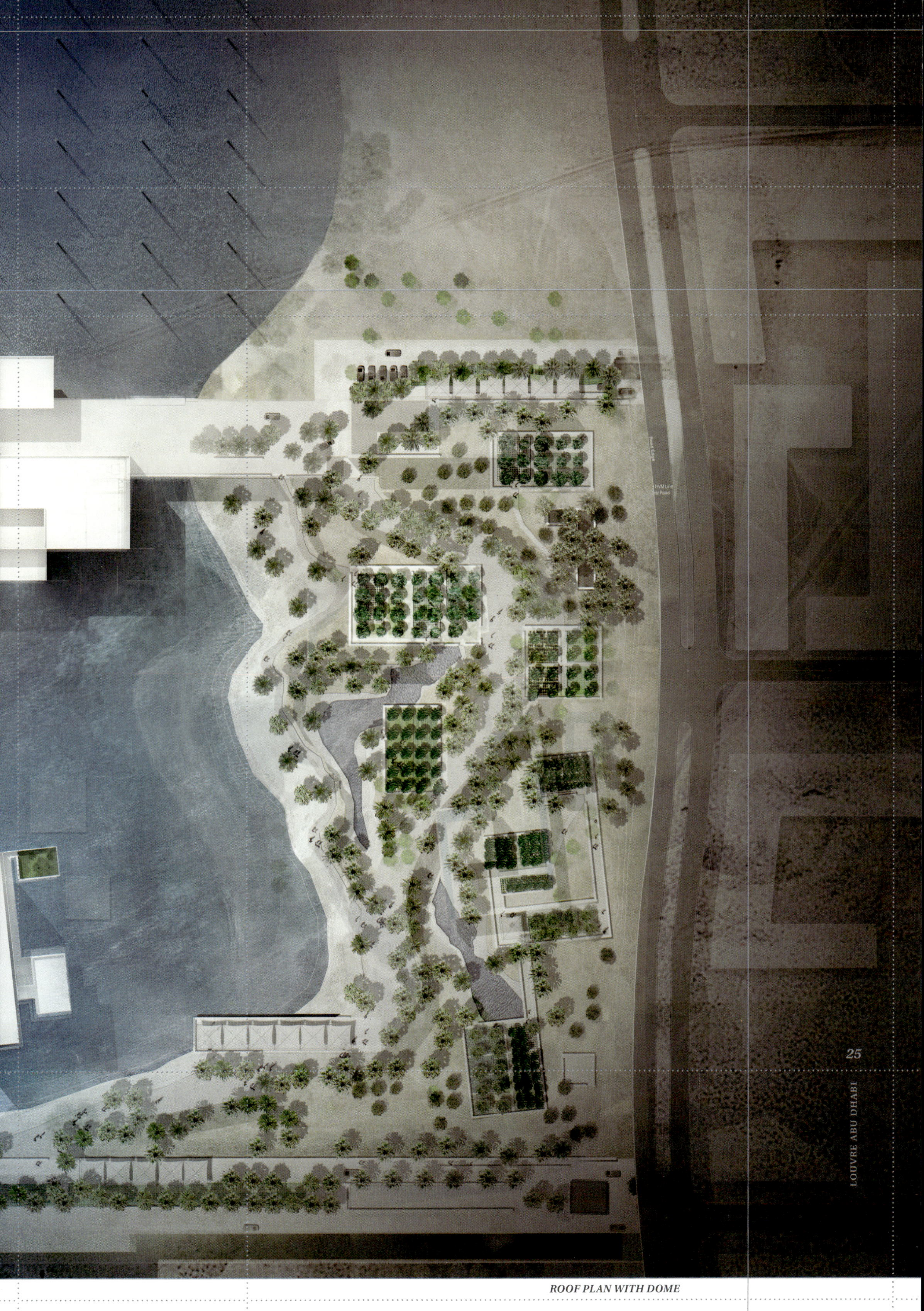

ROOF PLAN WITH DOME

"Emotion starts with bewilderment, when you no longer understand what is happening".

An urban neighbourhood beneath a parasol. In its simplicity, the image suggested by the architect for his project is very fitting when seen as a whole from a certain distance: a large shield of shining metal floating above a conglomeration of white, geometrical volumes.

After the vast and light-filled entry sequence, everything is very different: a space out of all proportion for which no-one is prepared. Even the figures can hardly do it justice. A gigantic dome 180 metres in diameter, a plaza 120 metres in length that seems to be bounded only by the horizon, edifices on vastly different scales without the slightest degree of transition – unless we consider the cyclopean layout created building by building – and the huge exhibition hall of 67 × 47 × 13 metres all combine to cause a feeling of giddiness. Here visitors experience unprecedented visual and perceptual shocks, like the contrast of the density of the permanent collection galleries and their closely-meshed maze to the south of the plaza with the sudden openness of the expanse of water from the Gulf that separates the Big Box from the café and extends to the north beyond the restaurant pavilion. The only object on a human scale is the Rodin on its column, but probably because it is a small work. We are astonished by the architecture, the deft and magnificent handling of volumes, and above all the light that bathes everything.

MAGIC

It is also on the plaza that we find the magic of the spectacle designed and presented by the architect: sunlight filtering through the different layers of the dome and falling through an atmosphere laden with moisture and fine dust from the desert that makes its shafts visible and indeed almost tangible. The "rain of light" cascades over the stone floor and the white walls of the different buildings in a host of glowing puddles of light that appear and slowly vanish, following one another without contact in an astounding and uninterrupted carousel.

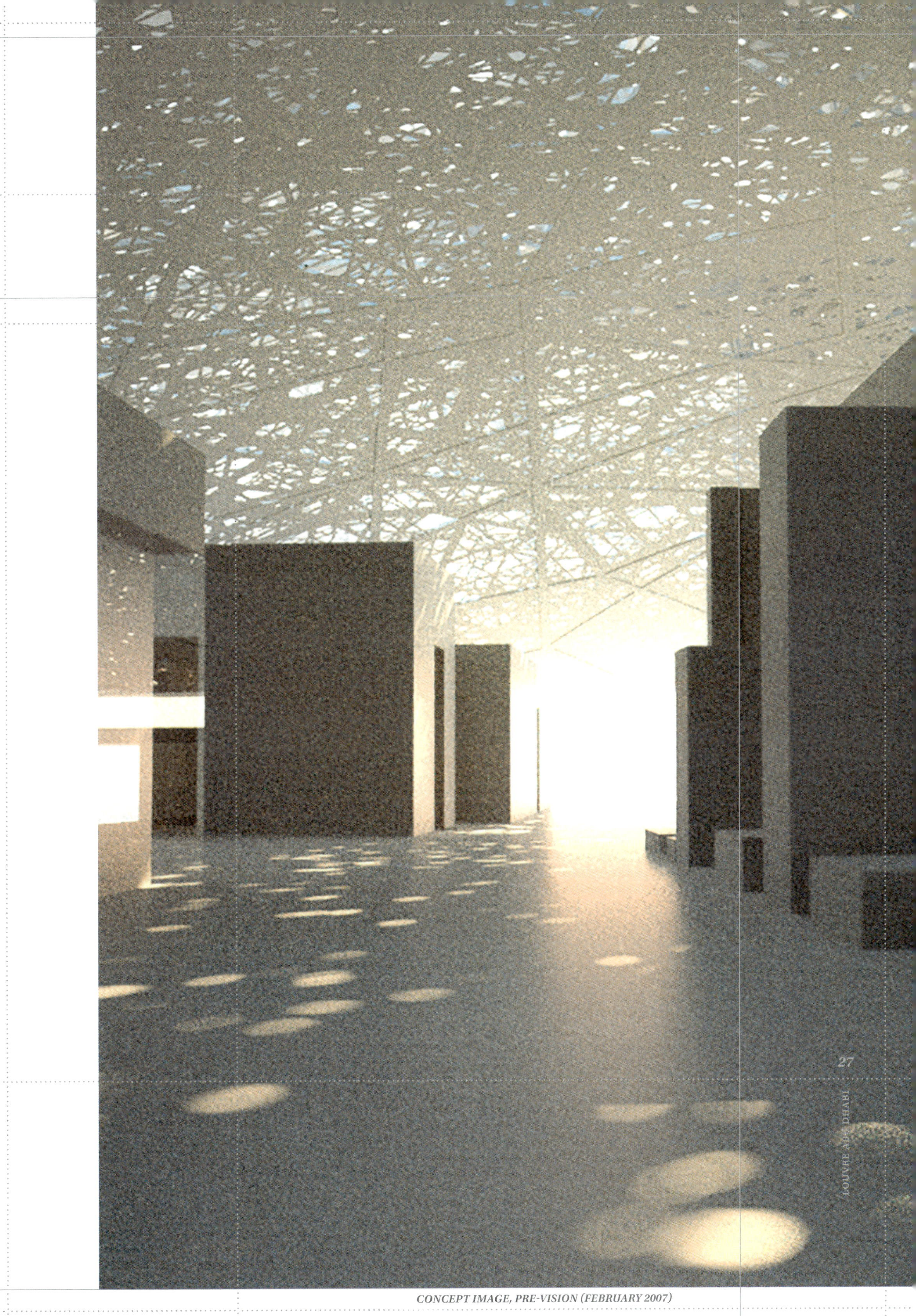

CONCEPT IMAGE, PRE-VISION (FEBRUARY 2007)

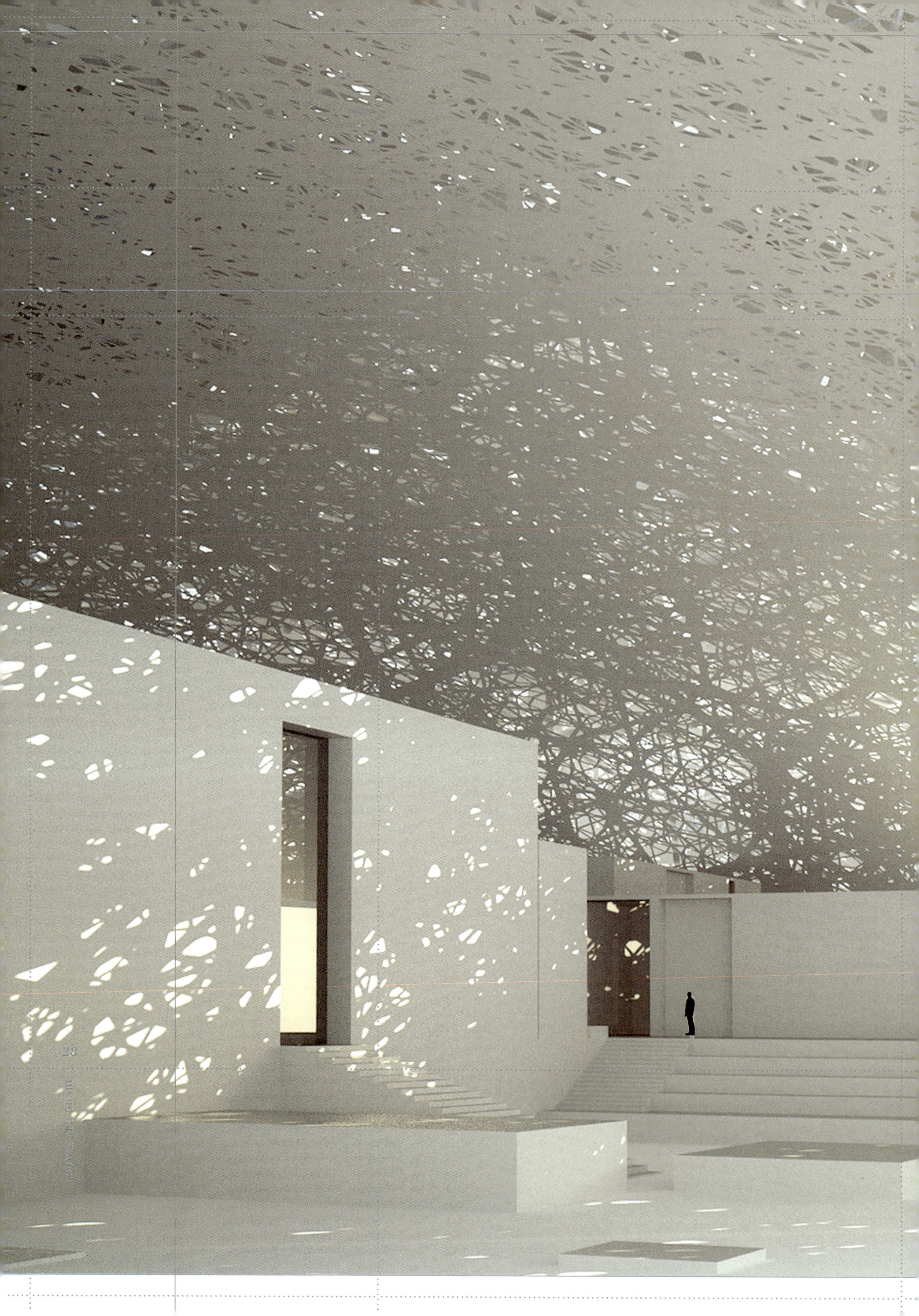

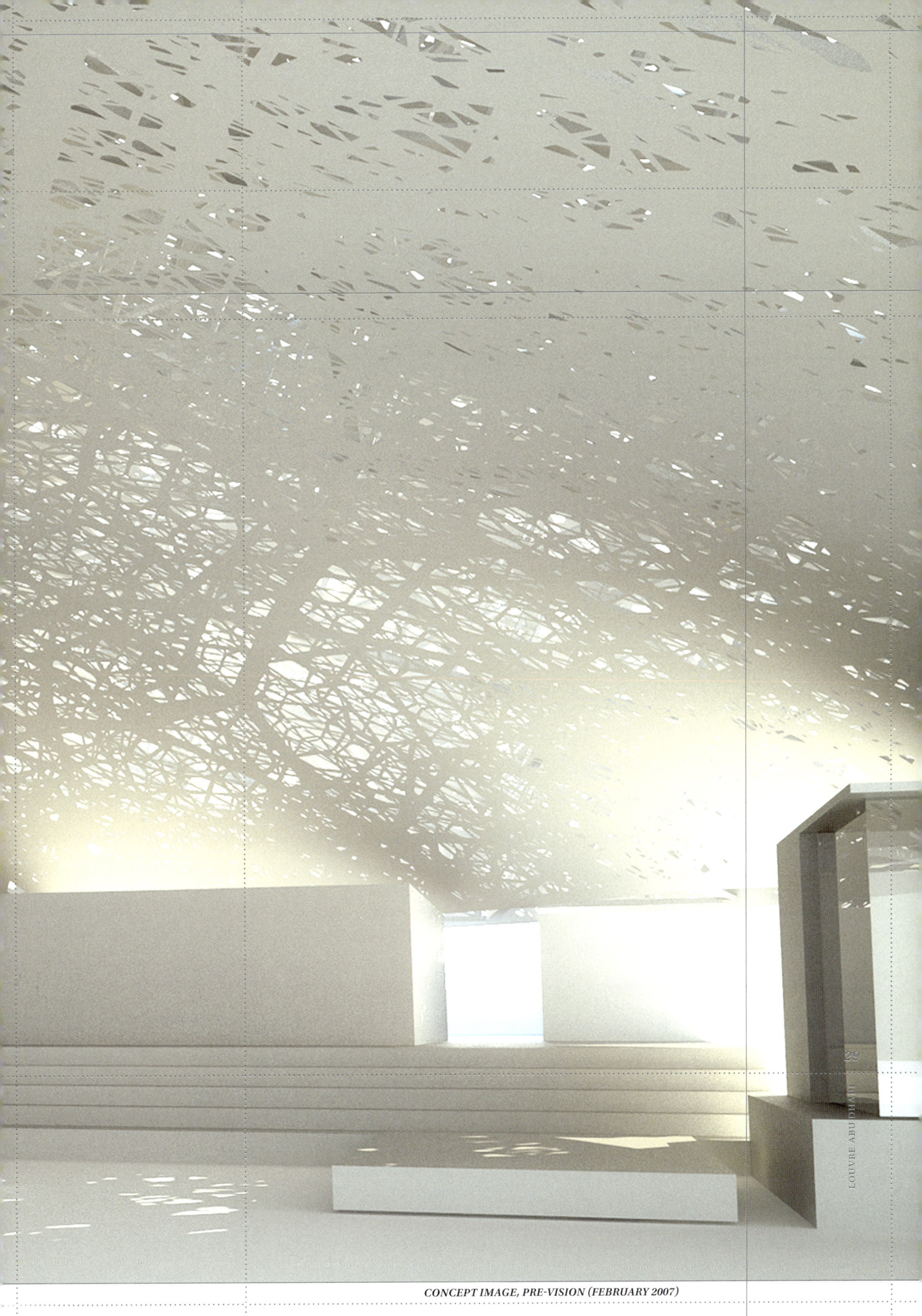

CONCEPT IMAGE, PRE-VISION (FEBRUARY 2007)

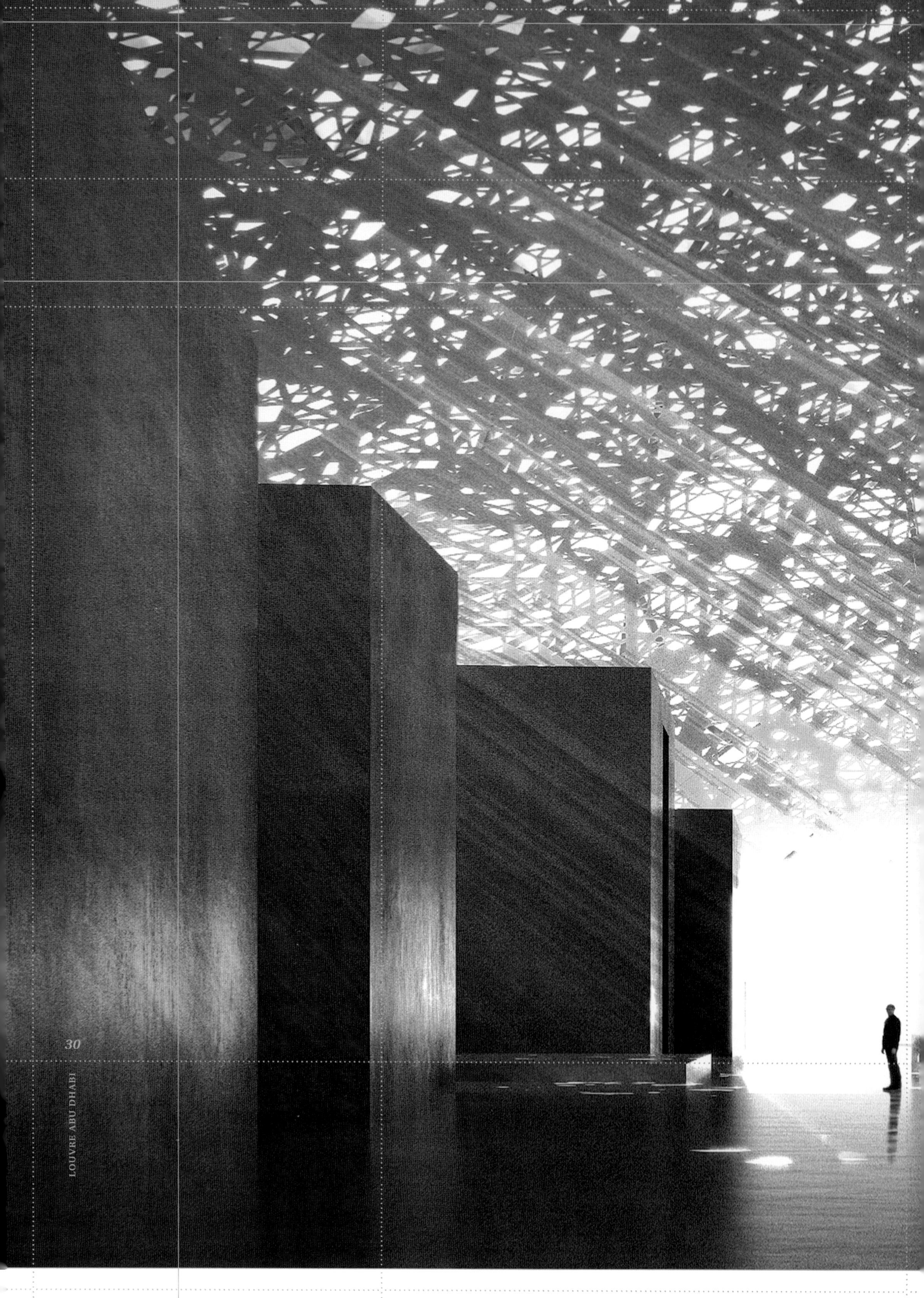

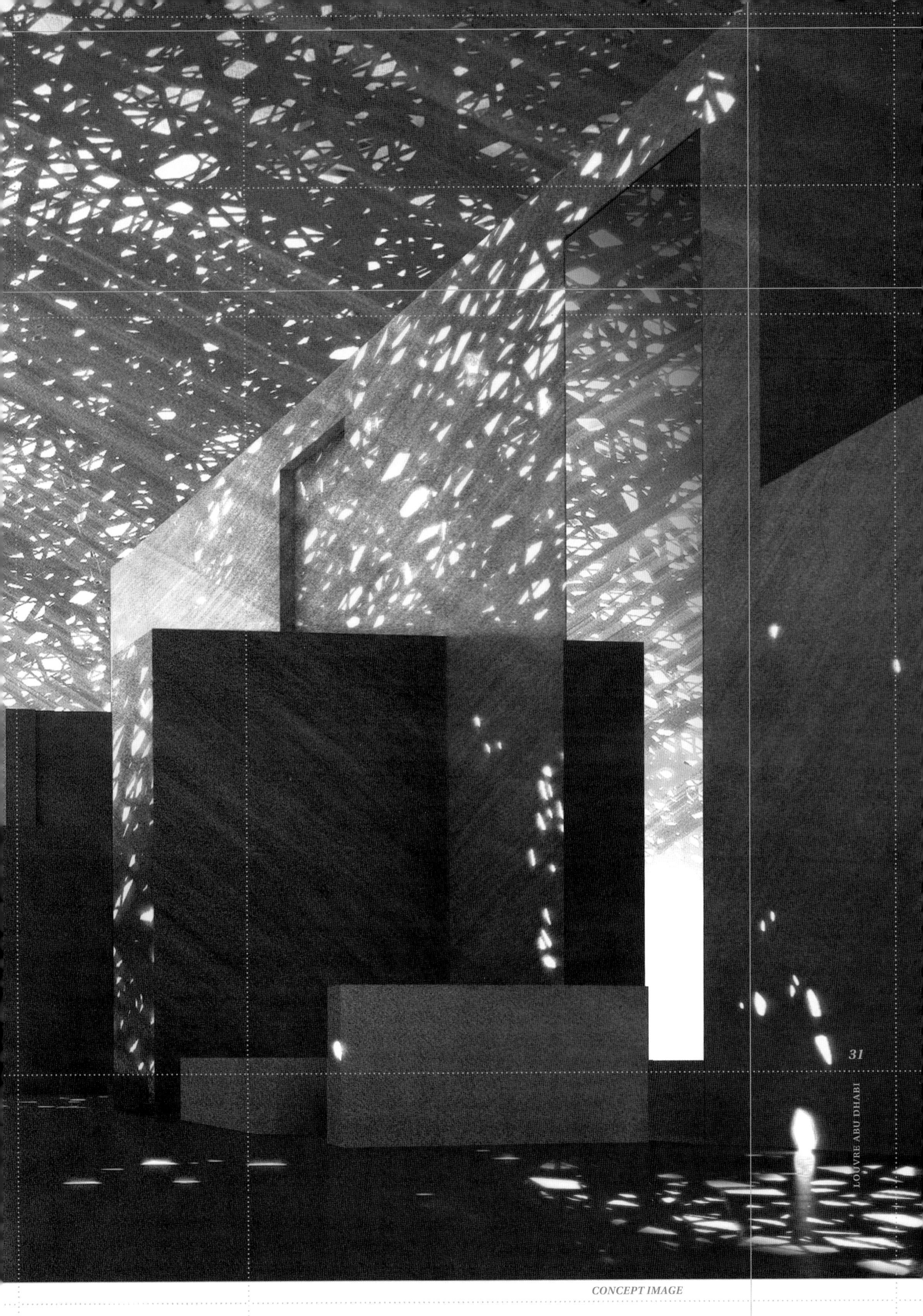

CONCEPT IMAGE

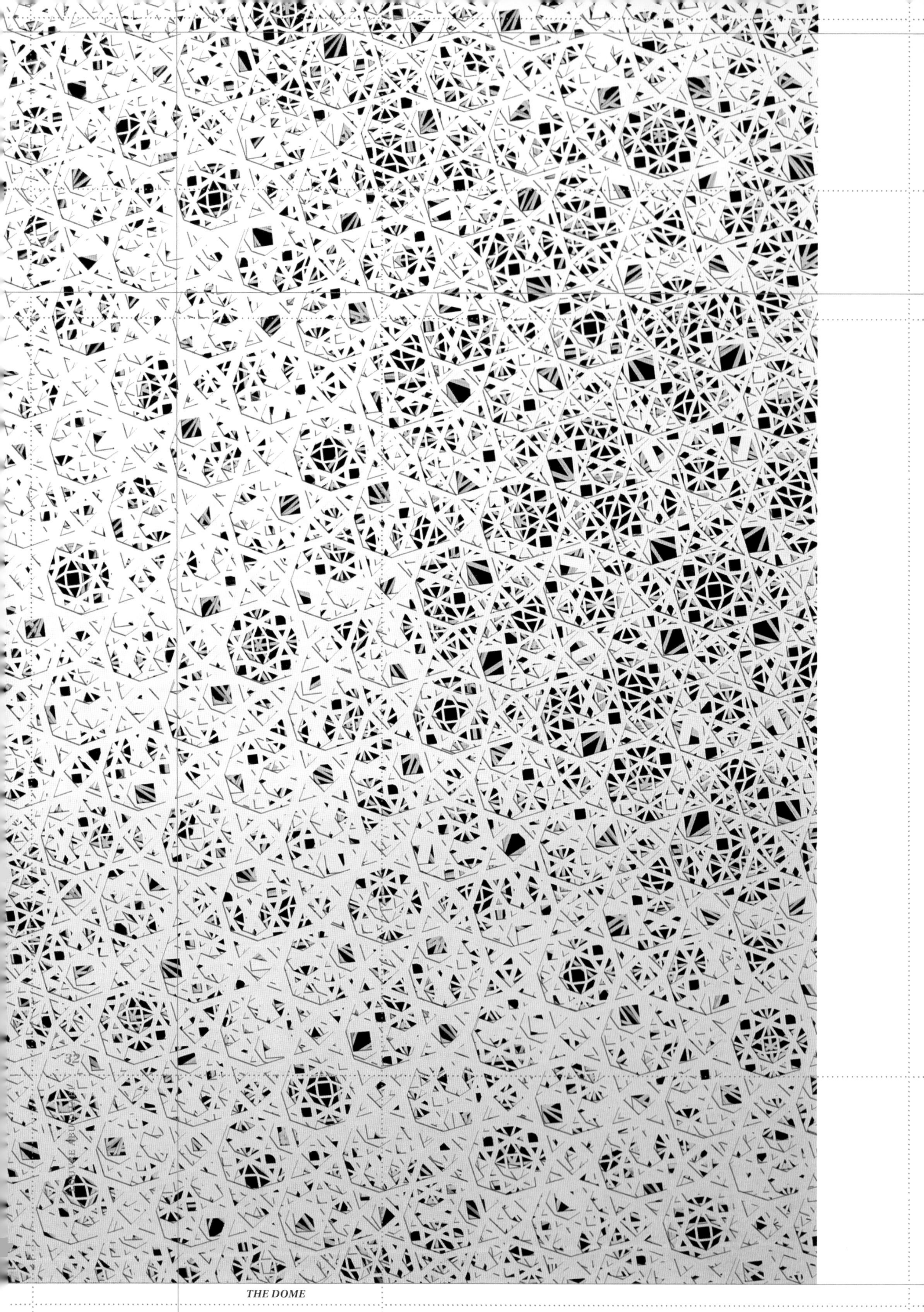

THE DOME

By adopting the idea and the form of the dome, "one of the archetypes of Arab architecture", to cover and protect the Louvre Abu Dhabi, Jean Nouvel gave Saadiyat Island a singular landmark that contrasts with the array of skyscrapers adorning the new cities that line the shores of the Gulf. With its curve glistening on the horizon, Nouvel's age-old form asserts a simultaneously apparent and discreet presence.

ROOTS

More than a sign of complicity with Arab architecture and culture can be detected in Jean Nouvel's work over the years. First of all in terms of a taste for decoration: in an early manifesto, the young architect urged his colleagues to "dare to decorate" once again in defiance of the modernistic taboo formulated by Adolf Loos in his essay *Ornament and Crime*. Then there is his propensity to use square and complex orthogonal frameworks, which attest to a fascination with obsessively reiterated geometric patterns and abstraction that is also deeply rooted in the Arab culture. (Consider the great mathematician Alhazen, whose works of the early 11th century indirectly paved the way for the invention of perspective by the Western artists of the Renaissance.) Mention should also be made of Nouvel's tireless investigation of the reflection and refraction of light, and the contrast between darkness and brightness, small and never exhausted miracles at work in the dome.

UNIQUE

The dome of the Louvre Abu Dhabi is unique. We would look in vain for a precedent. It presents itself as a large circular disk, convex on top and concave on the underside, resting on four pillars only slightly taller than the buildings nestling beneath and easy to confuse with them, camouflaged as they are by the same "cyclopean" slabs of smooth, white ultra-high-performance concrete. From a distance, the dome thus gives the impression of floating or levitating above the platform.

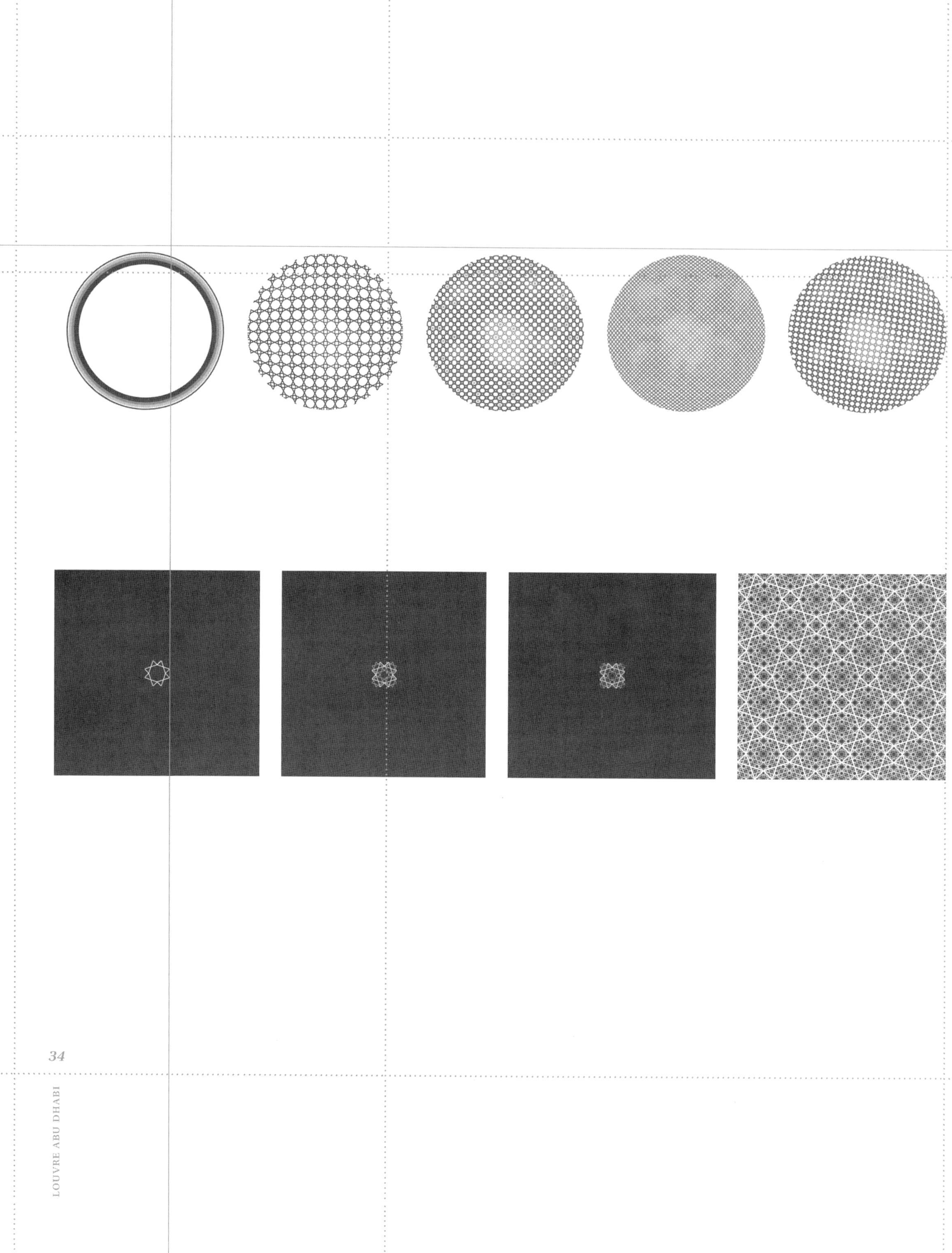

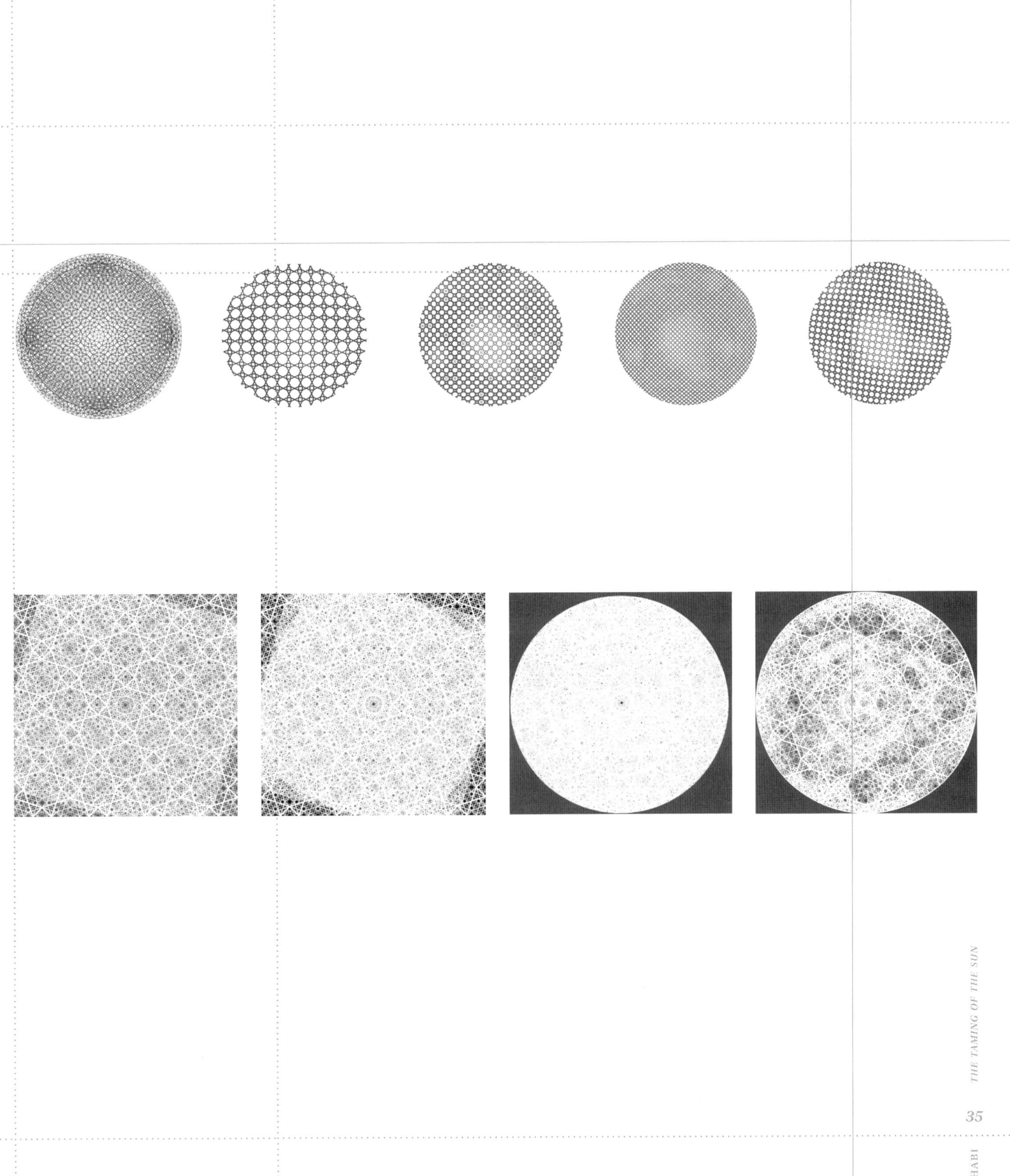

THE DOME AND THE CUPOLA, CONCEPT DRAWINGS

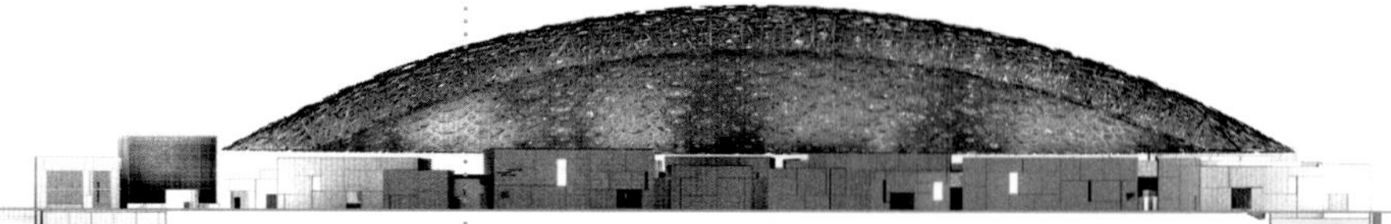

COMPOSITION

The dome consists of eight thin layers of metal in two shells, stainless steel for the outer shell and aluminium for the inner. The two shells are separated by a three-dimensional structure of square tubular steel, 5 metres deep, which constitutes another layer in the pattern. The eight layers consist of metal struts assembled to form a pattern of stars based on a square with four triangles, a basic motif comparable with the traditional *girih*. The voids in the motif are controlled by the thickness of the struts, which can be varied to increase the density of the pattern in areas where less direct light must penetrate the dome, such as the external public spaces, and decrease it where more natural light is required, as in the case of the skylit exhibition galleries. The superimposition of subtly staggered layers thus filters the rays of sunlight, which pierce the tracery of these surfaces and their assemblage. The shifting of alignments and the angle at which the sun strikes the outer surface of the dome create the fleeting motion of patches of light that appear and disappear as though by magic on the floor of the platform and the walls of the medina. The dome could thus be described as a gigantic horizontal and curved *mashrabiya* with a three-dimensional *girih* motif. The effect beneath the dome is comparable to the multi-layered ornamental vaulting known as *muqarnas*, described by Alhazen as a rough skin. The dome is simultaneously a medium and a filter of the ever-changing light that pierces it. The vibration simulated on the rigid surface of the walls symbolises the movement of the cosmos.

SCIENCES

Mention must be made of the complexity of the dome, for which the architect called in the greatest specialists of the day. There is nothing new under the sun. For the Pantheon in Rome and the imperial villa near Tivoli, Hadrian had his architects work together with astronomers to design an alignment programmed for the anniversary of his coronation on 11 August, when the niche containing his throne was struck by a shaft of sunlight for a few moments. In the Louvre Abu Dhabi, studies and simulation trials on models were developed for several years before the construction of the dome in order to ascertain the effects of the sunlight penetrating the eight curved layers in relation to the solar angle of incidence through the seasons and the hours of the day.

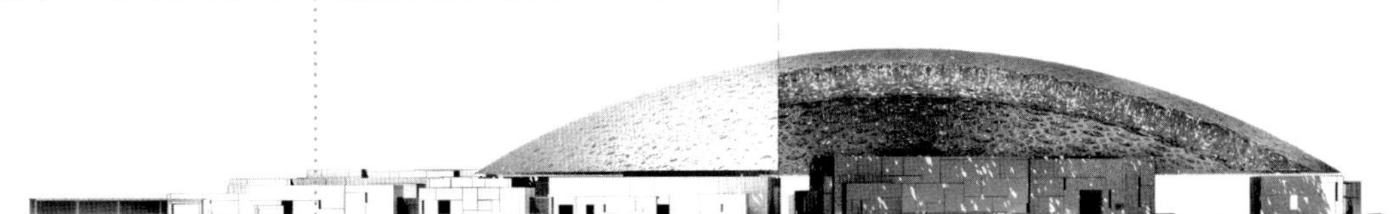

The dome responds to various competing requirements that it proved necessary to reconcile. The priority laid down by Jean Nouvel was to endow the plaza and the various buildings of the museum constituting the medina with a microclimate ensuring optimal thermal comfort for visitors in the extreme conditions of the region. This called for the maximum opacity of the parasol. At the same time, however, the space was required to offer visitors a unique aesthetic experience through the interplay of shafts of sunlight in accordance with the ambitions of a new museum with a universal vocation. It was the pursuit of this balance (or the resolution of this contradiction) that gave rise to the studies undertaken with all the specialists concerned – architects, structural engineers, experts in IT and virtual simulation, lighting specialists and large-scale model makers – working in close cooperation.

GIRIH

The size of the dome made its fragmentation and the search for an operational module necessary from the very outset. The basic motif was developed in the model-making department of the Ateliers Jean Nouvel through the laser-cutting of simple sheets of cardboard. It consists of an assemblage of four isosceles triangles around a square to form an octagon. The triangle, square and octagon were to constitute perforations through which the sunlight was to be filtered. The size of the perforations varies in relation to the width of the metal struts delimiting the triangles and squares, and therefore the octagons thus formed. These motifs are reiterated side by side over the entire surface of the dome to form a vast layer. The design initially envisaged ten layers and then eight, four for the upper shell and four for the lower, connected by a three-dimensional structure. A slight rotational shift of the layers controls the opacity of the whole to attain the limit of 1.8% luminosity set for thermal comfort while establishing alignments meticulously selected to create the effect of a shifting rain of light.

PROCESS

In each phase of the project, the different objectives regarding temperature, aesthetics, structure and museography, as well as feasibility in terms of manufacture, assembly and

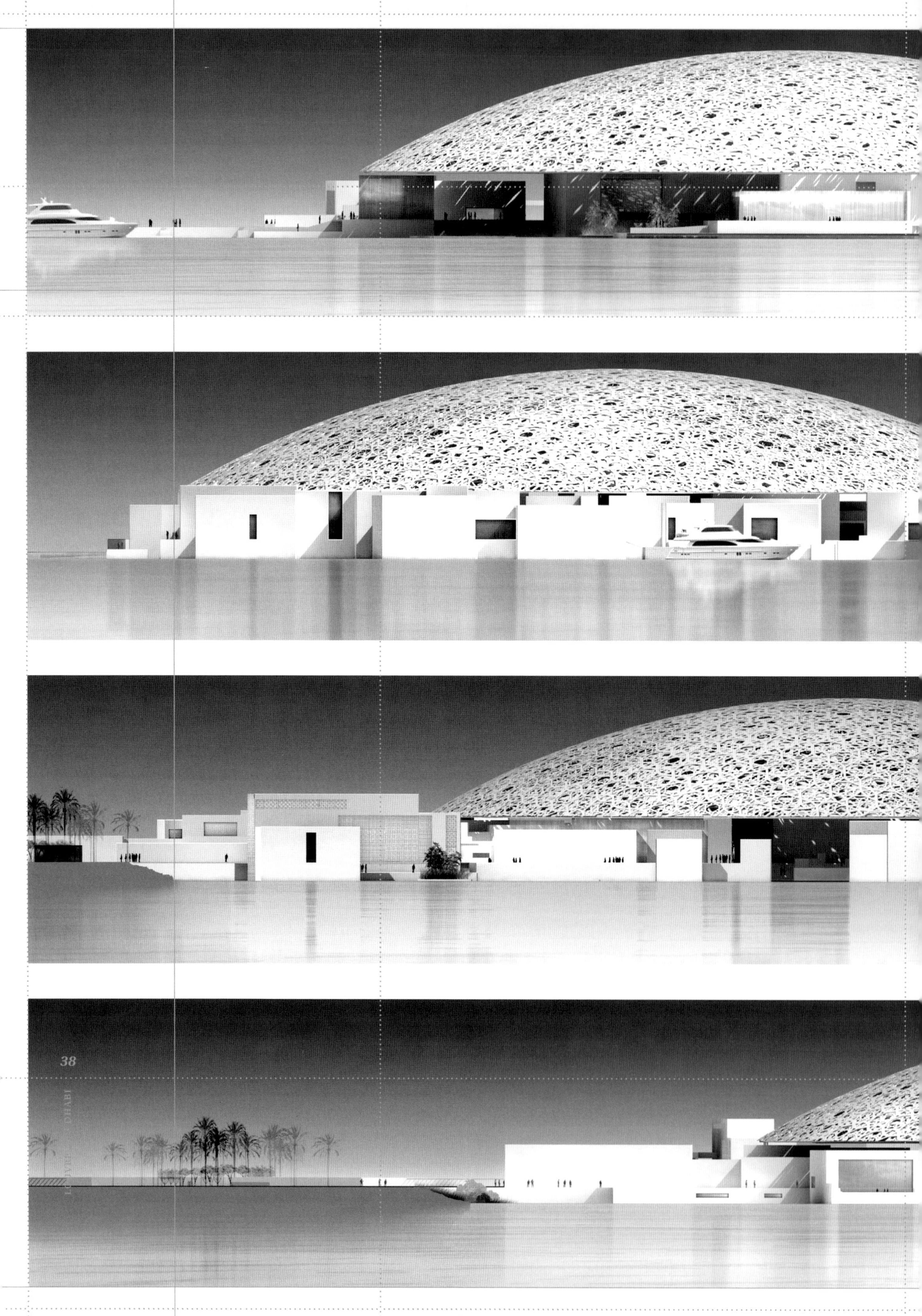

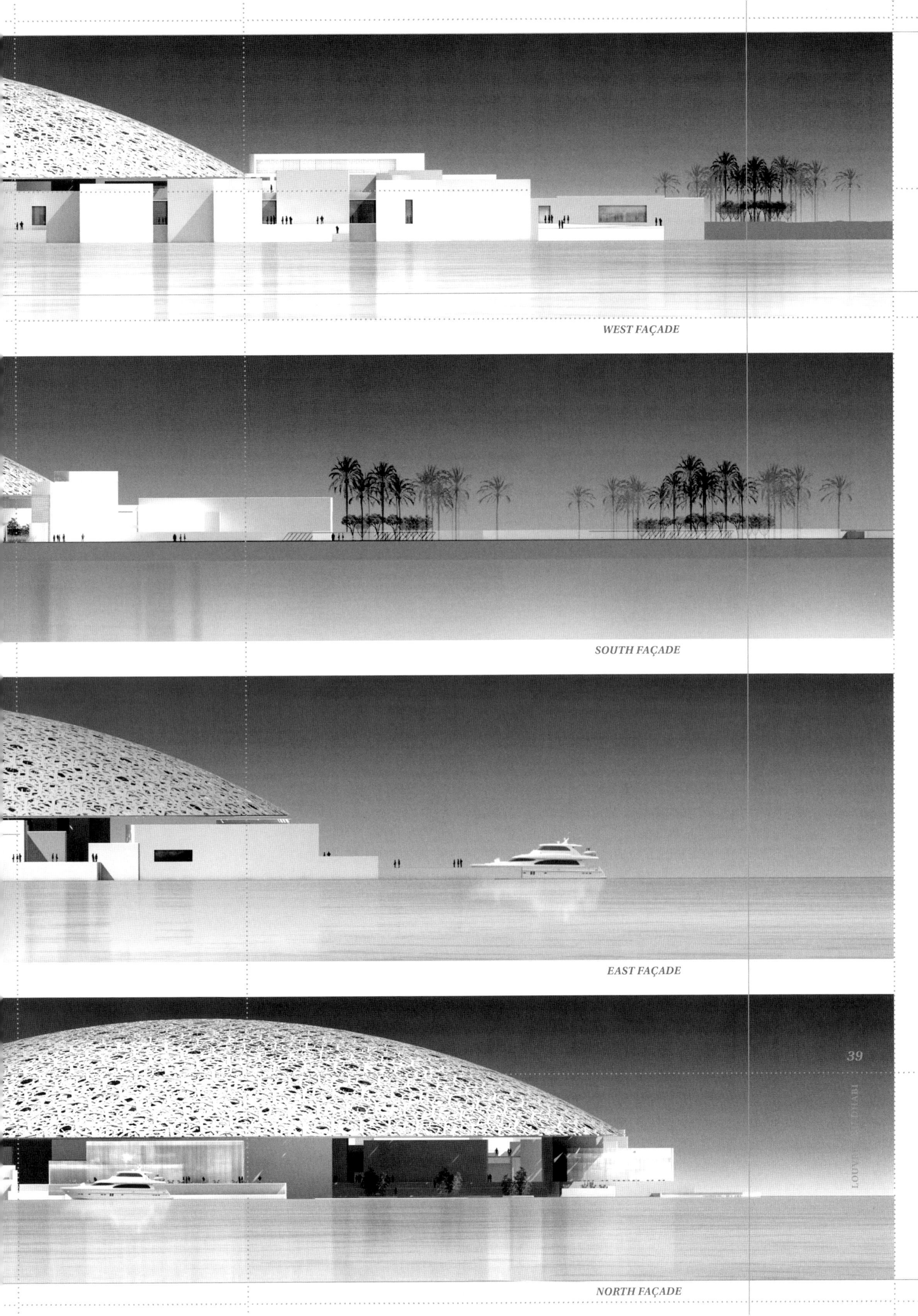

WEST FAÇADE

SOUTH FAÇADE

EAST FAÇADE

NORTH FAÇADE

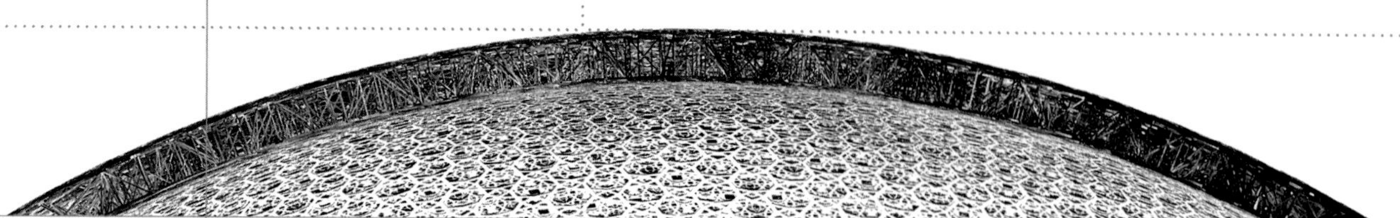

maintenance, were examined by means of simulations, analyses and exchanges of views between the different parties concerned.

This process involved a number of stages:

The first was a phase of geometrical definition and experimentation carried out by modelling using a virtual parametric 3D model, with which the architects and engineers carried out scale tests on the motifs and the rotation of the layers, as well as on the percentage of perforation and of correlation between the structure and the shells.

This virtual model was subjected to fine-tuning through the integration of data obtained from the testing of a 1:20 physical scale model, a wind-tunnel model, a 1:33 scale model and two scale 1 prototypes, one to test the behaviour of light and one to test the architectural and constructive details.

The 1:20 model for calibration of the geometric and microclimatic parameters, which made a "sensitive" approach to the project possible, was tested beneath an artificial sun in a laboratory of environmental engineering. The data obtained made it possible to calibrate certain geometrical parameters of the virtual 3D model of the dome. The direct light is controlled by the percentage of perforation of the dome, a value of 1–3% being deemed sufficient, and the indirect light by the albedo value of the finishing materials used beneath the dome (the floor, walls and roofs of the museum).

The 1:33 model for overall physical experimentation on-site was an authentic "project within the project", and its 5-metre dome required a specific construction study. The structure of the model was made of stainless steel and aluminium, and the shells were thin sheets of aluminium lightly pressed and cut by water jet. Various albedo values for the roofs and the floor beneath the dome were tested in the sun of Abu Dhabi, thus making it possible to establish values for the cladding to be chosen for the roofs of the buildings and certain paving stones of the medina beneath the dome.

The scale 1 model for partial physical experimentation on site provided the last data on temperature and light for final calibration of the virtual models. The distance of more than 5 metres between the layers of the upper and lower shells produces patches of light with changing contours, which move quickly enough to be perceived by the naked eye. Measurements taken with a laser thermometer show that they move too quickly to allow the surfaces to store the heat of the direct sunlight.

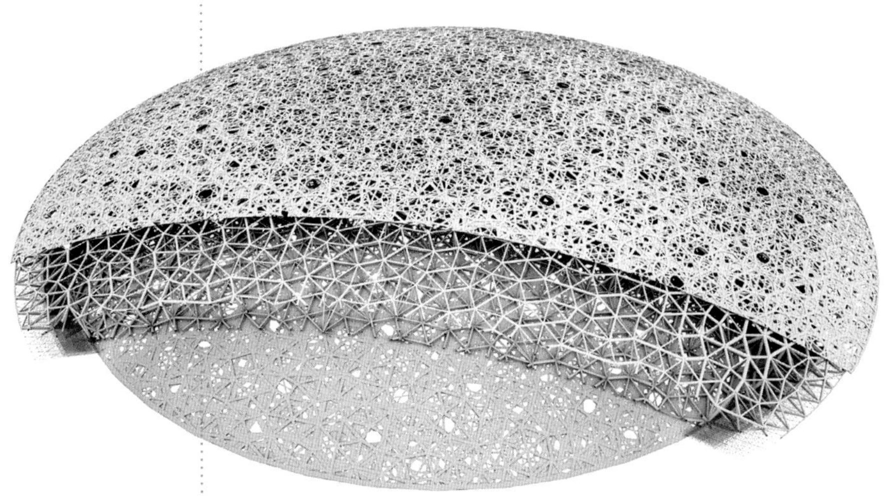

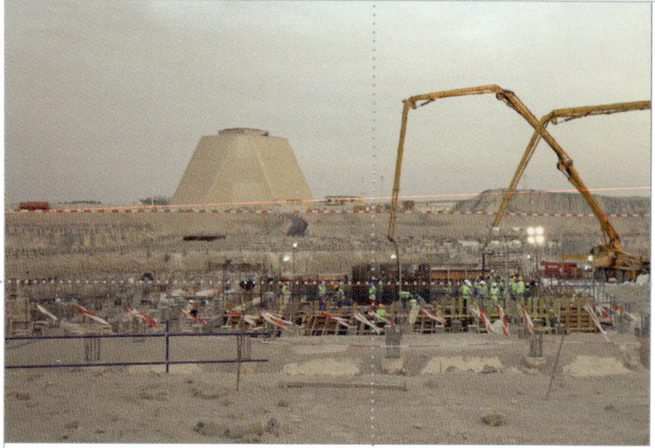

APRIL 2013
**CASTING OF THE FIRST CONCRETE PILLAR
TO SUPPORT THE DOME**

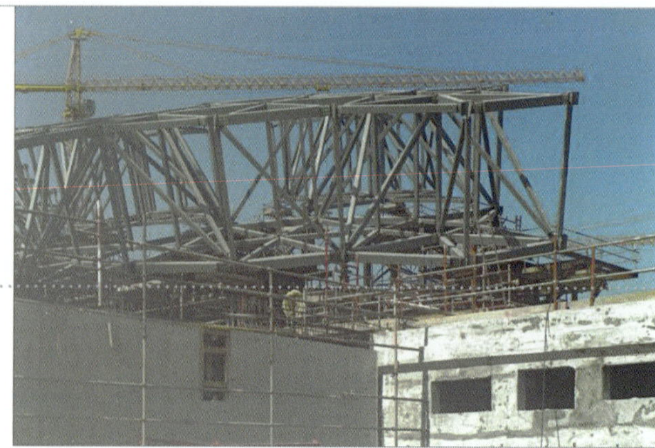

DECEMBER 2013
LIFTING OF THE FIRST OF THE SUPER-SIZED ELEMENTS

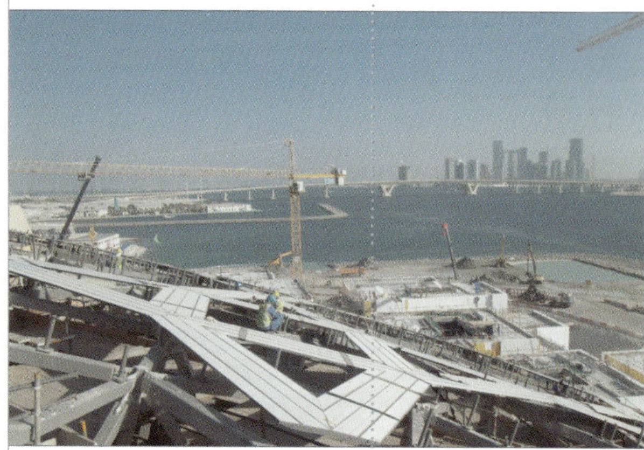

JULY 2014
INSTALLATION OF THE FIRST STAR OF THE DOME

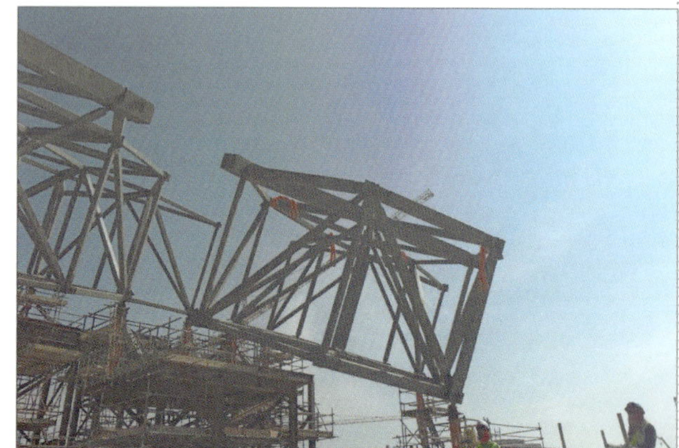

SEPTEMBER 2014
INSTALLATION OF THE LAST SUPER-SIZED ELEMENT

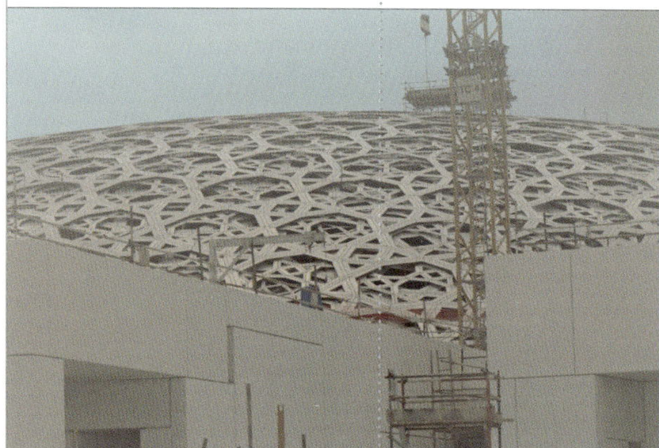

NOVEMBER–DECEMBER 2014
**LIFTING OF THE DOME, INSTALLATION OF THE DOME BEARINGS
AND POSITIONING OF THE DOME**

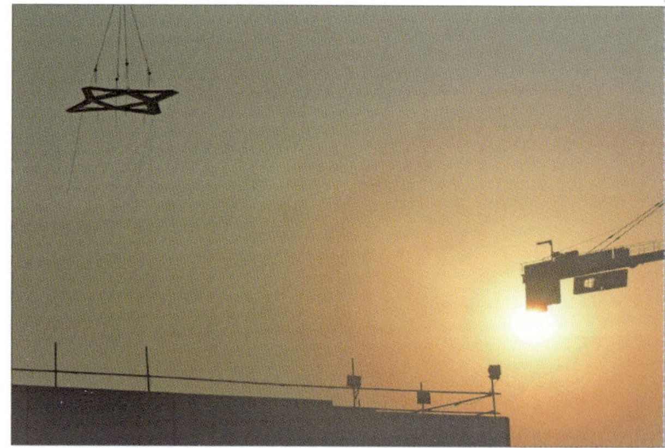

SEPTEMBER 2015
INSTALLATION OF THE LAST STAR ON THE EXTERIOR CLADDING

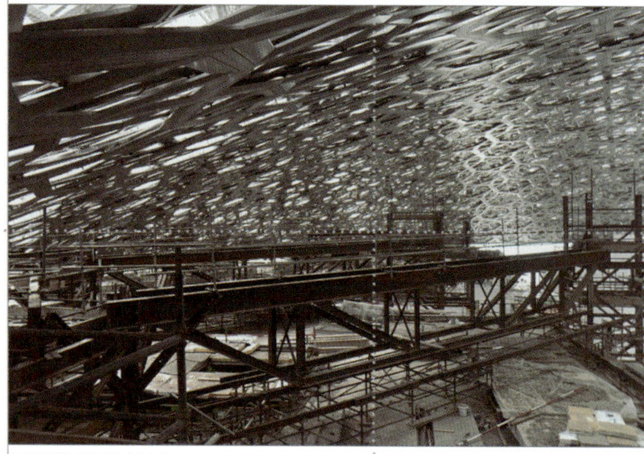

DECEMBER 2015
INSTALLATION OF THE LAST STAR ON THE INTERIOR CLADDING

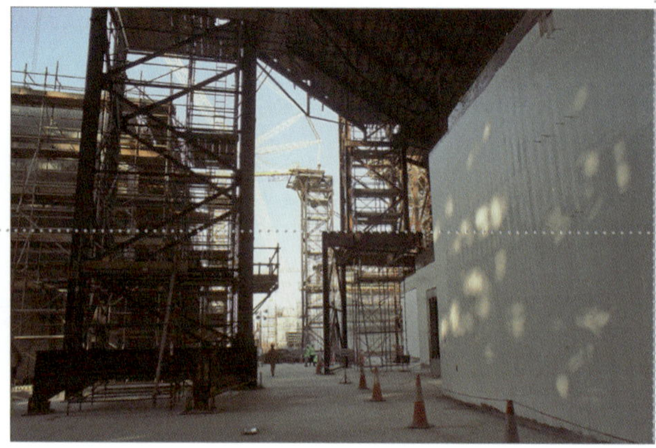

FEBRUARY 2016
DISMANTLING OF THE LAST TEMPORARY SCAFFOLDING TOWERS

The various components of the dome were manufactured in the neighbouring emirate of Dubai on the basis of digital files provided by the architects and engineers. The assembly was performed on site in Abu Dhabi in accordance with a long and complex process.

TOTAL WEIGHT OF THE DOME: 7500 tonnes

5200 tonnes of steel structure + 2000 tonnes for the 8 extruded layers

+ 300 tonnes of gratings, walkways, mesh and miscellaneous elements

DIAMETER OF THE SPHERE INTO WHICH THE DOME FITS: approximately 350 m

DIAMETER OF THE DOME: 180 m

CIRCUMFERENCE: 565 m

HEIGHT OF THE DOME ABOVE THE GROUND: 29 m

MAXIMUM HEIGHT OF THE DOME: 40 m above sea level, 36 m above ground-floor level

THICKNESS OF THE DOME: 7 m (layers + structure)

NUMBER OF SUPPORTING PILLARS: 4 at a distance of 110 m from one another

NUMBER OF LAYERS: 8 (4 above and 4 below)

DISTANCE BETWEN THE LAYERS: 80 mm

STRUCTURAL ELEMENTS: 85 super-sized elements, 3600 connecting elements

MATERIALS: structure of hollow structural steel + polyurethane paint; layers of the shell in extruded aluminium + powder coating; outer surfaces of the 4 upper layers in sheets of stainless steel 0.8 mm in thickness

COMPOSITION OF THE LAYERS: 158,250 elements

OVERALL PERCENTAGE OF PERFORATION OF THE DOME: 1.8%

THERMAL PERFORMANCE

Reduction in temperature in relation to exposure to sunlight: 42%

Saving on energy for air-conditioning of the buildings: 27.2%

Saving on water: 27%

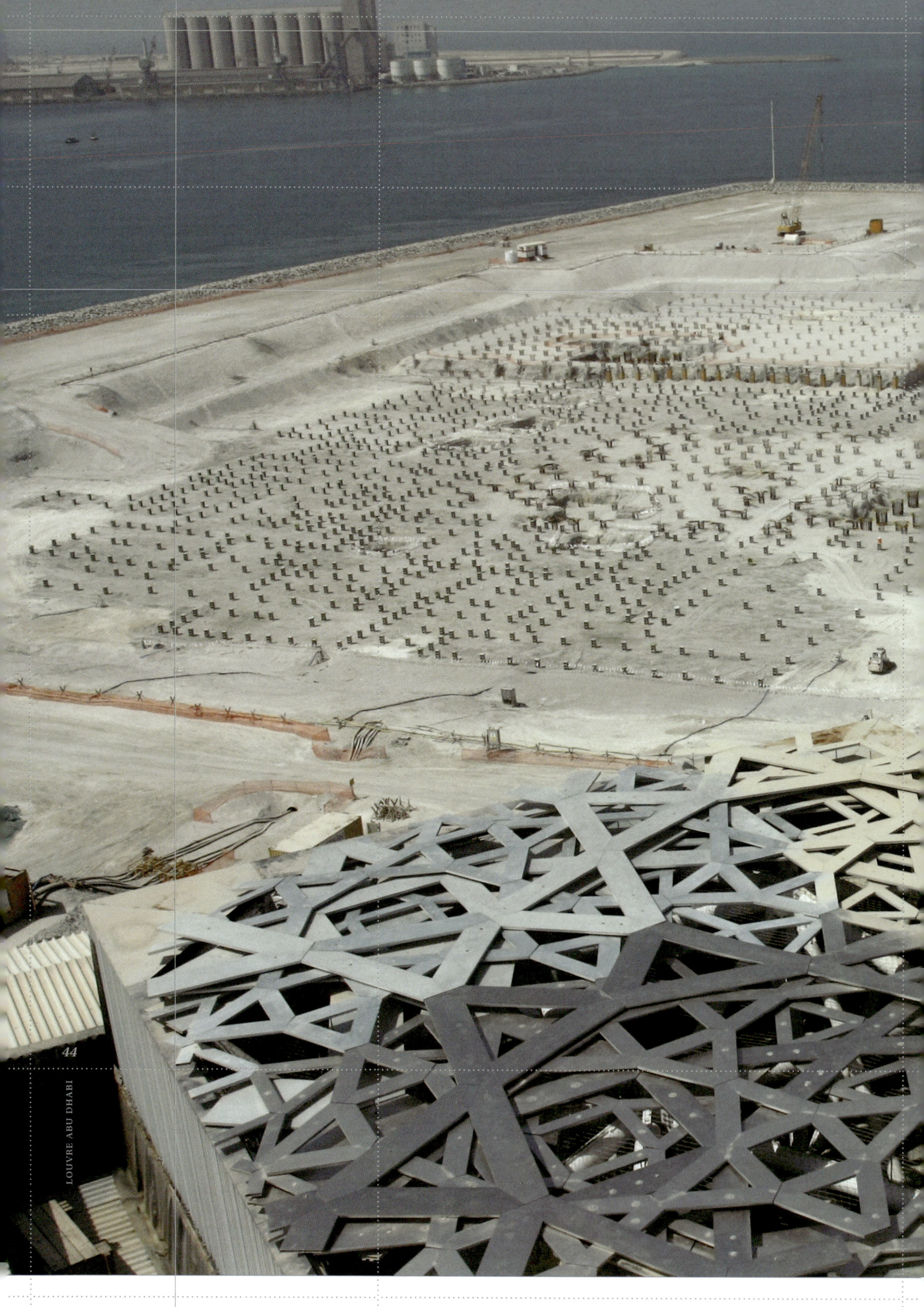

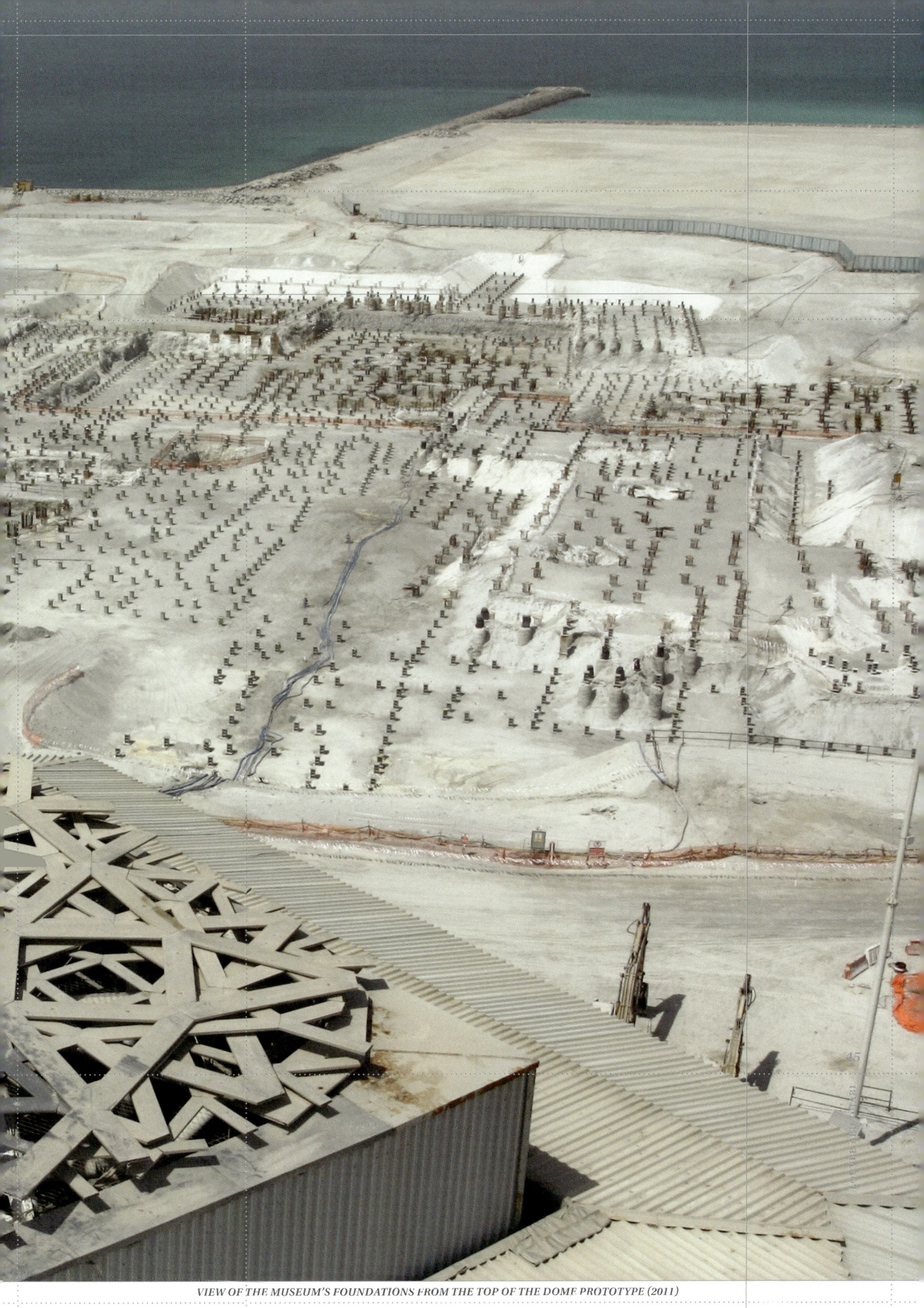

VIEW OF THE MUSEUM'S FOUNDATIONS FROM THE TOP OF THE DOME PROTOTYPE (2011)

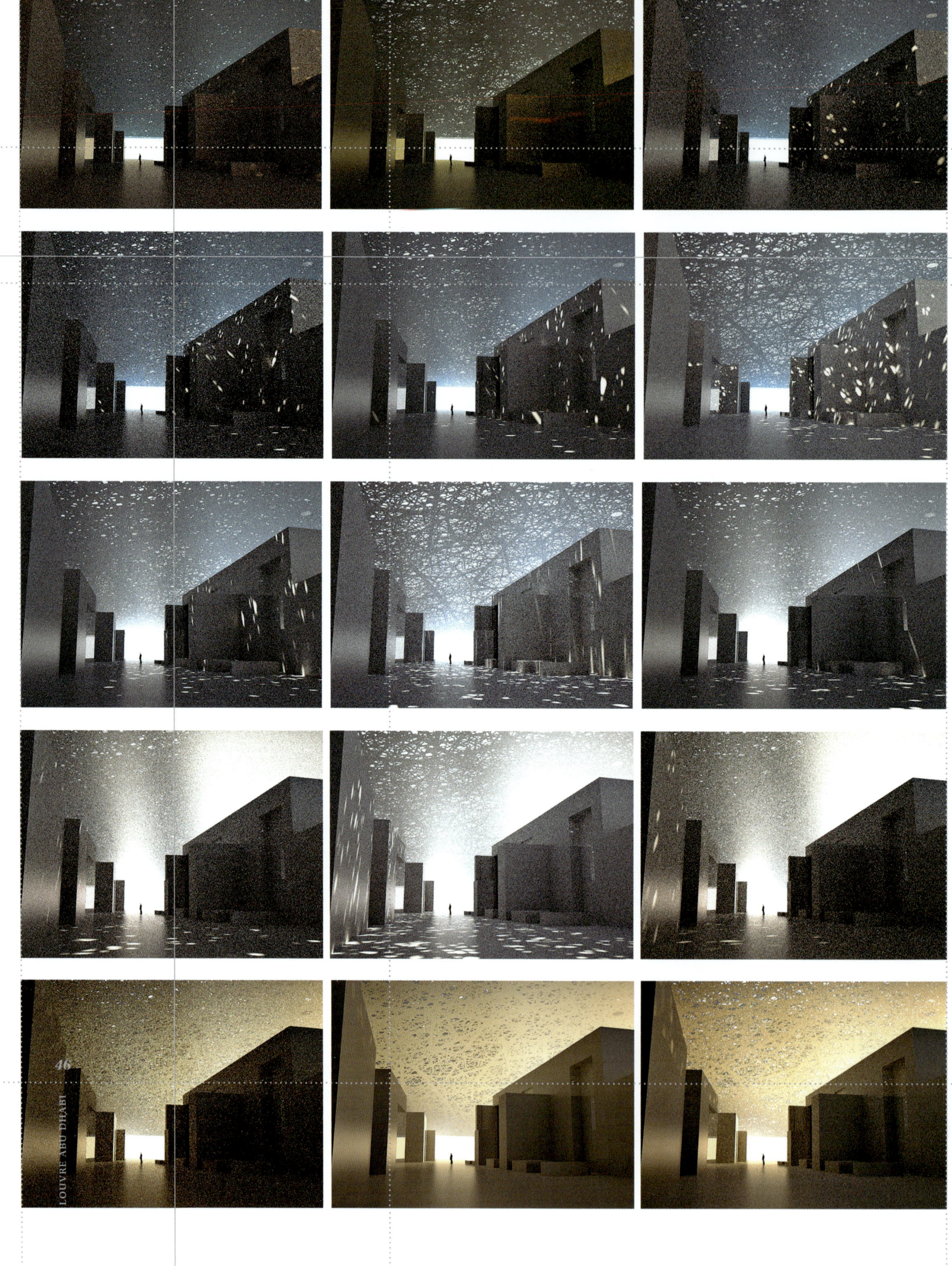

46
LOUVRE ABU DHABI

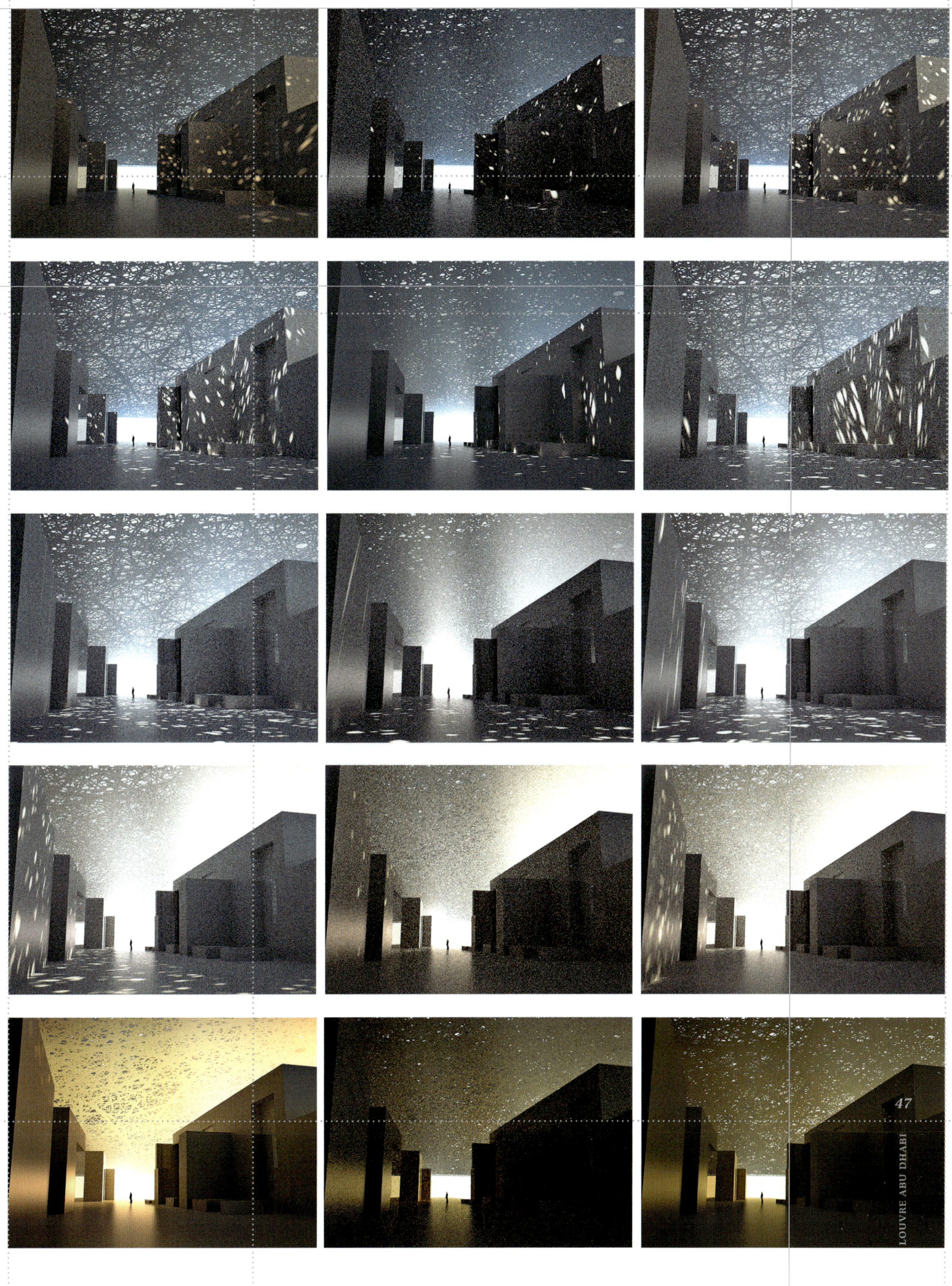

47
LOUVRE ABU DHABI

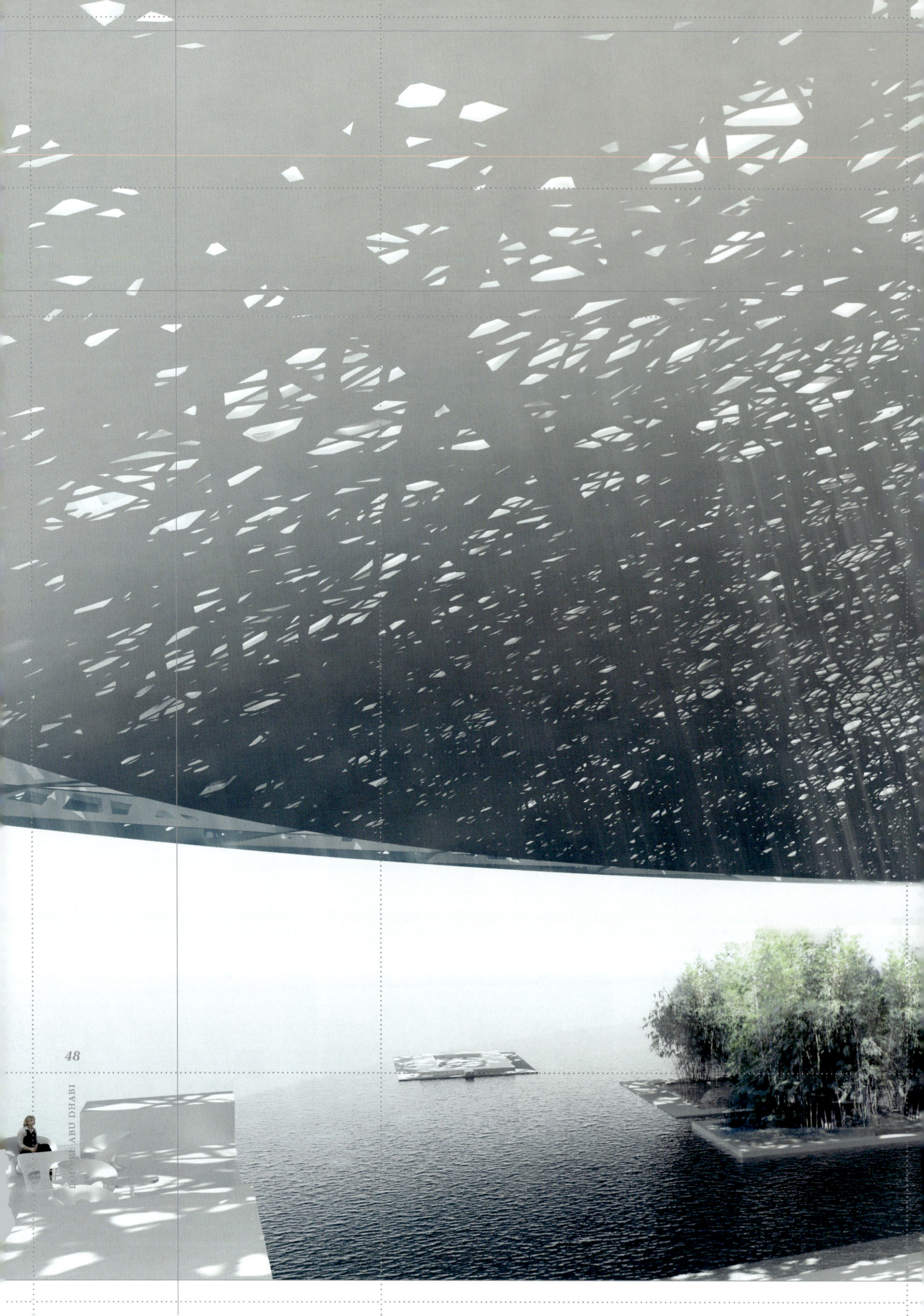

48
LOUVRE ABU DHABI

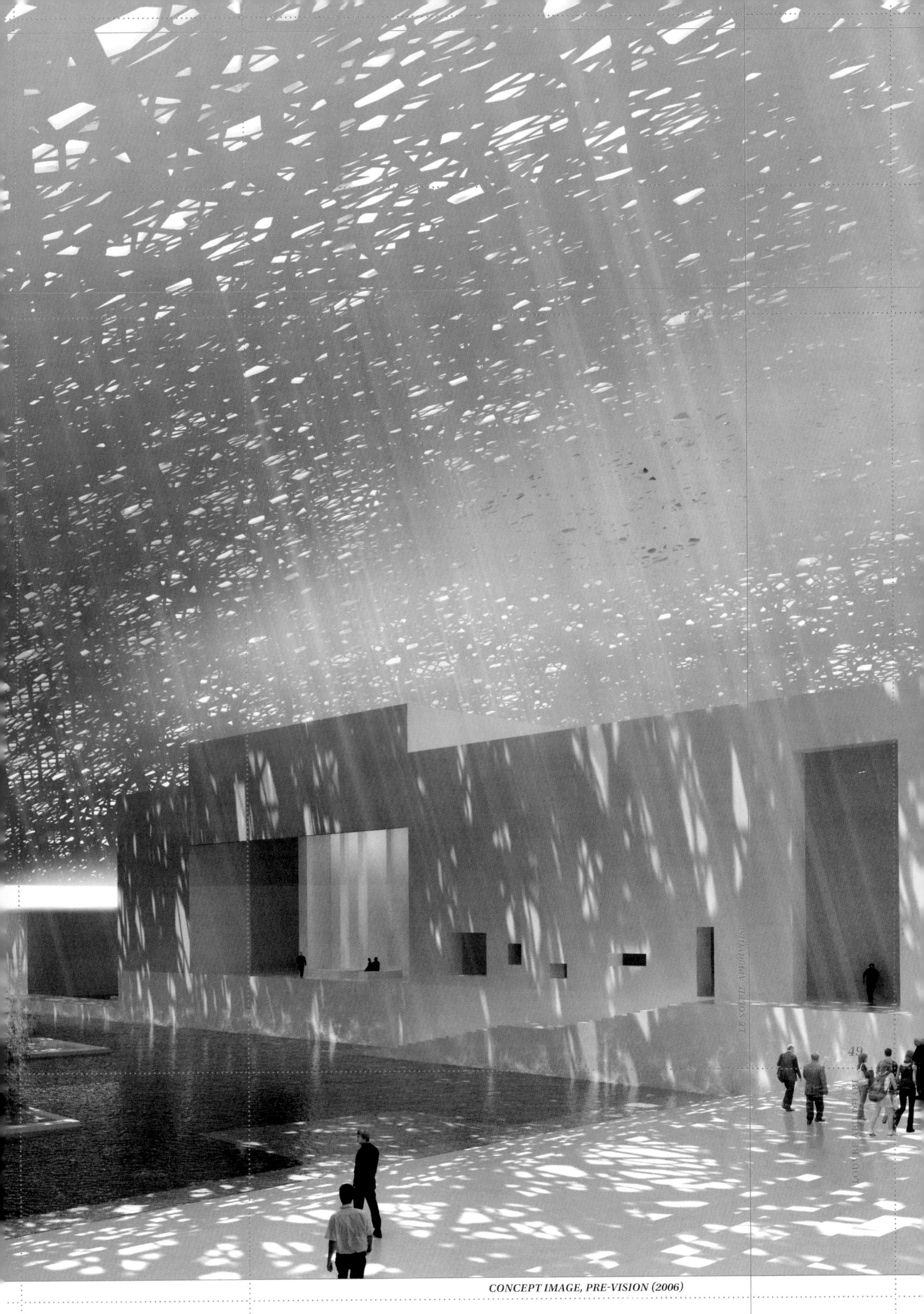

CONCEPT IMAGE, PRE-VISION (2006)

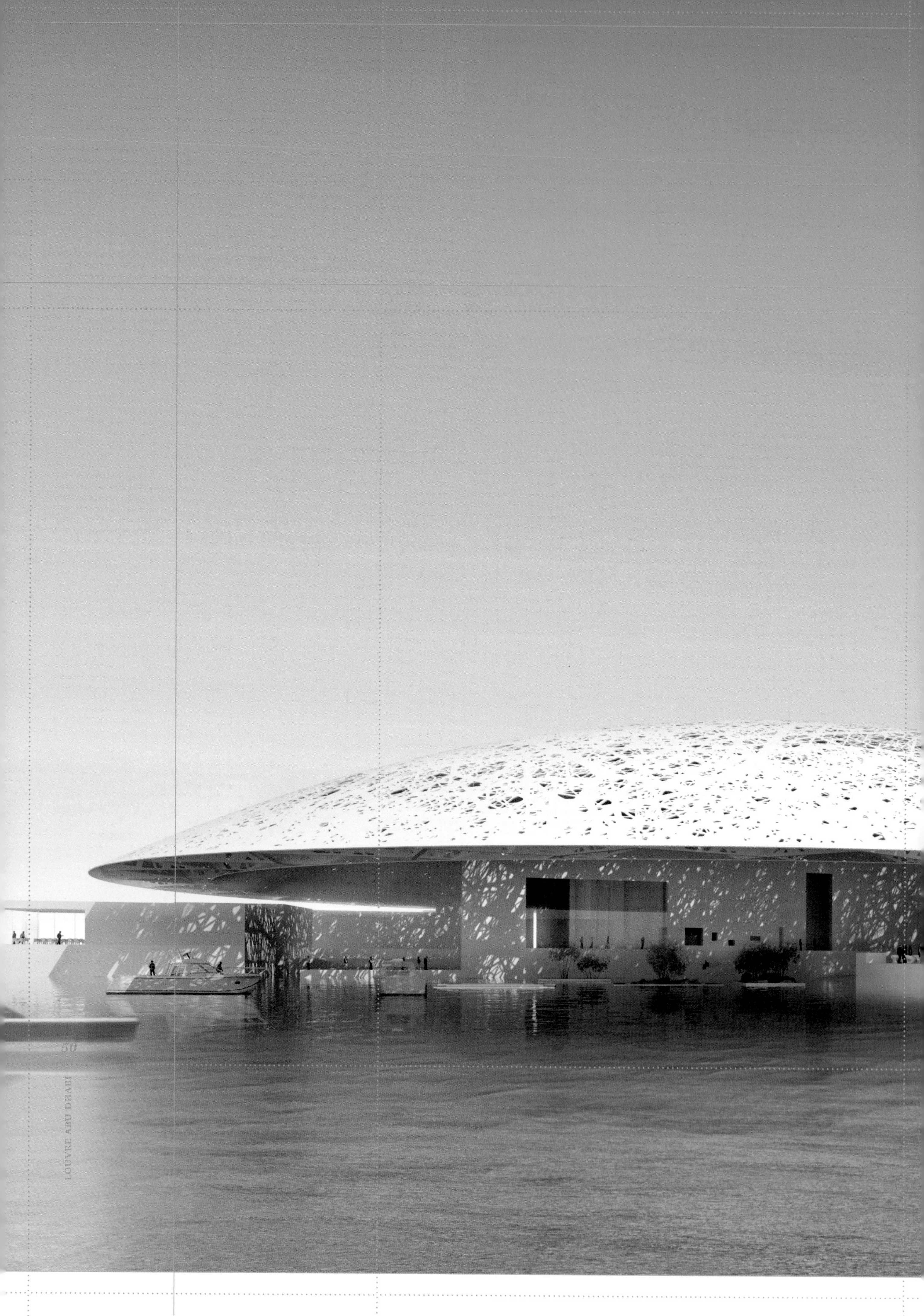

LOUVRE ABU DHABI

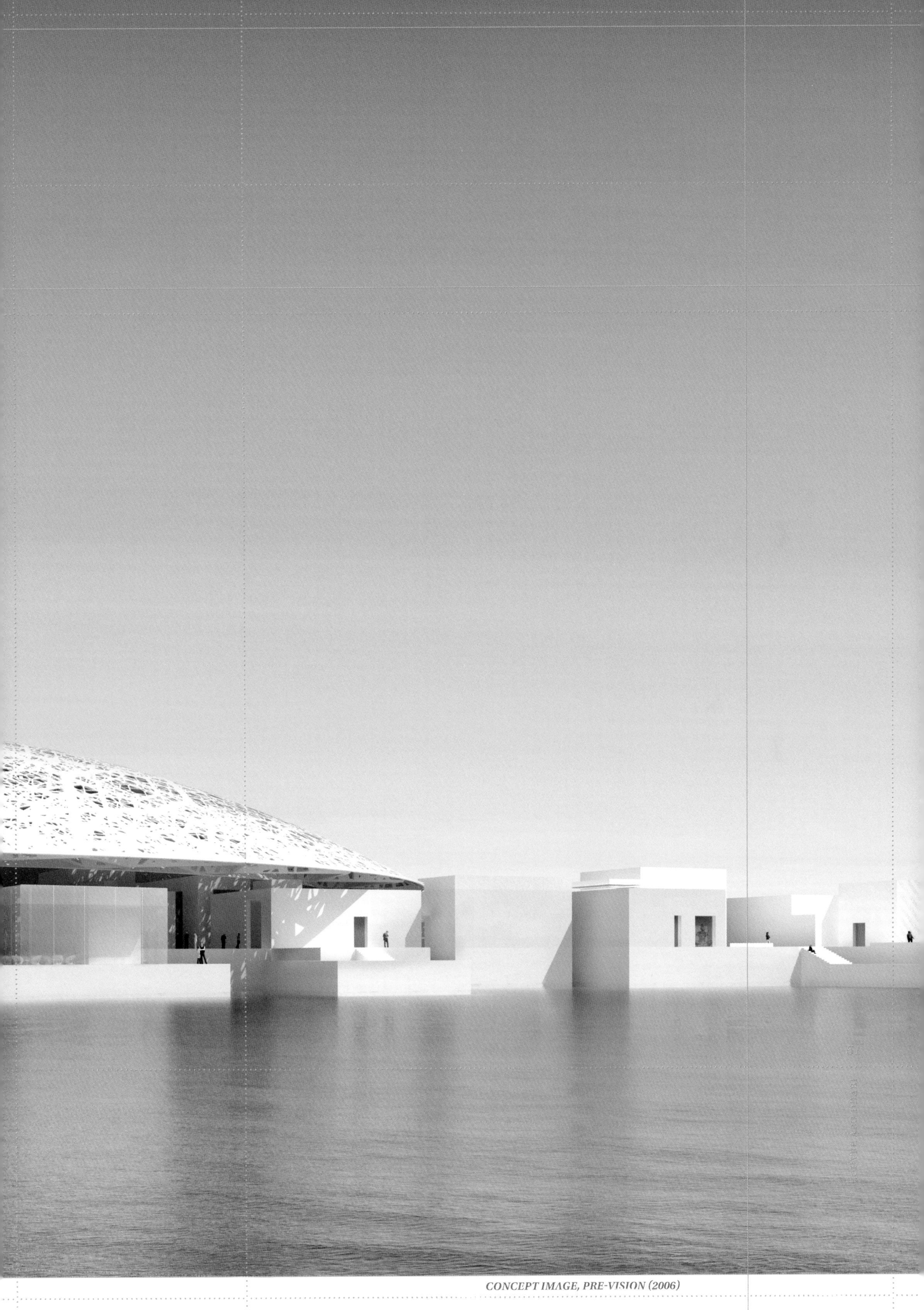

CONCEPT IMAGE, PRE-VISION (2006)

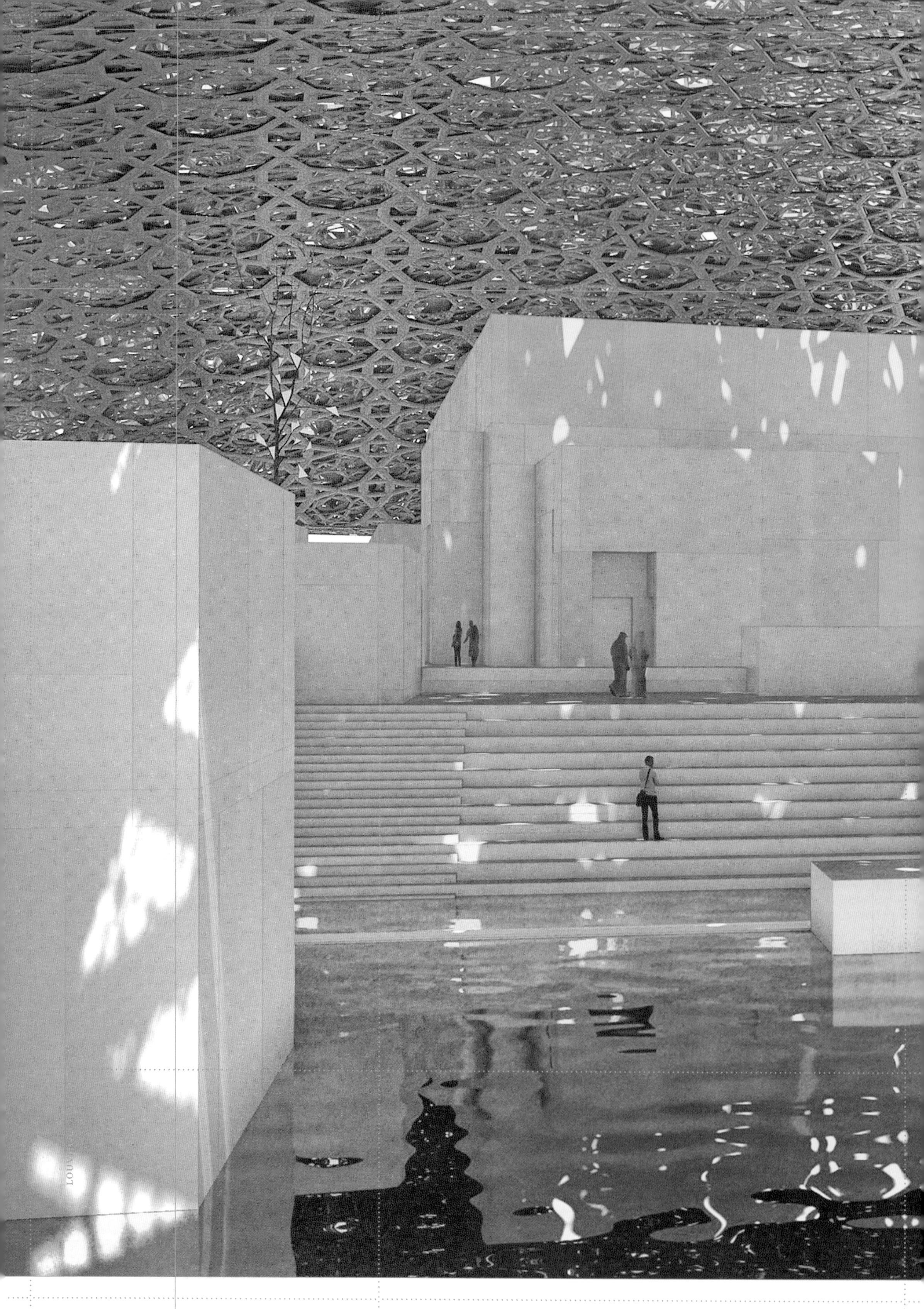

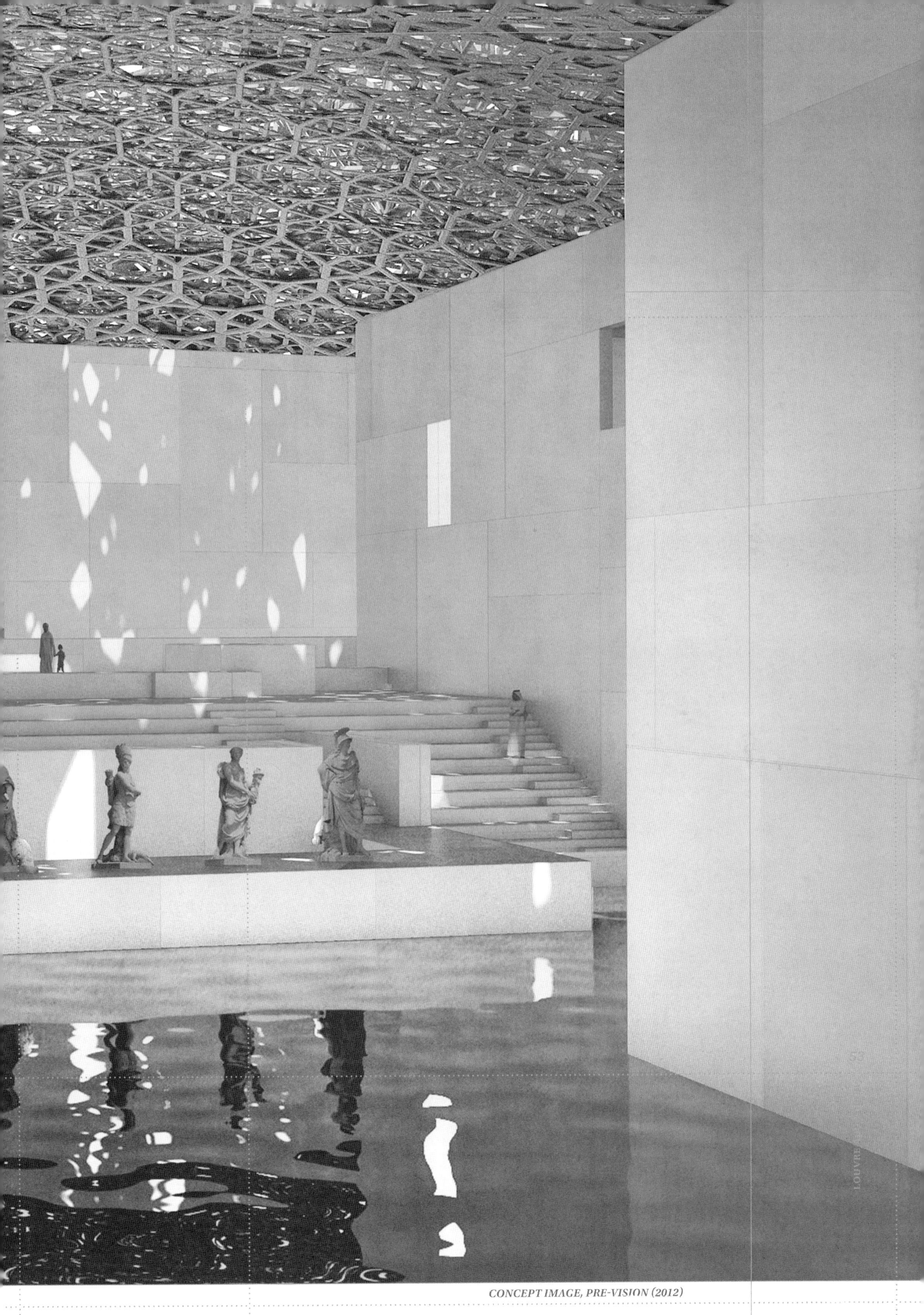

CONCEPT IMAGE, PRE-VISION (2012)

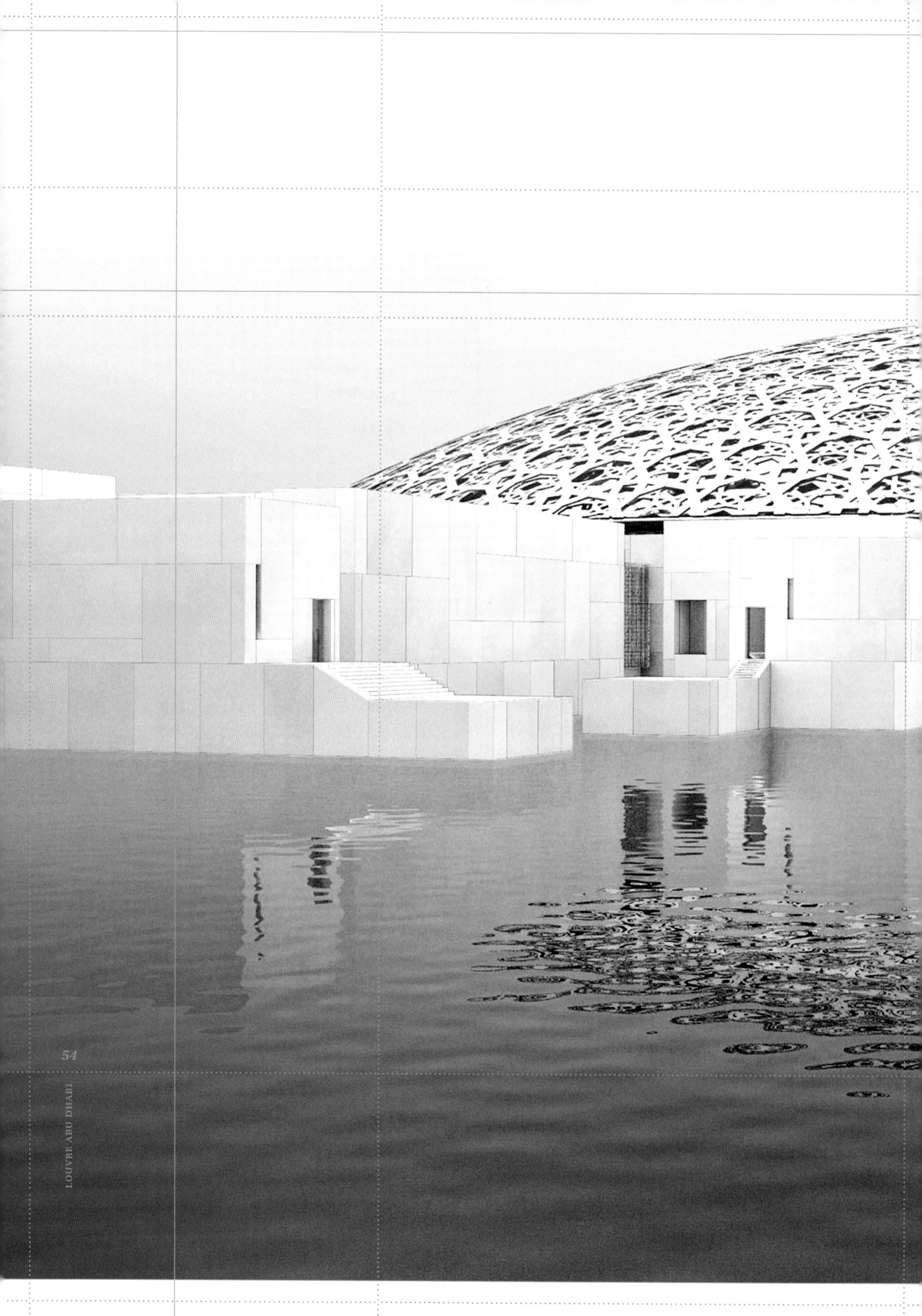

LOUVRE ABU DHABI

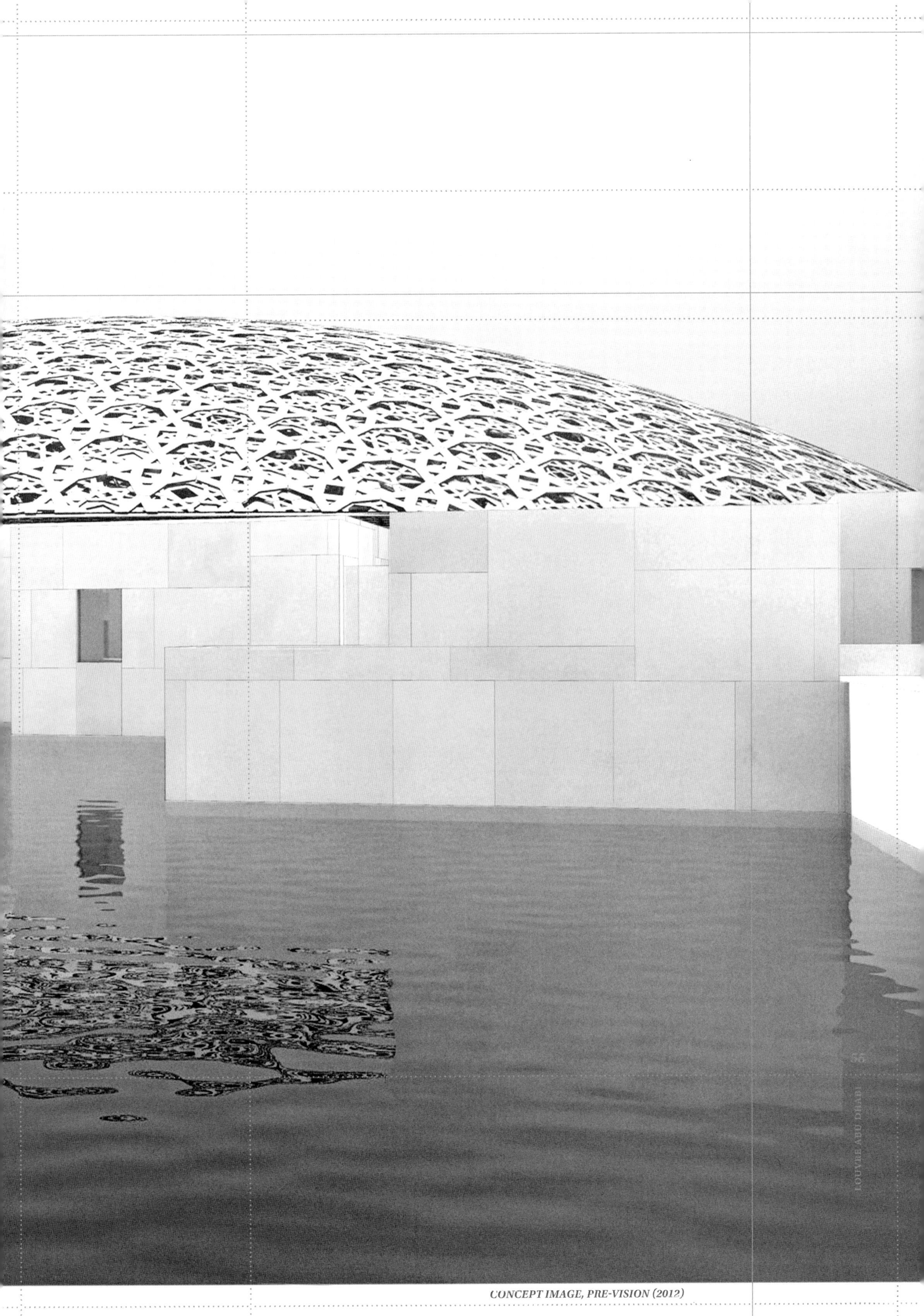

CONCEPT IMAGE, PRE-VISION (2012)

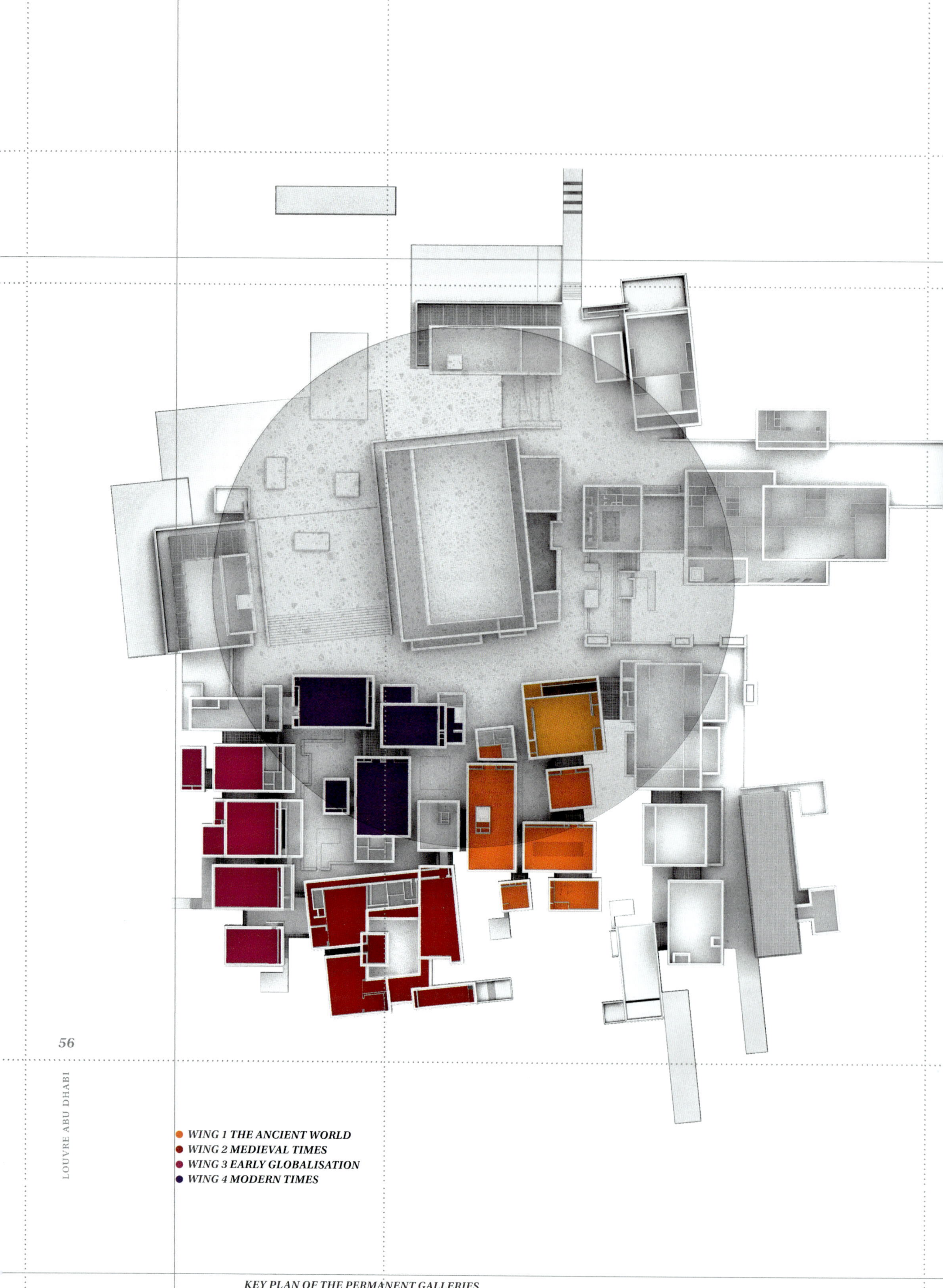

LOUVRE ABU DHABI

KEY PLAN OF THE PERMANENT GALLERIES

Since his experiences and projects in the theatrical field at the dawn of his career, Jean Nouvel has made it a rule to place the viewer in optimal conditions of sensitivity and receptiveness. The approach and entrance to a place of culture gain from being accompanied by a certain ceremony capable of arousing a general feeling or indeed a quiver of anticipation through an atmosphere of serene dignity and radiant hospitality.

Before arriving at the doors of the museum, the visitor proceeds along a pathway sheltered by a canopy and a masharabiya echoed in the façade of the administration building opposite. After passing through the security gates, today a prerequisite for any public building, the usual services in a museum entrance follow one another: the information desk, ticket office, cloakroom, audio headsets and admittance in a setting of linear counters and storage spaces in black and white that is sober without being intimidating.

"The intention here is to dissimulate – thanks to the colour black – any technical and logistical equipment so that only the main rhythms created by the lines of composition are apparent, highlighted by noble white materials (Corian or ultra-high performance concrete, depending on the situation; a colour in the same tones as the walls). As technical equipment usually comes in dark colours, it may be updated without causing any aesthetic disruption. This approach will also be implemented in the front halls and behind the white information desks: the hostesses' area, its storage, surfaces and equipment melt into a symphony of glossy, satin and matt blacks." **JEAN NOUVEL**

The linear pathway leading from the museum entrance to the point of access to the exhibition galleries finds its equivalent on the lower level for groups of visitors. This elongated space also houses complementary facilities such as the documentation centre, activity spaces and two prayer rooms. It leads to the forum, an orientation crossroads, and then to the galleries or towards the plaza, another meeting place and public area.

GRAPHIC DESIGN OF THE FLOOR OF THE GRAND VESTIBULE

THE GRAND VESTIBULE

Antechamber to the galleries of the museum's permanent collections, the Grand Vestibule occupies a key position in keeping with its function of introducing the concept of universality, the raison d'être of the Louvre Abu Dhabi, a subtle task intended only to arouse the visitors' curiosity at this stage. The vestibule is certainly not a "summary" of the museum and clearly refuses to reveal its secrets in advance.

Beneath a huge glass skylight that offers glimpses of the tracery of the dome, a vast and light-filled gallery presents a series of small puzzles seemingly suspended in mid-air inside tall display cases: modest arrays of tools, objects, artefacts and works made by human hands in faraway places and distant eras. Each small group presents disconcerting similarities between its members in their approach to eternal themes like motherhood, death, water, writing, aesthetics, prayer or faith, the sacred and the horse, everything that has brought human beings together at one time or another in their history and forged their customs, habits, mores and traditions. However, no detailed explanations of these similarities are yet offered.

The meandering line of the large design on the floor recalls an ancient nautical chart of the coast of the United Arab Emirates. The exotic names of the cities and countries bordering it are, however, those of the different places of origin of the objects in the museum's collection. This presentation is a way to prepare visitors for exploration and discovery, and to spark their curiosity to find out more.

MAZE

Beneath its apparently random configuration, the series of buildings that house the permanent collection forms a slightly chaotic loop, sometimes linear and sometimes zigzagging, yet it is not by chance that the route leads in a clockwise direction.

The permanent exhibitions are laid out in four wings corresponding to four great eras in human history.

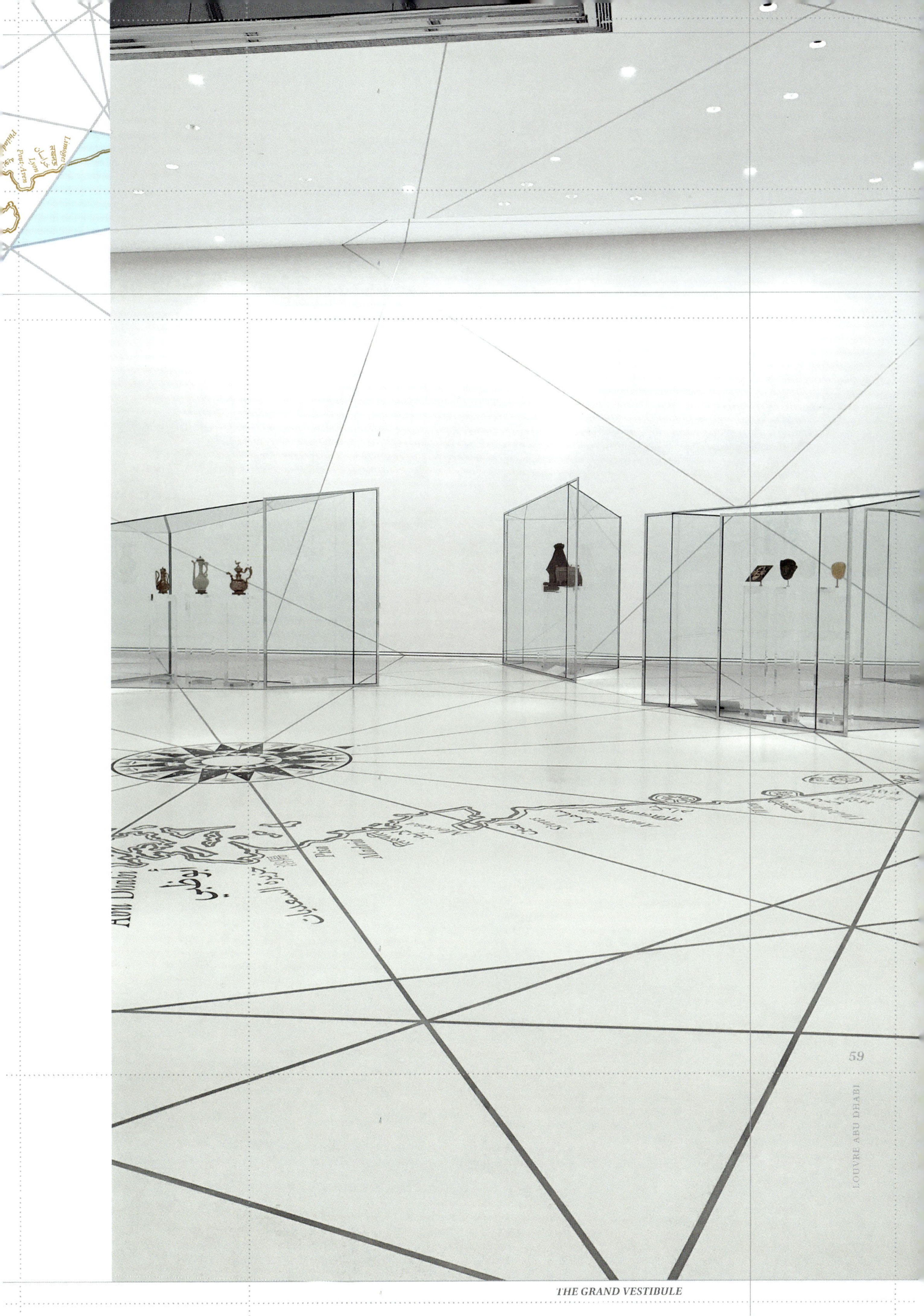

THE GRAND VESTIBULE

The 12 thematic stages are divided into a total of 23 galleries that present the story of humanity's long progress. This small labyrinth takes a free, winding, naturally guided course through history and the world. It is interspersed with short, glazed passages that connect the galleries and offer visitors interludes with views of the landscape, a square or an expanse of water. They express the architect's constant concern to convey the sense of the here-and-now, to remind visitors that they are in this museum palace on the shores of the Gulf at a certain hour of the day. They also offer visitors the opportunity to rest and refresh the eye in preparation for the next stage of the visit.

VESTIBULES

Three vestibules mark the transition between the four wings of the permanent exhibitions. They offer the opportunity for a pause but also to deepen our understanding of what has just been seen in the galleries already visited rather than to prepare us for the next wing. Interactive desks invite visitors to discover various key works of the collection as well as the relationships between the works. The halls are furnished with seats and sofas specially designed for the museum by Jean Nouvel and their comfort is augmented by a leather carpet. Equipped with consoles and sophisticated information devices, they fully perform their role as places for rest and study during the visit to the museum.

THE PERMANENT EXHIBITION GALLERIES

Despite their apparent unity, which already contradicts the suggestion of cyclopean structural elements proportional to each of them, the buildings on the platform all differ in size. For example, among the 23 permanent exhibition galleries,

GALLERY 4: measures 10.7 X 10.7 X 7 m, GALLERY 15: 15.7 X 8.7 X 8 m,

GRAND VESTIBULE: 26.82 X 26.82 X 10 m,

GALLERY 5: 37.7 X 17.2 X 9 m, and GALLERY 19: 28.6 X 18.7 X 7.7 m.

The spaces they contain differ not only in size and shape (square, rectangular or trapezoidal, height of ceiling) but also in terms of material. The floors, ceilings and walls differ and are

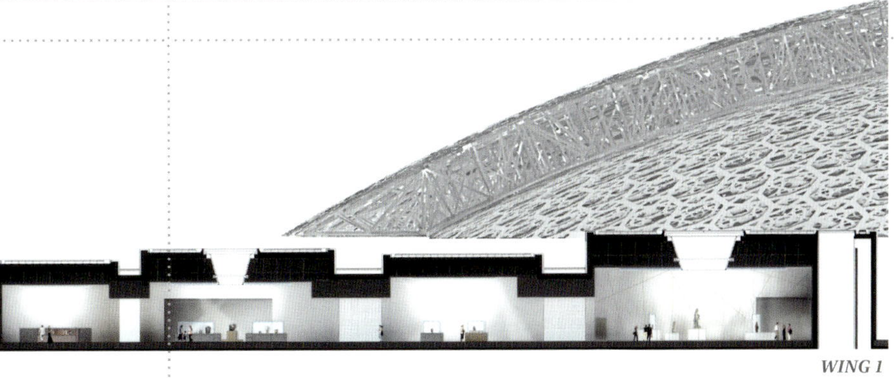

WING 1

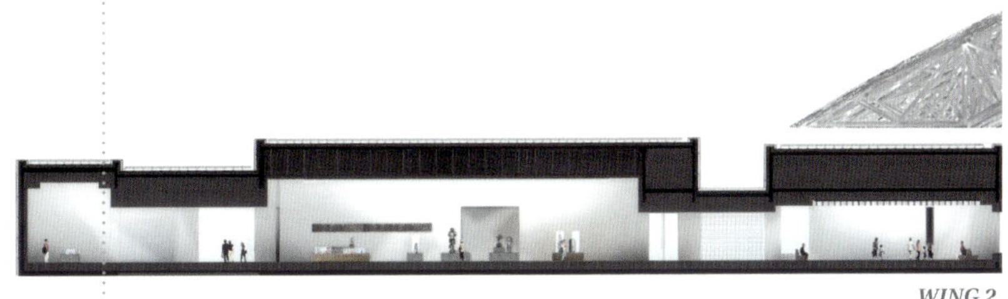

WING 2

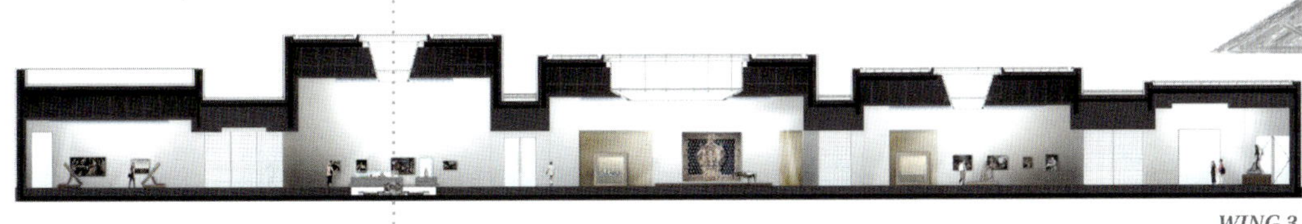

WING 3

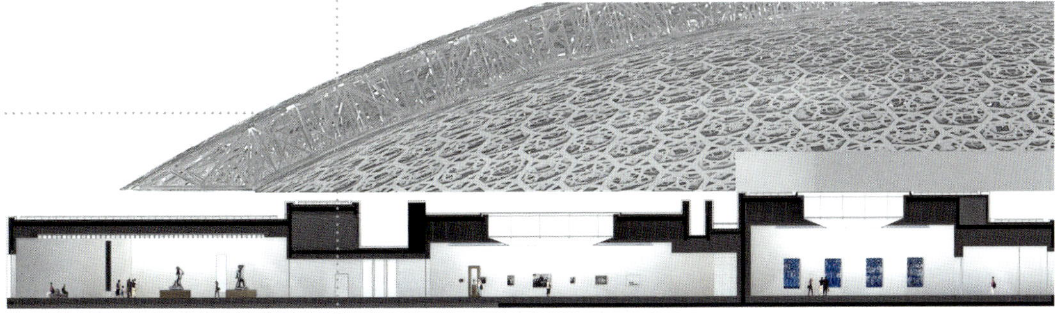

WING 4

combined so that each gallery presents an individual appearance, atmosphere and character that even the least sensitive cannot but perceive.

"The floors, walls and ceiling surfaces of the museum areas are directly linked to the architectural expression of the Louvre Abu Dhabi and must participate in the creation of the character of the building, and reinforce the palatial dimensions of this particular place. This objective should be achieved by responding comprehensively to the programmatic demands directly associated with the three key elements of the museographical systems. The required flexibility remains the primary constraint and should be set out in such a way as to camouflage the different operational systems, access panels, electrical cabling for flooring systems, the ventilation in the walls and the ceilings, as well as the complexity of the lighting in the ceilings above. We are in search of the very essence of these three elements (floors, walls, ceilings). We propose that they be calm, noble and in direct relation with the colours and materials expressed outside and underneath the dome." **JEAN NOUVEL**

THE FLOORS are paved with stone in large modules. The primary module of 140 × 23.3 cm is set in a thin frame of bronze. In the case of connections, the basic module gives way to a more complex form of 16 stone modules inside the same bronze frame. It is thus possible to install an electrical connection at any point in the set of floors by creating a sophisticated layout that offers no indication whatsoever of the floor's technical aspects.

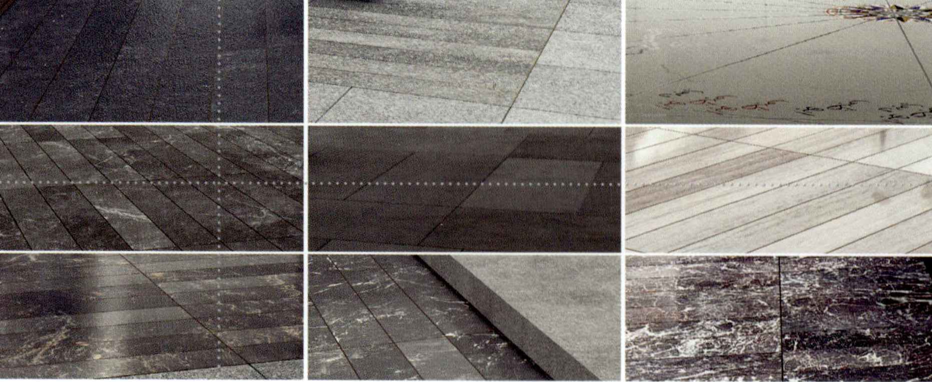

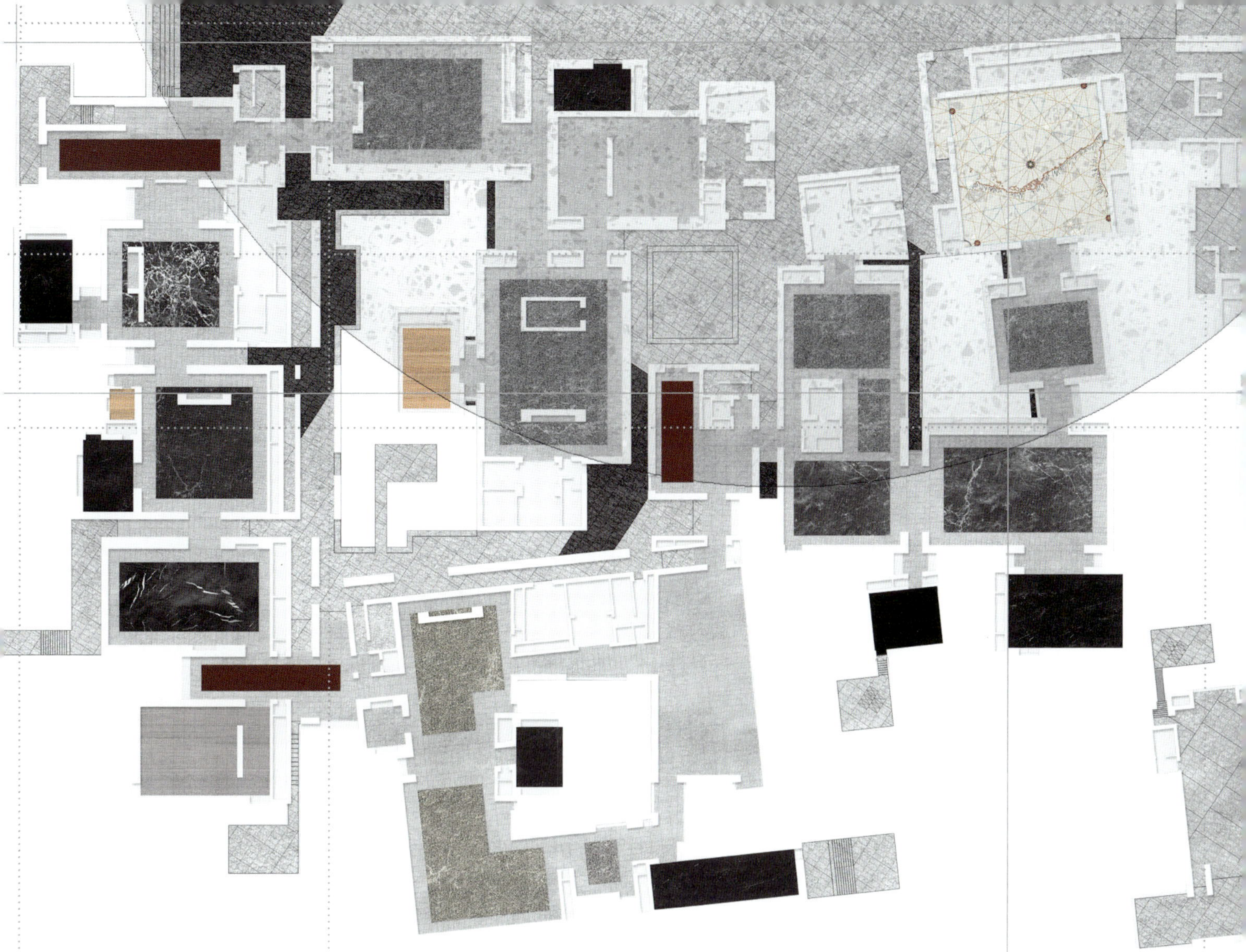

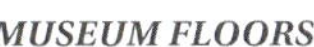

MUSEUM FLOORS
STONE CARPETS

 BLACK OMANI

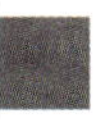 DARK OMANI

DARK VEINED OMANI

 BAOLITE

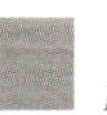 MARQUINA

 BLACK SAINT LAURENT

 RED LEVANTO

MUSEUM PERIPHERY

 BLEU DU HAINAUT

OTHER FINISHES

RESIN AND METAL
INSERTS IN THE STONE

 EBONY

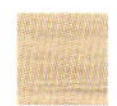 LIGHT OAK

 LEATHER

GLASS CEILINGS, CONCEPT IMAGE

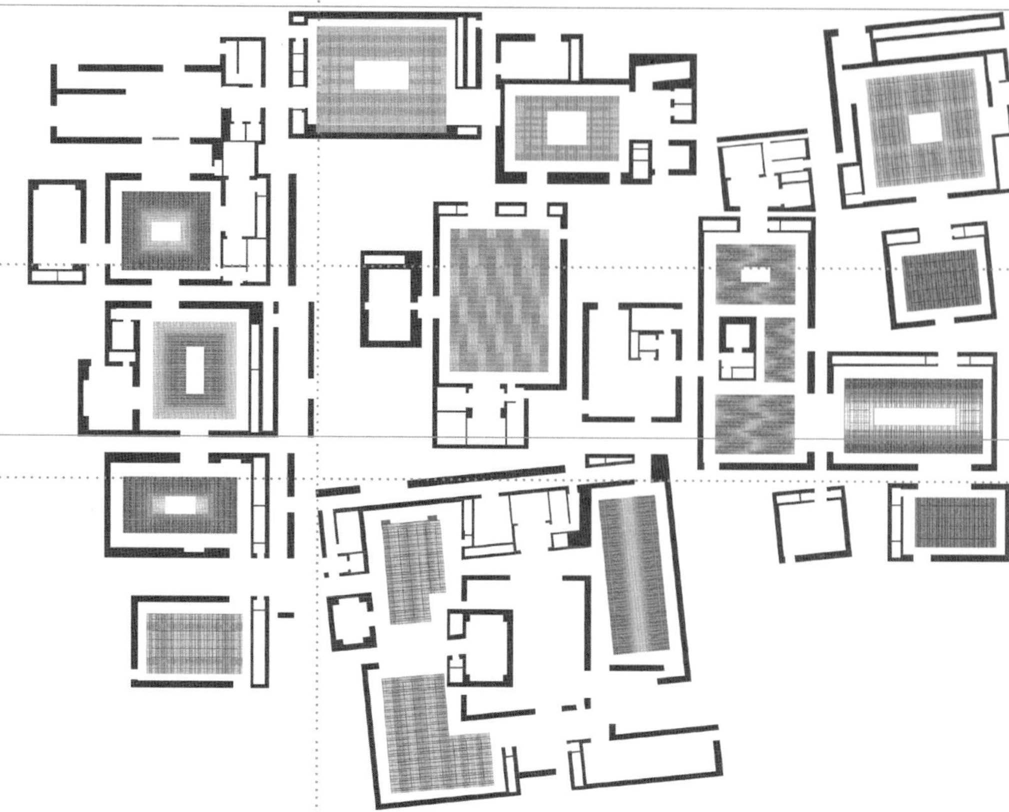

CEILINGS are often the hallmark of an institution. Here they are the place from which overhead light arrives but they also house the system that illuminates the works. In about half of the large galleries, a central panel of clear and mirror glass frames the dome. Around this, a ceiling of thick, white acid-etched glass is composed in various patterns and textures adapted to the museum's lighting system fully incorporated within it. The nature of the lighting, specially adapted to each gallery, is what determines the layout of matte and opaque ceiling surfaces. These are delicately translucent in varying degrees in relation to the intensity of the light, extending all the way to exceptional transparencies (e.g., for spotlights). When there is no glass panel, the ceiling covers the whole of the central part of each gallery. Additionally, one-third of each wall that forms the perimeter of the galleries is made of stucco.

Different kinds of glass were used for the ceilings, generally superimposed in twos at 90 degrees to form a grid, the element famously identified by the art historian and critic Rosalind Krauss as the fundamental motif of modernism, paradoxically constituting an absolute constraint while open to infinite variation at the same time.

THE WALLS are essentially of stucco (hard and perfectly planimetric plaster). Two narrow lines of 15 mm in width define a shock-resistant skirting board of stone, identical to the floor, to ensure perfect solidity and facilitate maintenance. Where required, the same type of wall can be thickened to create useful spaces for museum purposes. The walls thus clearly express their function as supports for hanging art. If other volumes exist in the space, they form part of the museographical displays.

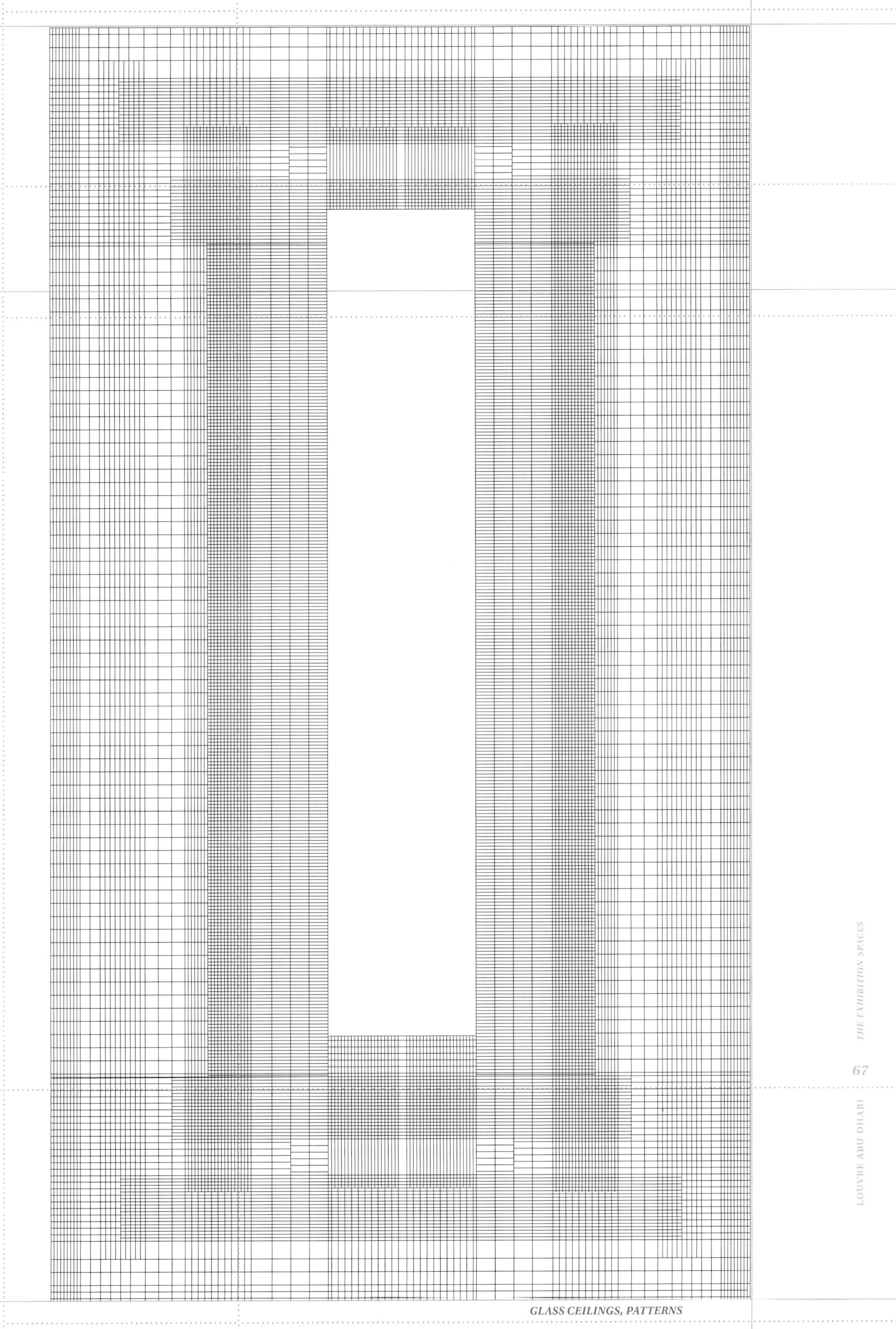

GLASS CEILINGS, PATTERNS

BRONZE

An age-old alloy, probably one of the first indications of human ingenuity, bronze has been recognised for centuries as a noble metal of ancient lineage.

Its use in the Louvre Abu Dhabi is particularly concentrated in the galleries addressing themes of a certain gravity connected with metaphysics (existence and death), faith and violence. Its physicality offers a contrast with lightweight forms in places where the lighting must be less intense so as to preserve works of greater fragility. Visitors will note its use to frame the paving modules, the edges of certain display cases and the podiums of sculptures and artefacts. Logically, it is used in the gallery that houses the dialogue between Rodin and Antiquity.

THE BREATH OF SACREDNESS

Wing 2 of the Louvre Abu Dhabi addresses the key moment in the history of mankind and human cultures when the concepts of faith and transcendence emerged, elements that impinge in their various aspects on the different monotheistic religions.

The associated objects, images and writings are ancient, subtle in terms of expression and often physically fragile. They require special precautions with regards to exposure to light and an atmosphere conducive to concentration, attention and contemplation. The spaces of the galleries concerned are dimmed through the use of bronze panels on the walls, an age-old material clearly in harmony with the sense of eternity, together with low, diffuse lighting that helps to create a serene atmosphere in which murmurs or whispers are barely tolerated and the need for silence is strongly felt.

COSMOGRAPHIES

This particular space halfway through the permanent galleries is devoted to the year 1500, the symbolic date of the great turning point that led to an extraordinary acceleration in the history of the world. *Cosmographies* recounts the progress achieved in science, mathematics, astronomy, cartography and shipbuilding that opened the way to the great discoveries. For the first time in history, human beings travelled around the world and visited previously unknown continents, traded with them and established trading posts and bases for future conquests. *Cosmographies* bears witness to this era with instruments, astrolabes, globes, maps and images of previously unknown lands and peoples. These splendid, ancient instruments and maps, that to us seem today to come from an imaginary world can only fill us with wonder at the remarkable and fearless explorers like Ibn Battuta, Zheng He and Vasco da Gama, who opened up the horizons of our world in their day.

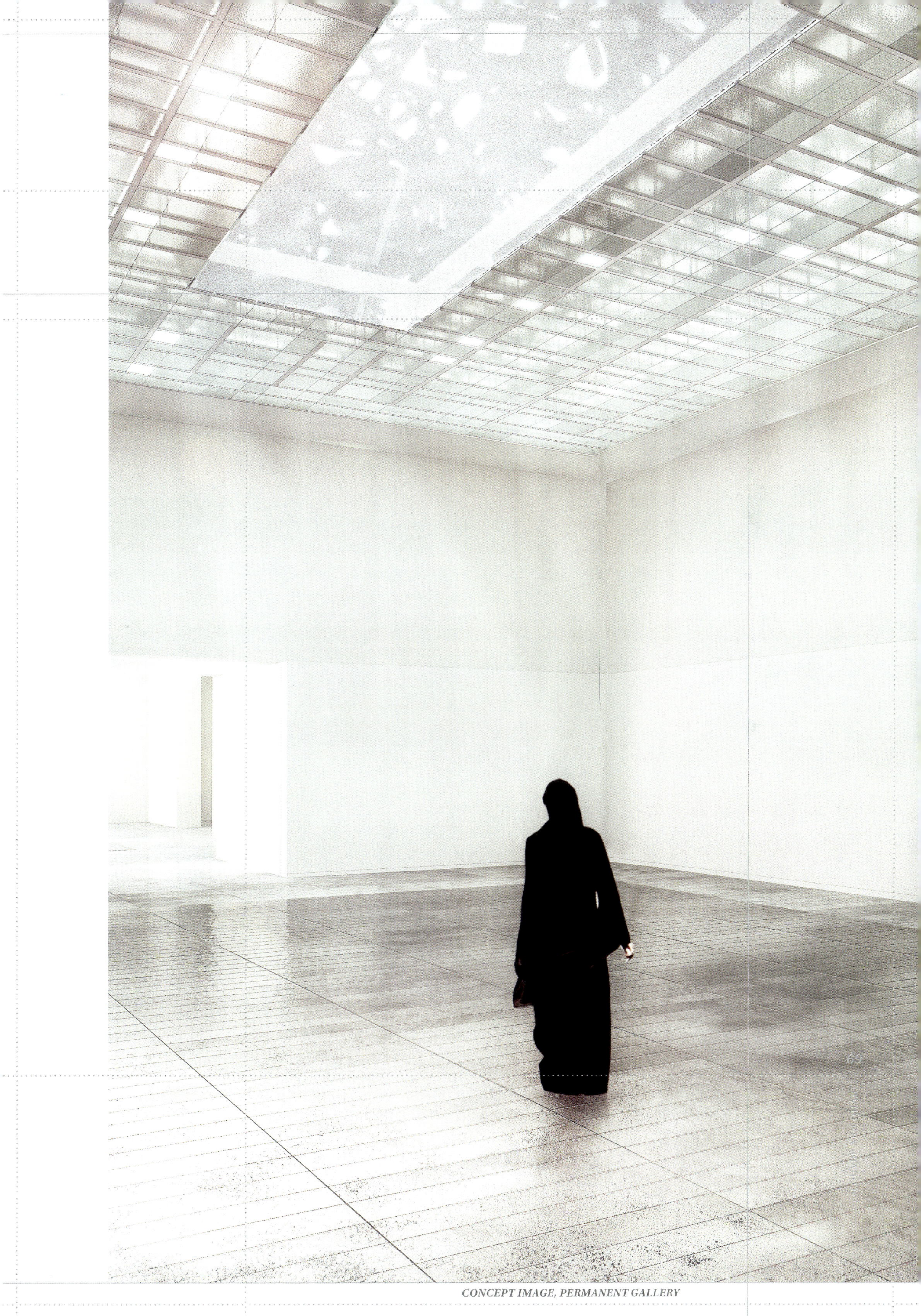

CONCEPT IMAGE, PERMANENT GALLERY

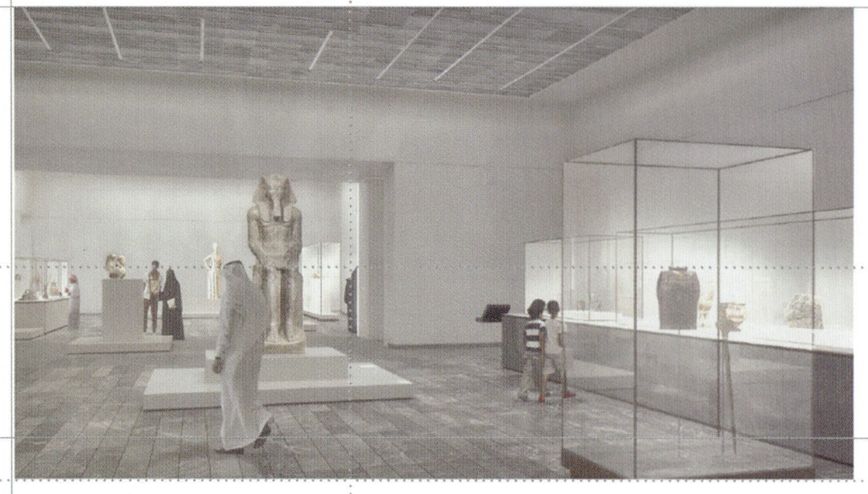
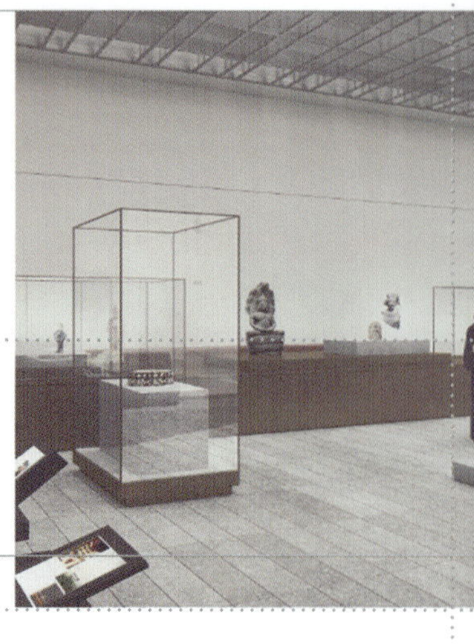
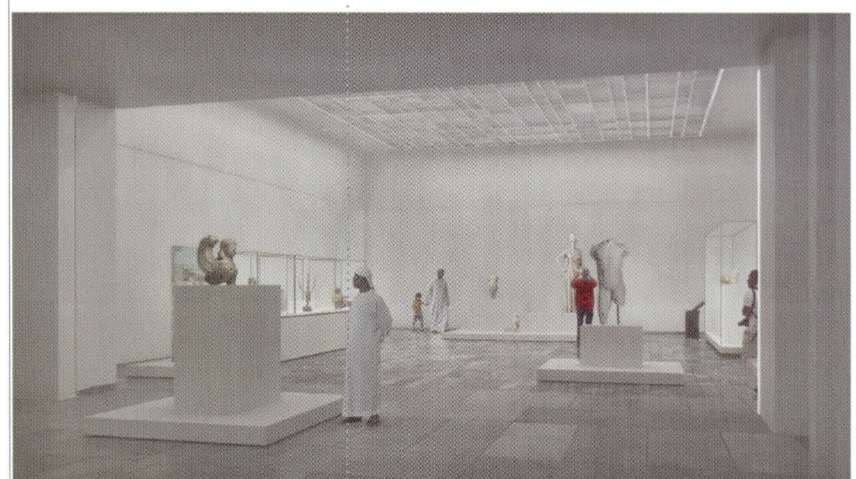
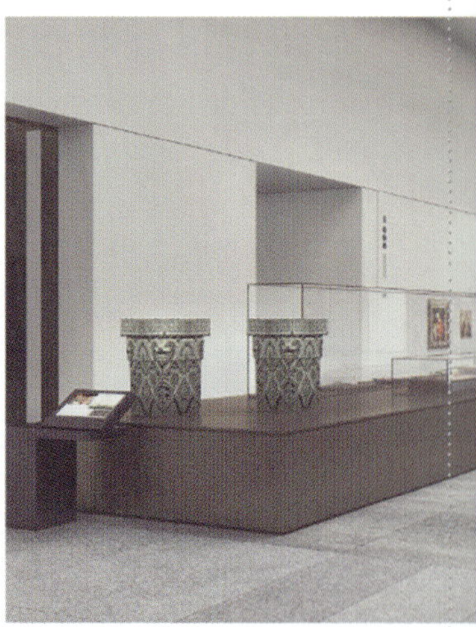
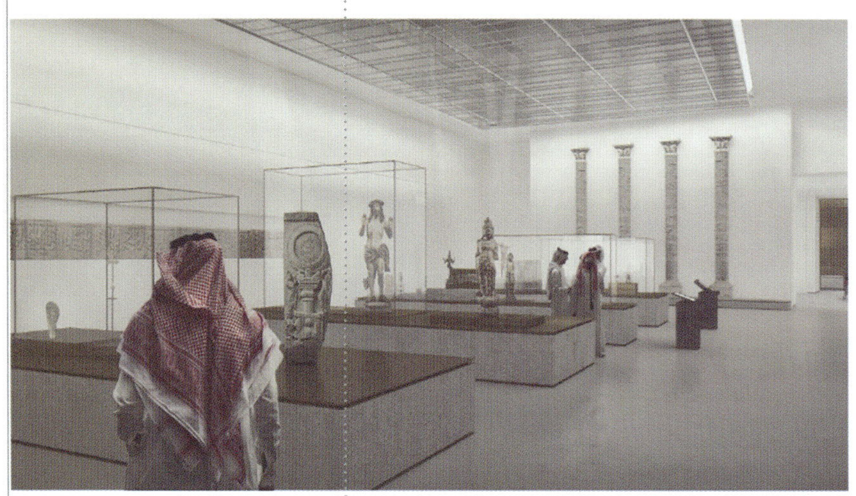
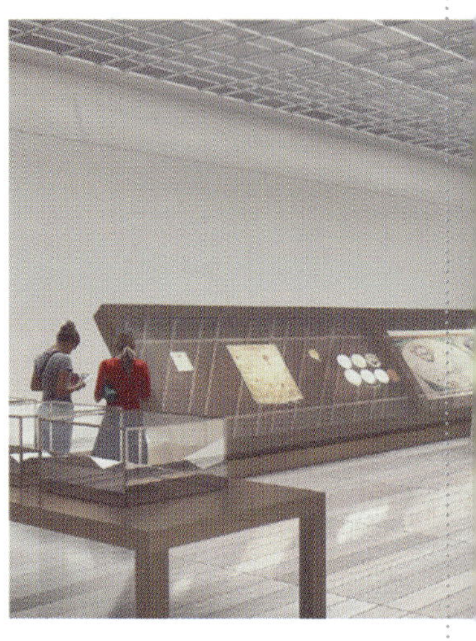
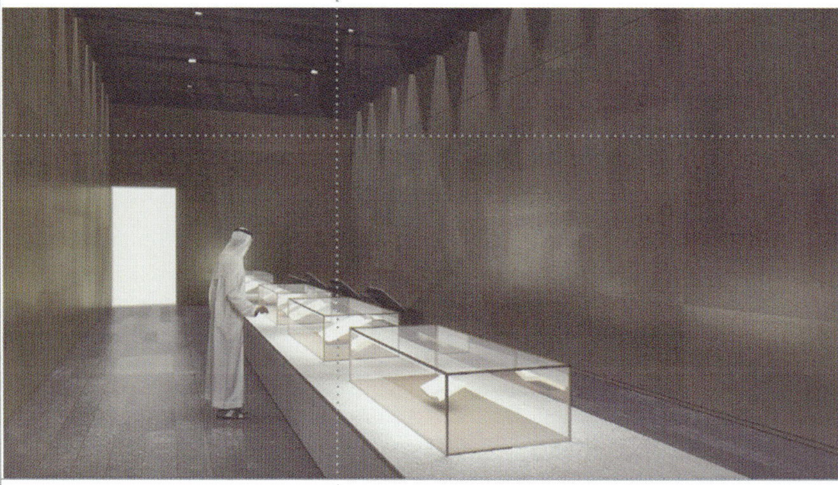

THE MUSEUM SPACES AND MUSEOGRAPHY AS A WHOLE WERE CONCEIVED AND DESIGNED BY JEAN NOUVEL AND HIS TEAM,

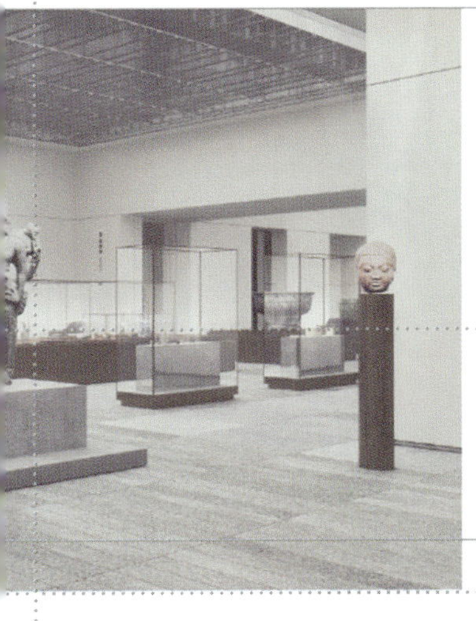 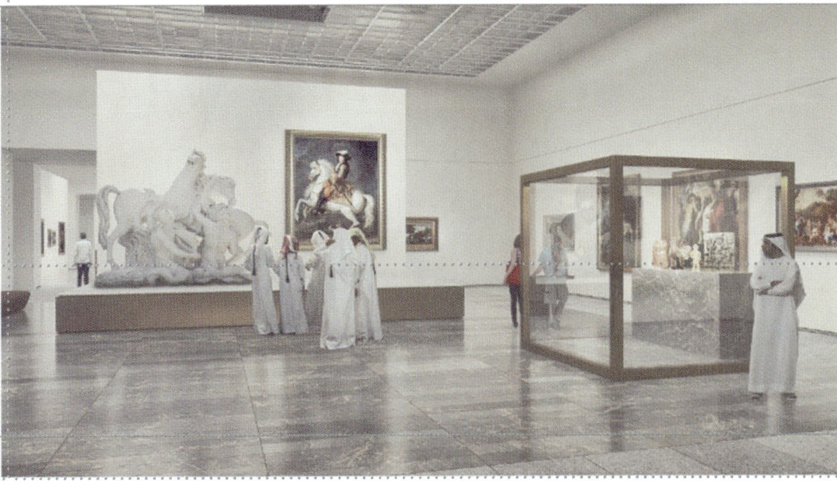

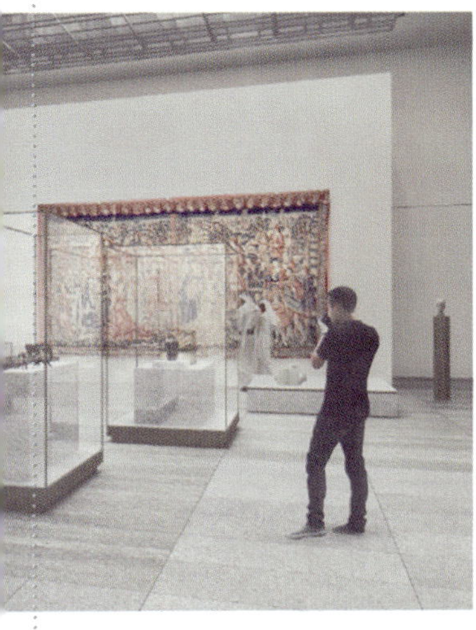 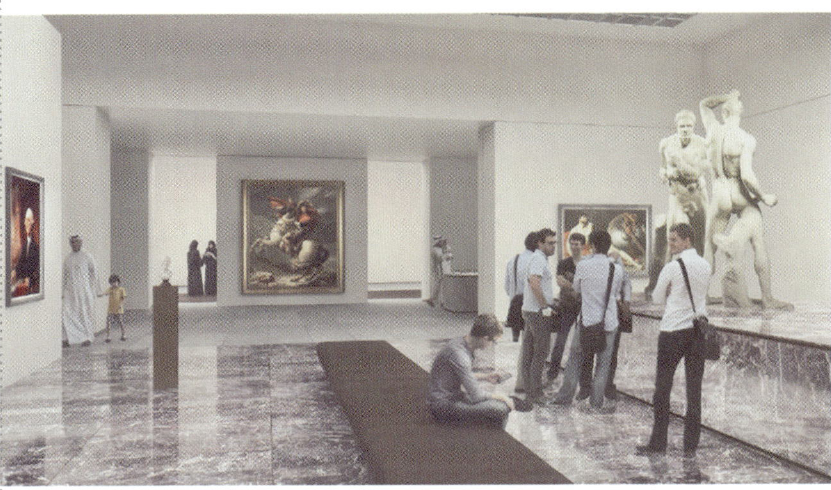

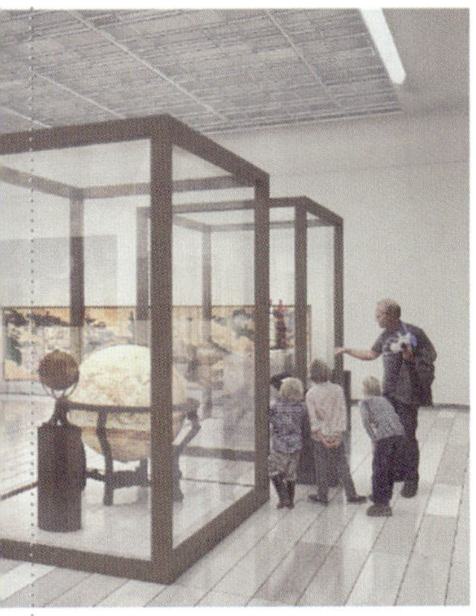 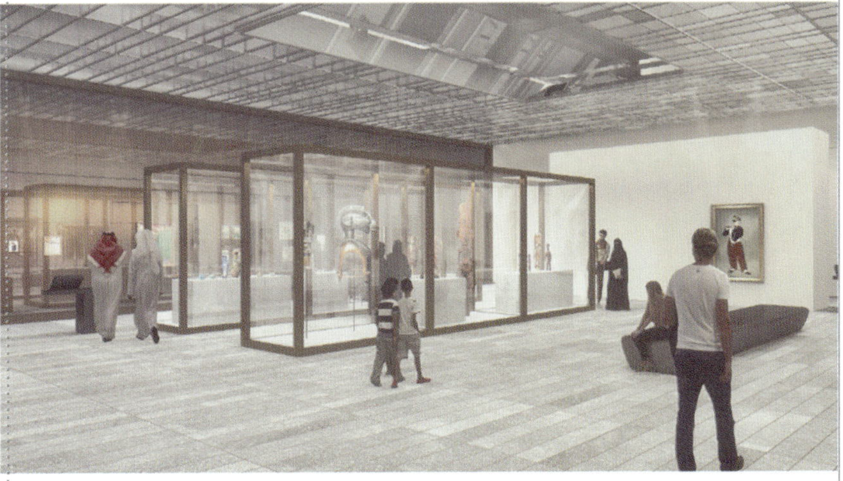

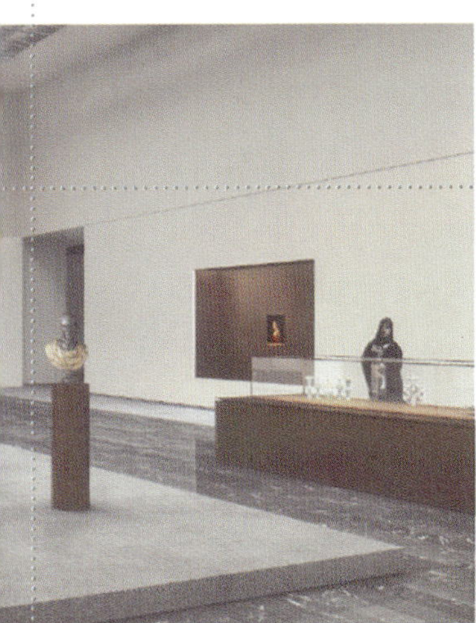 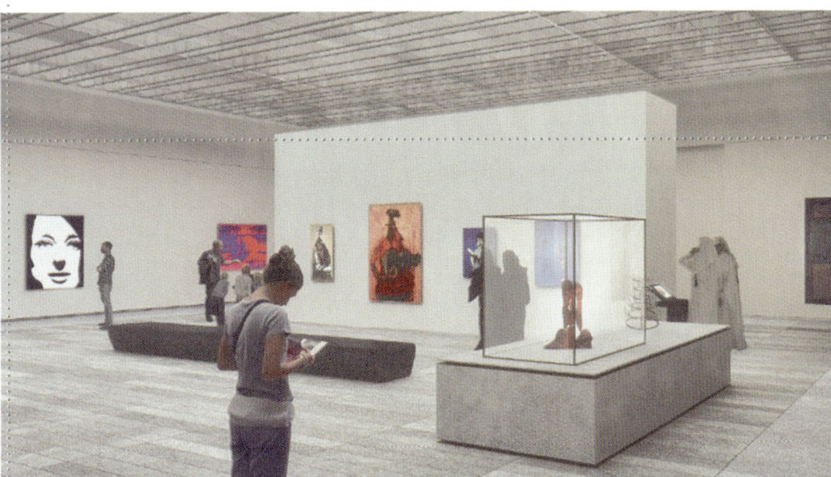

RENAUD PIÉRARD, HALA WARDÉ, ANNA UGOLINI & ATHINA FARAUT

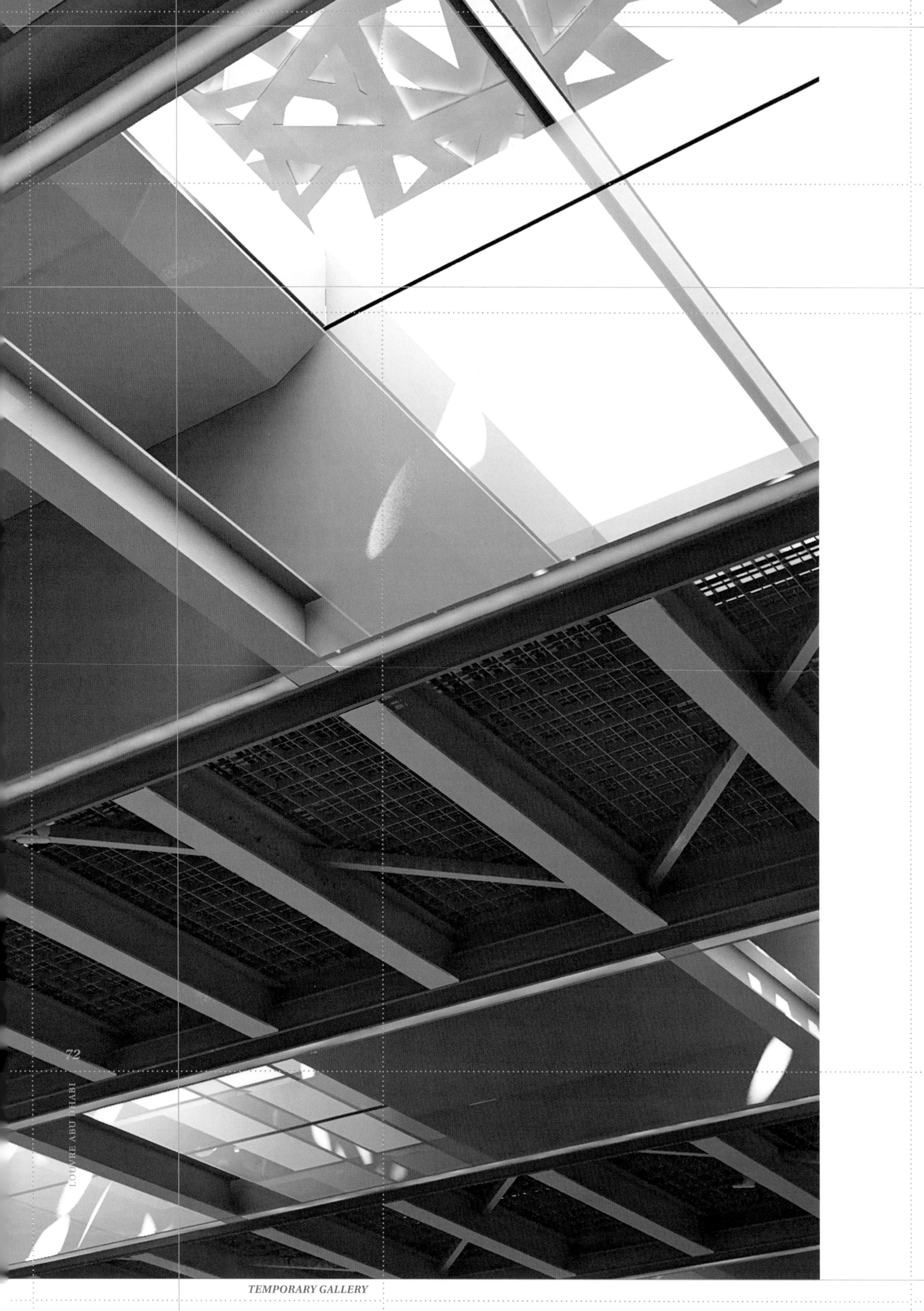

TEMPORARY GALLERY

It was once a luxury before becoming a necessity and soon a norm. From midway through the 20th century, in addition to spaces and galleries to exhibit their collections, new museums were all equipped with places of considerable size to hold temporary exhibitions of varying duration capable of attracting a large public. The initial model was provided by the German *Kunsthalle*, designed for exhibitions of contemporary art in towns or areas with no museum or permanent collection (albeit often with plans to build a museum at a later date).

The trend gathered momentum with the conversion of practically disused premises briefly used to house national exhibitions and World's Fairs, or abandoned factories that culture alone could bring back to life. Examples include the Grand Palais in Paris and Tate Modern in London.

These huge spaces generally serve to present major thematic exhibitions or solo shows of work by famous artists capable of drawing the crowds, the "blockbuster" events of which more than one curator dreams. In the Louvre Abu Dhabi, temporary exhibitions are assigned a major role in asserting the museum's identity and its determination to take its place among the world's greatest institutions. These events will make it possible to stimulate the museum's cultural activities and to develop relations of international cooperation at the highest level. The Louvre Abu Dhabi's exhibitions will put forward a vision of the history of art with a new slant and a more global approach to subjects, exploring areas off the beaten track or attempting to explore phenomena on a broader scale than is usually the case. The aim is to generate a new way of looking, of arousing the curiosity and thirst for knowledge of a new and young public.

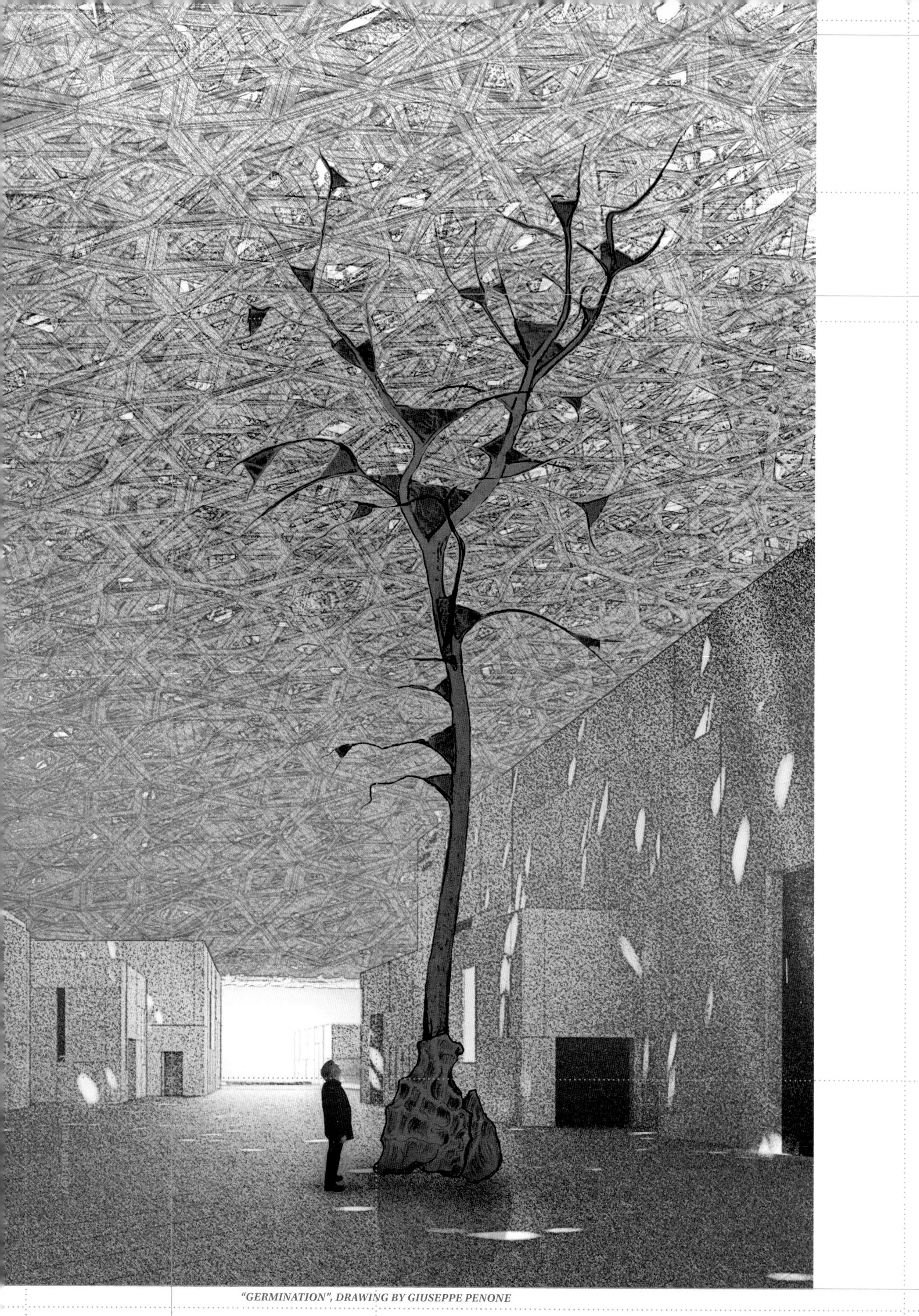

"GERMINATION", DRAWING BY GIUSEPPE PENONE

In addition to its permanent and temporary exhibition galleries, the Louvre Abu Dhabi has external spaces on the platform partially shaded by the dome, sometimes open, as on the long plaza that runs east to west, sometimes enclosed between the outer walls of the various galleries on narrow streets, and squares with expanses of water shimmering with reflections from the "celestial vault" of the dome. This is where it was decided to exhibit works of public and urban art belonging to the Louvre Abu Dhabi collection – ancient, modern and contemporary. Indeed, some of the latter were specifically commissioned from recognised artists.

GIUSEPPE PENONE, *Germination*

Germination by Giuseppe Penone consists of four works that dialogue with the architecture of the museum and with its collections. The Italian artist explores the connections between mankind, art and nature. The print of a human hand is the starting point of "germinations" in the form of a tree, an anthropomorphic vase, handfuls of clay and a line of propagation stretching towards infinity. Symbolising the vital movement of birth, this work accompanies the blossoming of the Louvre Abu Dhabi. Born in 1947, Penone was part of the Arte Povera movement in the late 1960s, when, in opposition to the consumer society, with Jannis Kounellis, Giovanni Anselmo and Michelangelo Pistoletto he championed a return to "poor" materials. Deeply versed in Greek and Roman classical culture, he also draws on the wellsprings of Celtic and Eastern thought, and probes the links between the worlds of plants and animals, using his own body to apprehend nature on a human scale. Highlighting the similarities between mankind and nature, he reveals the invisible mysteries of life and art and the work in gestation. It is precisely this vital and creative movement that he explores in *Germination*.

Planted in the middle of the Louvre Abu Dhabi's plaza, the artist's tall tree stretches up very close to the dome as though supporting it as a pillar, an integral part of the building. This hybrid sculpture, a fusion of nature and technology, of the plant and mineral kingdoms, stands as a symbol of the spirit of our time. Its leaves, steel mirrors located at the intersection of the branches, reflect the sunlight, thus establishing harmony with the building and the rain of light streaming in through its dome.

The handful of earth transposed into bronze, and enlarged to serve as a basis for this tree, bears the imprint of the artist's hand. Encapsulating an age-old action, it reappears in *Earth of the World – Vase*, a work created with the Cité de la céramique de Sèvres, to support a porcelain vase covered with enamels. In *Earth of the World – Handfuls of Clay*, its enlarged shape is made up of lumps of clay from all over the world. The concept of geographical source reappears in the third work *Propagation*, again created with the Cité de la céramique, where lines radiate in centrifugal waves from the thumbprint of Sheikh Zayed, founder of the United Arab Emirates. The fingerprint or dactylogram, specific to all of mankind, is simultaneously universal and absolutely unique to every individual.

AUGUSTE RODIN *Walking Man on a Column*
France, 1900. Bronze, no 6/8 cast by Coubertin,
copyright 2006
(354 x 60 x 39 cm)

To coincide with the Paris World's Fair of 1900, Rodin organised an exhibition of his work in a pavilion erected on the Place de l'Alma. The exhibits included this small sculpture perched on a column with a Corinthian capital, for which he assembled two fragments of a *John the Baptist*, the torso leaning forward and slightly rotated on a pair of legs to impart dynamic movement to his *Walking Man*. While the figure, devoid of head and arms, recalls an ancient statue, the decision to preserve the torso in the form of a fragment and free the sculpture from any superfluous detail exemplifies the artist's very modern approach.

Perched on a Corinthian column and standing out against one of the cyclopean walls of the galleries, the work enters perfectly into dialogue with the architecture of the place in its relationship with Antiquity and its contemporary power of expression. Prescience on the master's part? The armless and headless anchorite was to take his first step into the sidereal void at the end of the century.

OCTAGONAL FOUNTAIN AND ITS FLOORING

This pavement provides a fine example of architectural decoration in the region of Syria in the 12th century. The alternation of white and coloured stone stretches back to an ancient stone-cutting technique initially used for courses of two-colour masonry in Byzantine buildings, and then in the geometrical decorations of the floors of the Arab-Norman palaces in the 12th and 13th centuries. Between the late 14th and the early 19th century, Syrian decorations developed through two complementary techniques, namely *ablaq* for mineral or stone elements and *ajami* for woodwork on walls and ceilings.

Designed for coolness during the hot season, the pavement and fountain were originally part of the inner courtyard or main hall of an 18th-century mansion in Damascus. In Syria, more than anywhere else in the Islamic world, inner courtyards occupied the central place in houses and palaces, with the rooms constituting its extensions. Here, in a contemporary setting flooded with light, the fountain regains some of its traditional symbolism as a mirror image of the celestial vault represented in architecture in the form of a dome or cupola.

JENNY HOLZER, *For the Louvre Abu Dhabi*, 2017
Marble and limestone reliefs

Created by the conceptual artist Jenny Holzer (b. 1950 in Gallipolis, Ohio, United States), *For the Louvre Abu Dhabi* (2017) celebrates the art and act of writing, the history of which covers a span of over four millennia. The work consists of three separate pieces installed on walls in different places in the museum.

Holzer employed advanced technological processes like three-dimensional digital scanning to transform three literary treasures, each representing a peak of past civilisations, into monumental stone reliefs. The first presents a cuneiform tablet copied by a young scribe in ancient Mesopotamia (c. 1250 BCE), the transcription of a creation myth in two languages. The second consists of pages from a remarkable ancient calligraphic manuscript of the *Muqadimmah*, a key treatise on history written during the Islamic Golden Age in the 14th century by Ibn Khaldun. The third presents Michel de Montaigne's final revisions of his *Essays*, completed during the last four years of his life at the end of the Renaissance in the late 16th century.

Marble relief of a text written in cuneiform script in Sumerian and Akkadian, from a Mesopotamian tablet of c. 1250 BCE

This poetic text recounts a myth of the creation of mankind as imagined by the inhabitants of Mesopotamia nearly four thousand years ago. After the sky, the land and the rivers, the gods created the first human beings, Ulligara and Zalgarra, by mixing clay with the blood of a sacrificed divinity. Discovered on the site of the ancient village of Assur in present-day Iraq, the clay tablet bearing the text is now in the Vorderasiatisches Museum in Berlin (Germany). The cuneiform signs, which constitute the earliest known form of writing, were imprinted on the clay using a stylus made from a reed. The text on the left is in Sumerian and the text on the right in Akkadian. While there are several versions of this text from ancient Mesopotamia, this tablet in particular was written by a young scribe as an exercise during his apprenticeship.

The work on transcription, translation and transmission forms part of a tradition that can be traced back to the birth of writing in Mesopotamia.

Limestone relief representing three pages
of a 14th-century manuscript
of the Muqadimmah by Ibn Khaldun

These walls present extracts from the *Muqaddimah*, widely regarded as one of the first texts to establish the methodological basis of history as a science, as is also the case for philosophy, theology and socio-cultural analysis.

Its author Ibn Khaldun (1332–1406) examines numerous subjects while examining the question of how we can grasp and understand the increasingly distant past, and thus presents a living image of human intellectual, aesthetic and scientific achievement. Written in the *naskh* style of cursive Arabic, these pages were reproduced from a 14th-century manuscript in the Atif Efendi Library, Istanbul.

The three pages selected by Holzer address the concepts of thought and language. In the text inscribed on the wall on the left, Ibn Khaldun discusses the mind, which is stimulated by the activity of the brain and perceptions of the physical world through the senses to create an almost uninterrupted stream of thought. He suggests that abstract thought is the highest and noblest human activity. The page in the middle addresses poetry, which he regards as inseparable from song. He suggests that language is intrinsically social, in that languages exist and develop as a means to facilitate communication between human beings. Language is conventional but can also lead to lofty works of art and intellectual contemplation.

The page on the wall on the right is a poem by the calligrapher Ibn al-Bawwab, regarded by Ibn Khaldun as an aesthetic model of the lyrical form. The poem explores the art of calligraphy, drawing a parallel between the subject and the form of its expression. Holzer has a longstanding interest in literature extending to the practice of writing, as illustrated by her choice of this page from the *Muqadimmah*.

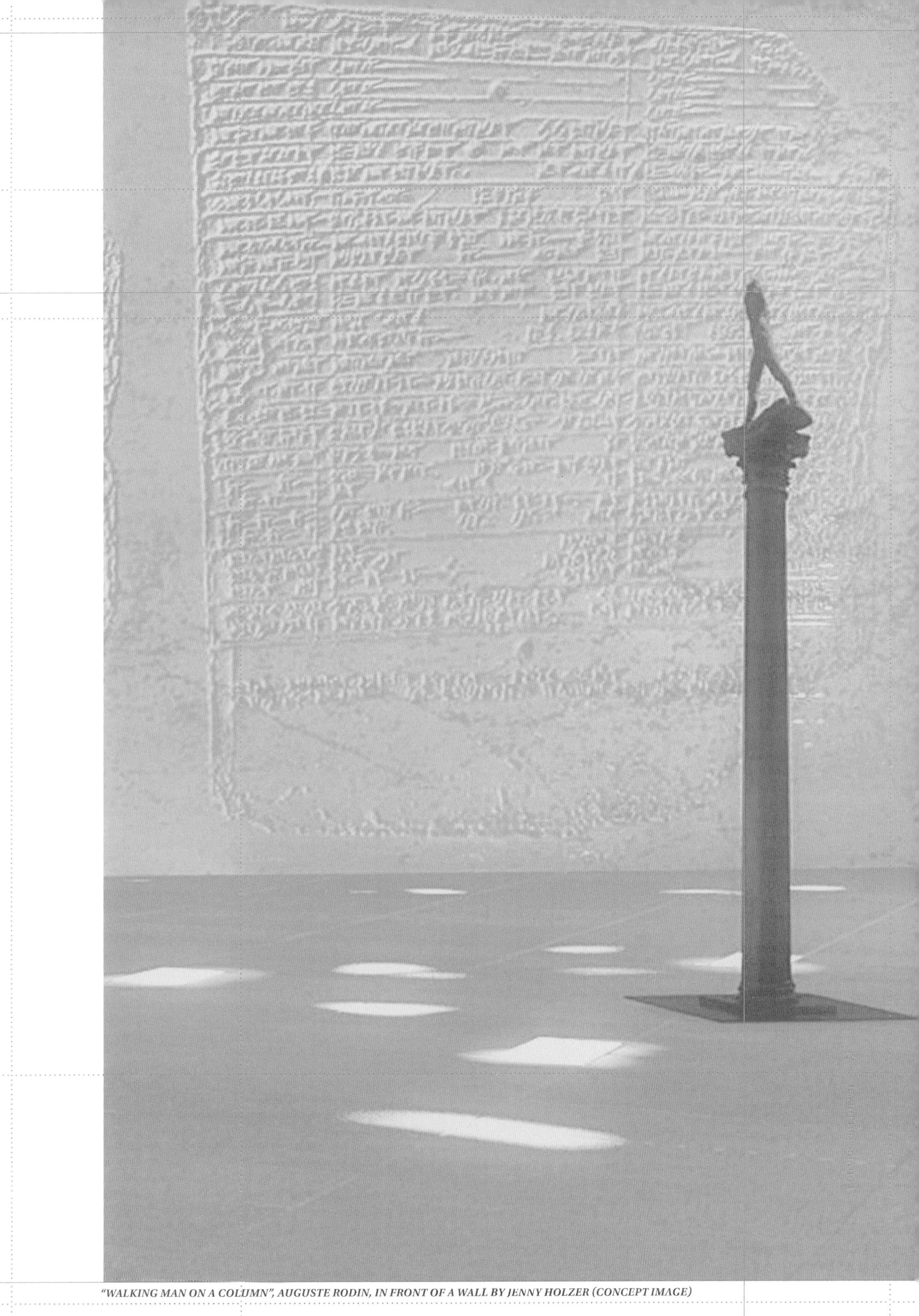

"WALKING MAN ON A COLUMN", AUGUSTE RODIN, IN FRONT OF A WALL BY JENNY HOLZER (CONCEPT IMAGE)

Limestone relief with three pages
from the Bordeaux copy of the Essays by Michel de Montaigne:
On Democritus and Heraclitus (Book I, chap. 50),
On Conversation (Book III, chap. 8), On Vanity (Book III, chap. 9)

Michel de Montaigne's *Essays* stand out in the long European literary tradition of autobiography, memoirs and confessions. First published in 1580, then expanded with thirteen entirely new essays as well as other additions and revisions in 1588, it was substantially increased again and annotated after this date – as can be seen from the three pages chosen by Holzer for her work – with additions accounting for approximately a quarter of the work hand-written by Montaigne during the last four years of his life. Posthumously published in 1595, the *Essays* are regarded as among the world's most original and important literary works, forming a bridge between Antiquity, the Renaissance and the modern era.

Holzer's work focuses on Montaigne's final revisions of three well-known essays on free will and self-determination, where he aptly compares the human mind to a racehorse, on the demanding challenges of writing, on criticism and the celebration of poetry. Above and beyond the physical beauty of these pages, as displayed in this copy from the municipal library in Bordeaux, we can see the mind of a writer at work, not only having the last word in a discussion with his younger self but also delivering the judgement of an artist of another time, culture and country, the support of which is again the written word.

MYTHS OF CREATION
What else are we going to do?
What else are we going to create?
O Annuneki, you powerful gods,
What else are we going to do?
What else are we going to create?

IBN KHALDUN

If you truly wish to master the art of writing,
ask your Master to help you.

MICHEL DE MONTAIGNE

I do not think that we are so unhappy as we are vain,
or have in us so much malice as folly.

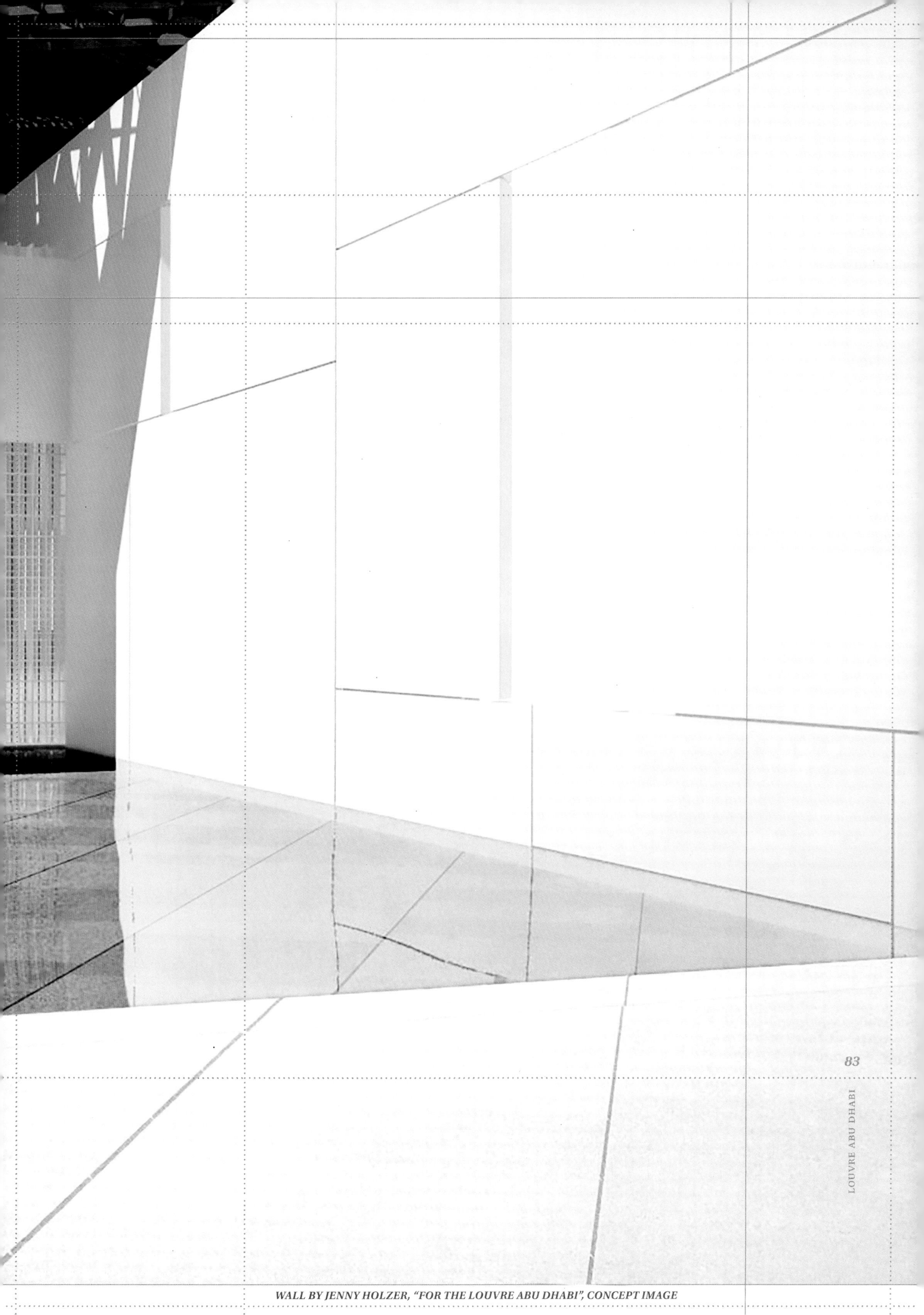

WALL BY JENNY HOLZER, "FOR THE LOUVRE ABU DHABI", CONCEPT IMAGE

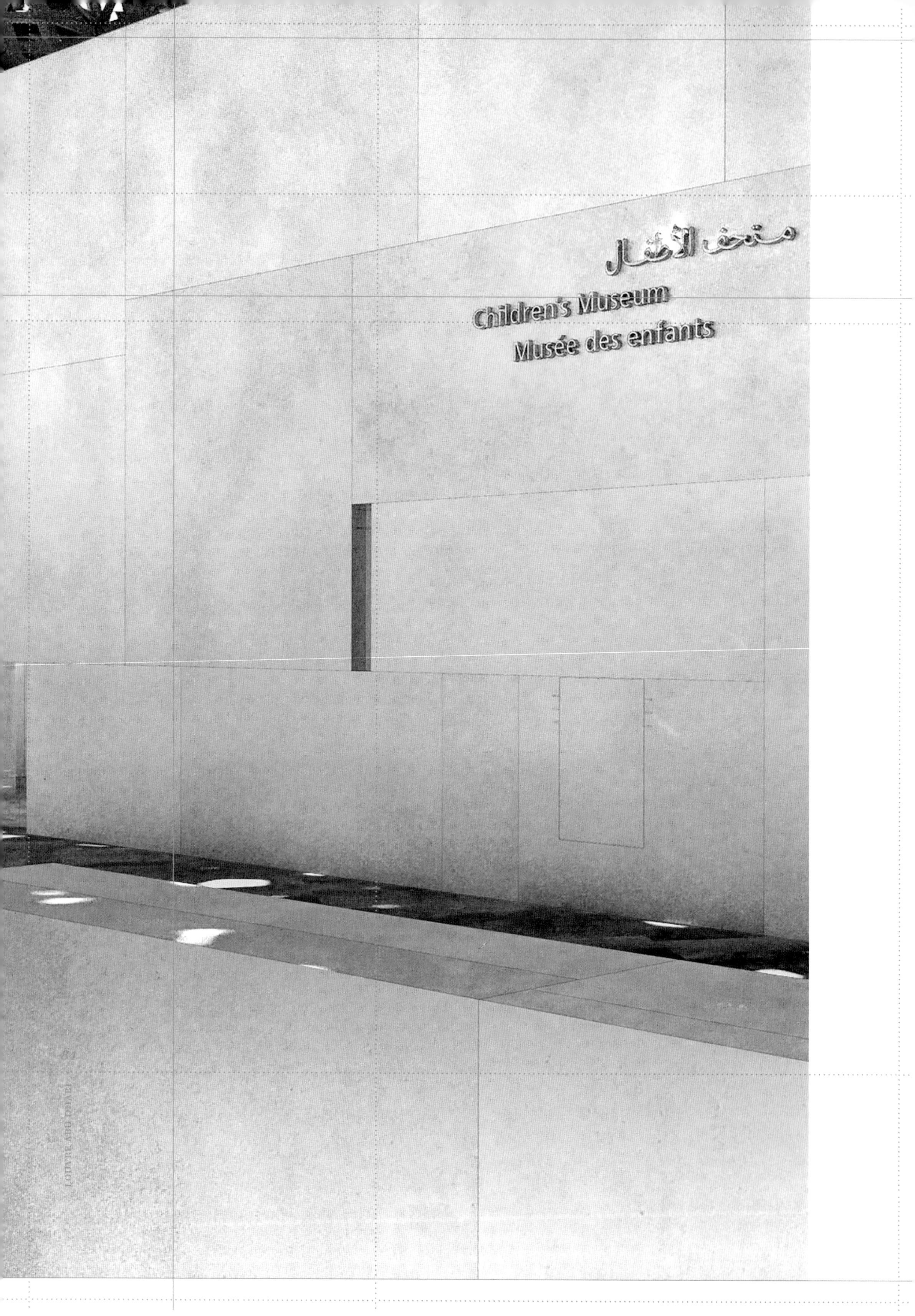
متحف الأطفال
Children's Museum
Musée des enfants

All the major museums today have spaces dedicated to children. One sometimes suspects, however, that this is a convenient place for parents to unload their offspring before going to visit a fine exhibition for adults.

This is not at all the case in the Louvre Abu Dhabi, whose Children's Museum is on an equal footing with the buildings of the medina between the temporary exhibition gallery and the auditorium. Proportionally sized in relation to the temporary exhibition galleries and readily accessible from the plaza or the forum, the Children's Museum is an integral part of the community.

In accordance with its universal vocation, the Louvre Abu Dhabi has adopted an original and innovative attitude. The space for children is an authentic museum on a smaller scale using a selection of works from the collection to introduce its young visitors to art and familiarise them with museum codes, while also giving free rein to their curiosity. The programme of activities follows the life of the museum in real time, focusing both on the themes addressed in the permanent galleries and on the events in the large neighbouring gallery.

Two temporary exhibitions a year are envisaged for the Children's Museum. The initial three-year programme develops general themes related primarily to the great subjects of art and representation, including *Forms and Colours*, *Landscapes from Here and Elsewhere*, *Real and Imaginary Animals* and *The Portrait*.

The scenography is laid out so as to provide the spatial flexibility required by the rotation of exhibitions, while the personnel have comfortable spaces at their disposal, as well as interactive tools of tried and tested validity.

THE SPACES

A ground floor of 200 square metres at the same level as the plaza; access from the forum or the plaza; an upper floor beneath the glass ceiling with a space for circulation around a light well, and two spaces of 60 square metres separated by a mobile partition to serve as educational workshops.

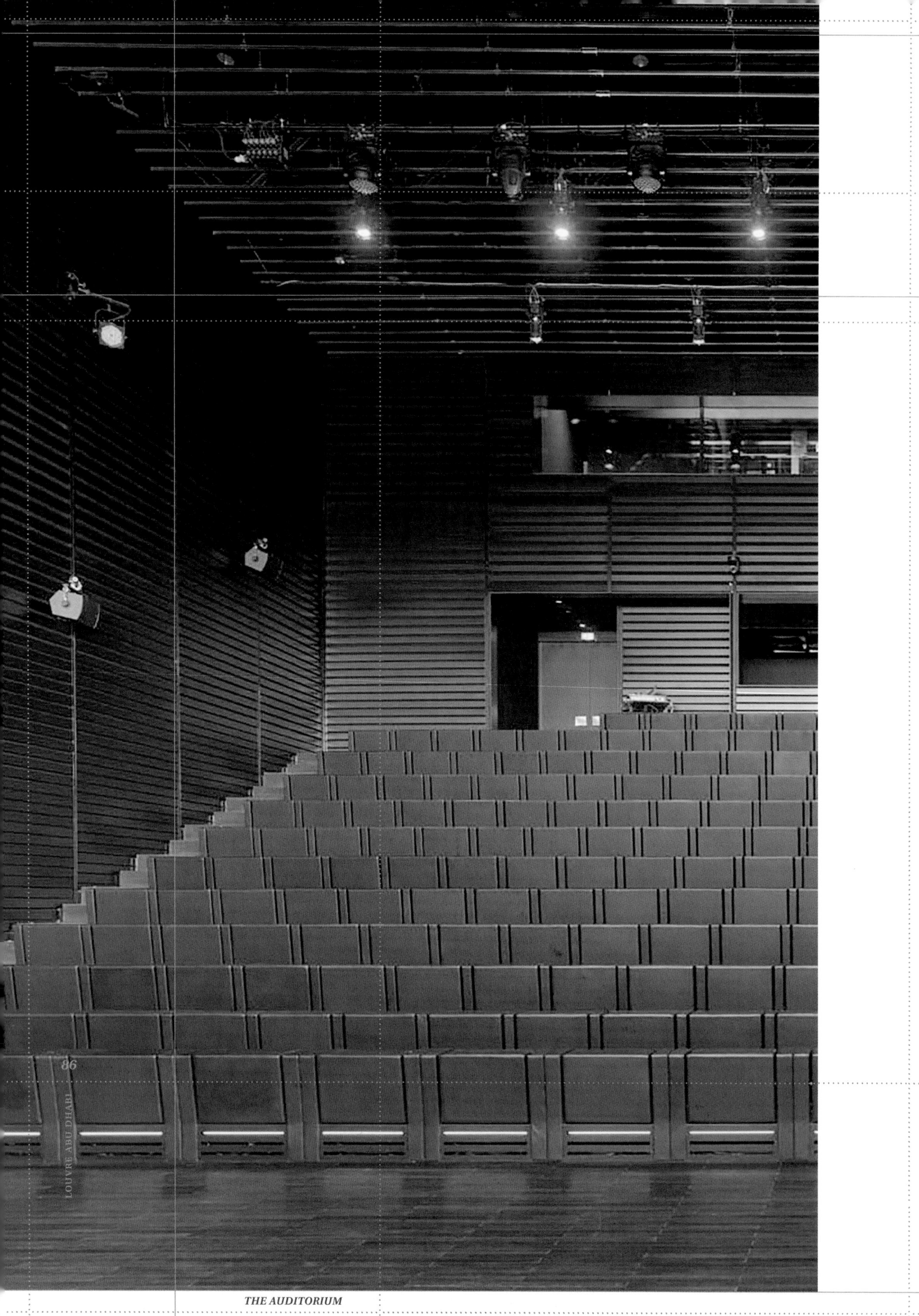

THE AUDITORIUM

Following the example of the world's great museums, the Louvre Abu Dhabi has an auditorium designed to shed light on subjects in the history of art, place them in perspective through commentary and discussion, and highlight their relationships with performing arts like music, dance and cinema.

The auditorium's programme establishes direct continuity with the life of the museum through lectures, debates and events closely connected with the themes addressed both in the permanent galleries and in the temporary exhibition gallery.

The auditorium displays the same rectangular proportions as the exterior of the buildings in the medina. Some of these modules can be opened to create the right acoustics for the events or to house spotlights. Others are acoustically transparent. Here, too, simplicity is synonymous with luxury. It is unquestionably the paradigm of simplicity/complexity, the essential hallmark of the present day, that characterises the fixtures and fittings of the Louvre Abu Dhabi. Comfort is guaranteed by the *Close* seating system specially designed for the Louvre Abu Dhabi by Jean Nouvel.

420 M2, A TIERED ROOM UNIFORMLY CLAD IN BLACK

A SEATING CAPACITY OF 268 IN 12 ROWS

NO PROSCENIUM OR WINGS. OUTSIDE THE SERIES

OF LECTURES, DEBATES AND SEMINARS, THE AUDITORIUM

IS RESERVED FOR "LIGHTWEIGHT" PRODUCTIONS

MOSTLY BASED ON IMAGES DUE TO CONSIDERATIONS

OF LANGUAGE (NO SUBTITLING) AND FEATURING MUSIC,

DANCE OR PERFORMANCE.

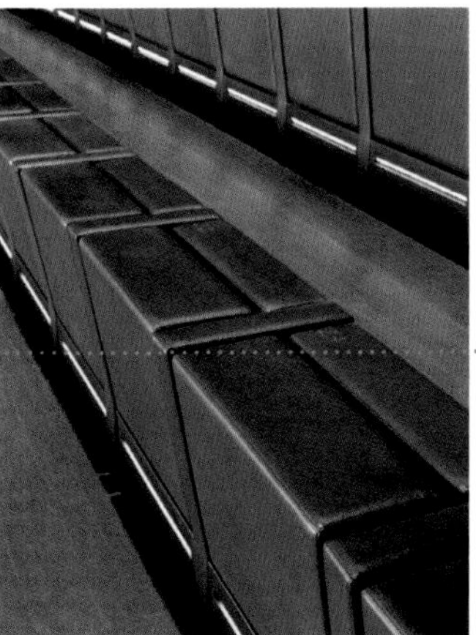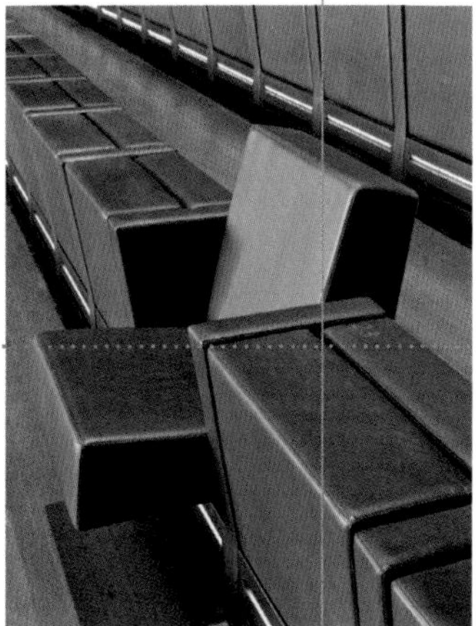

THE "CLOSE" SEATING SYSTEM OF THE AUDITORIUM, DESIGNED BY JEAN NOUVEL AND MANUFACTURED BY POLTRONA FRAU

The restaurant of a major museum must meet high standards of quality and sophistication with regards to its dishes, decor and location.

This is why the the restaurant has been placed close to the auditorium and just a few steps from the Majlis, a place for VIPs to gather and hold meetings, while also offering privileged access to the waters of the Gulf from the museum's marina. The restaurant is laid out in distinct areas. The main hall is divided into suites or salons separated by mobile partitions that can disappear into the arches of the ceiling to create larger spaces. There are thus seven consecutive suites that can be transformed into a large banqueting hall. The round tables can be extended if necessary by means of an ingenious system. The walls are decorated with subtle motifs that differ for each room, including variations on the general theme of the dome and star patterns with superimposed circles and octagons. A long terrace looks out onto the landscape on the north side and can be used for dining in the appropriate season. On the upper level, a bar decorated with black motifs serves aperitifs, cocktails and late evening drinks.

The seating is part of the classic *Elementary* line designed by Jean Nouvel and the modular tables are specially fitted with a complex and ingenious assembly system. The seven chandeliers, one for each room, were specially designed by the architect for the restaurant and produced in Paris by Mobilier National, a centuries-old institution that once provided tapestries, fittings and furniture for the royal palaces and now furnishes the buildings of the French Republic.

THE FURNITURE

INSIDE:

— *Elementary* seats in white leather.

— Round tables in white Corian with inserts of silver-coated and gilded resin fitted with a system for extension (from 120 to 160 cm in diameter) and assembly.

— *Elementary* seating in black on the upper level including two-seat sofas and high banquettes in the bar.

— Square tables in black Corian with inserts of silver-coated and gilded resin.

OUTSIDE:

— White *Elementary* sofas with a slender back, metal structure, gelcoat finish and removable cushions. Low tables with gelcoat finish and a marine plywood structure.

— Low tables with gelcoat finish and a marine plywood structure.

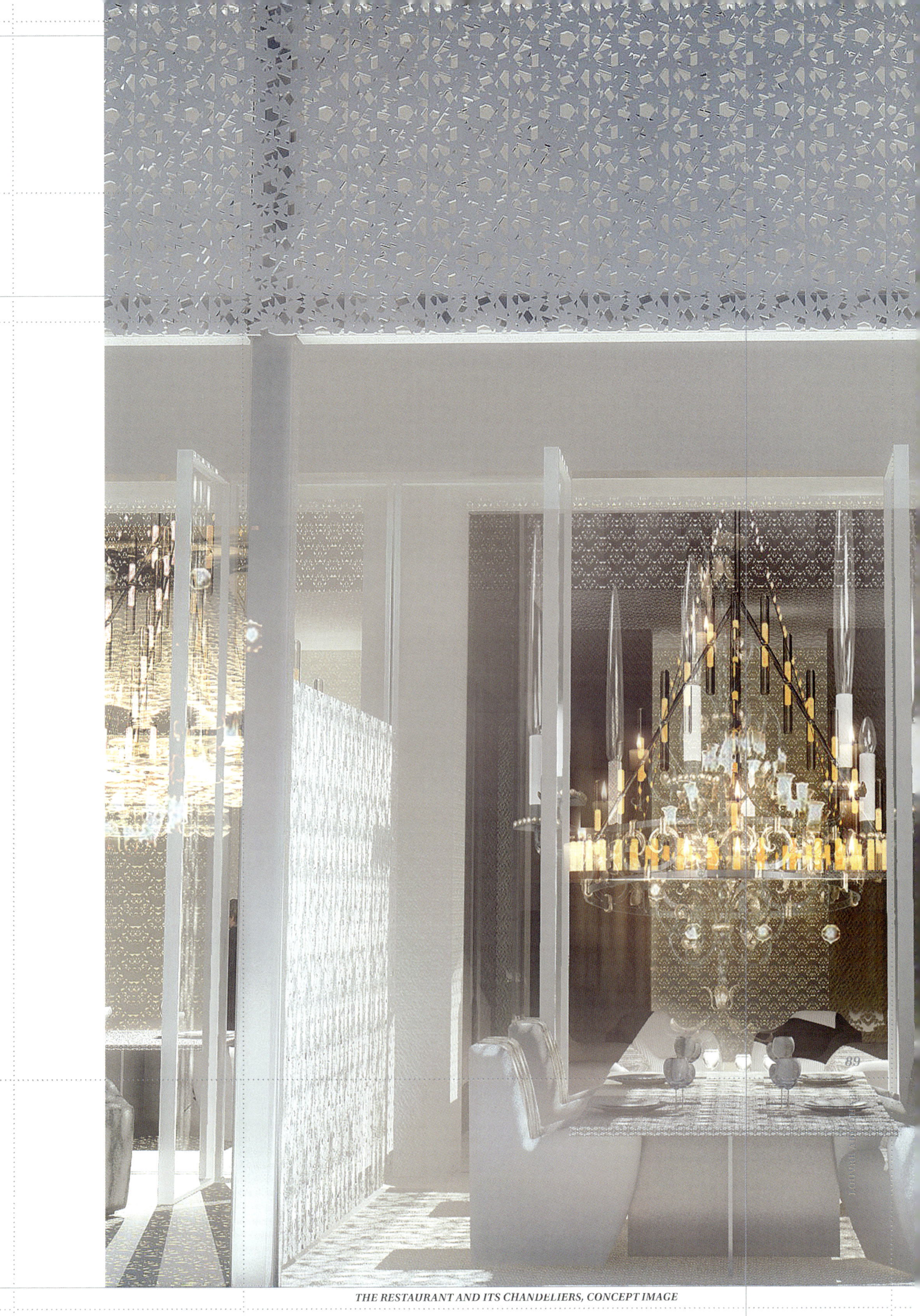

THE RESTAURANT AND ITS CHANDELIERS, CONCEPT IMAGE

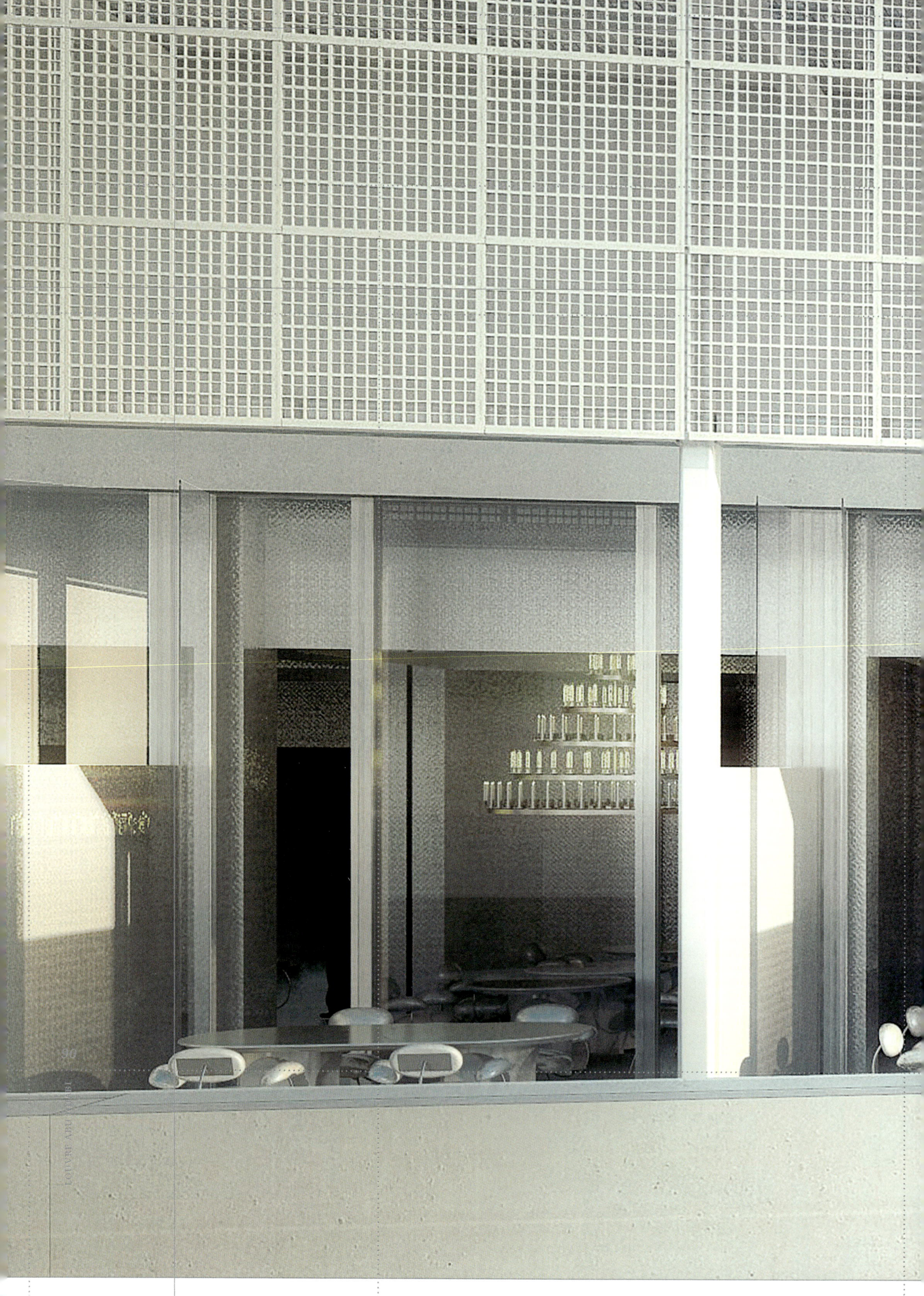
90
LOUVRE ABU DHABI

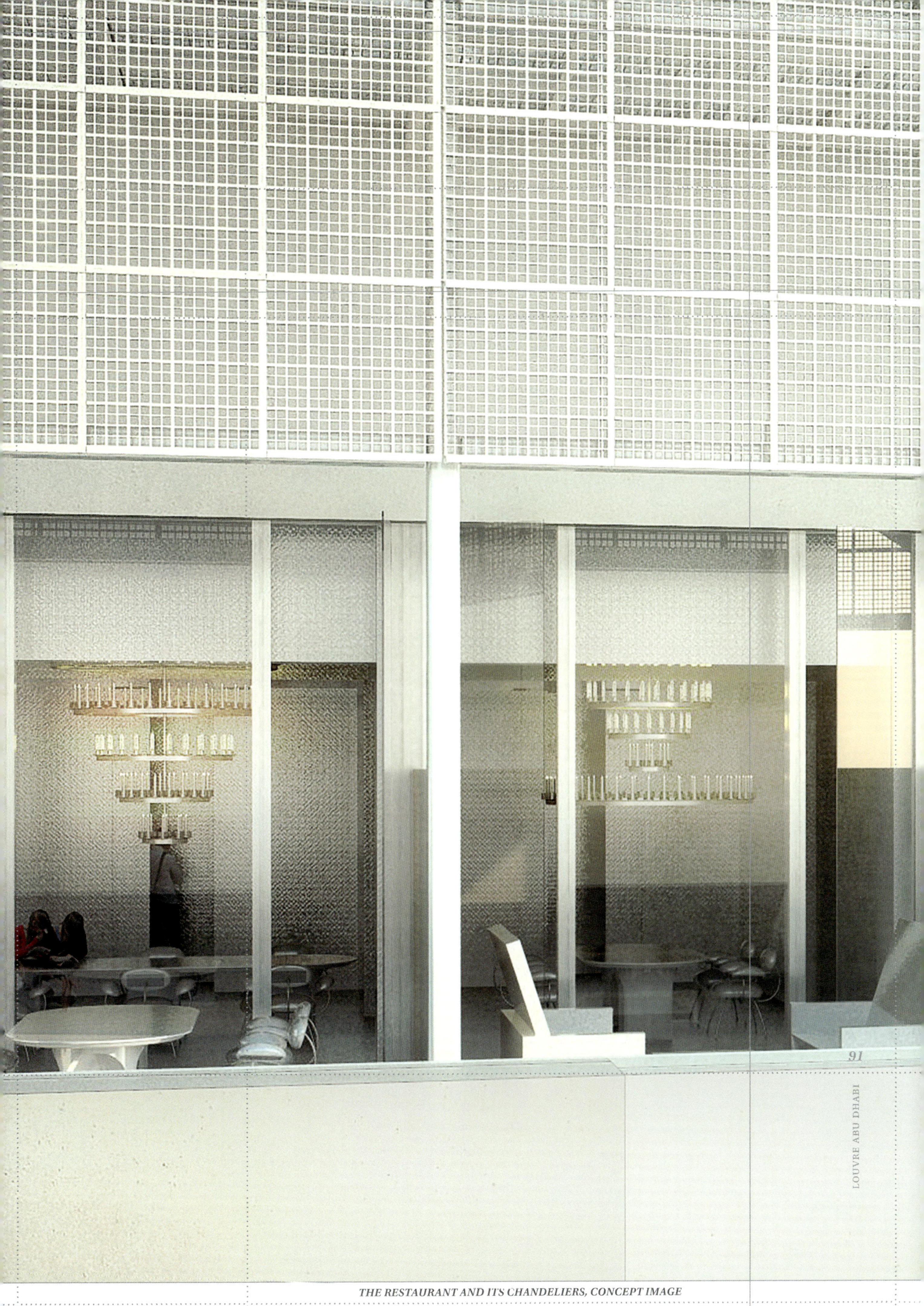

THE RESTAURANT AND ITS CHANDELIERS, CONCEPT IMAGE

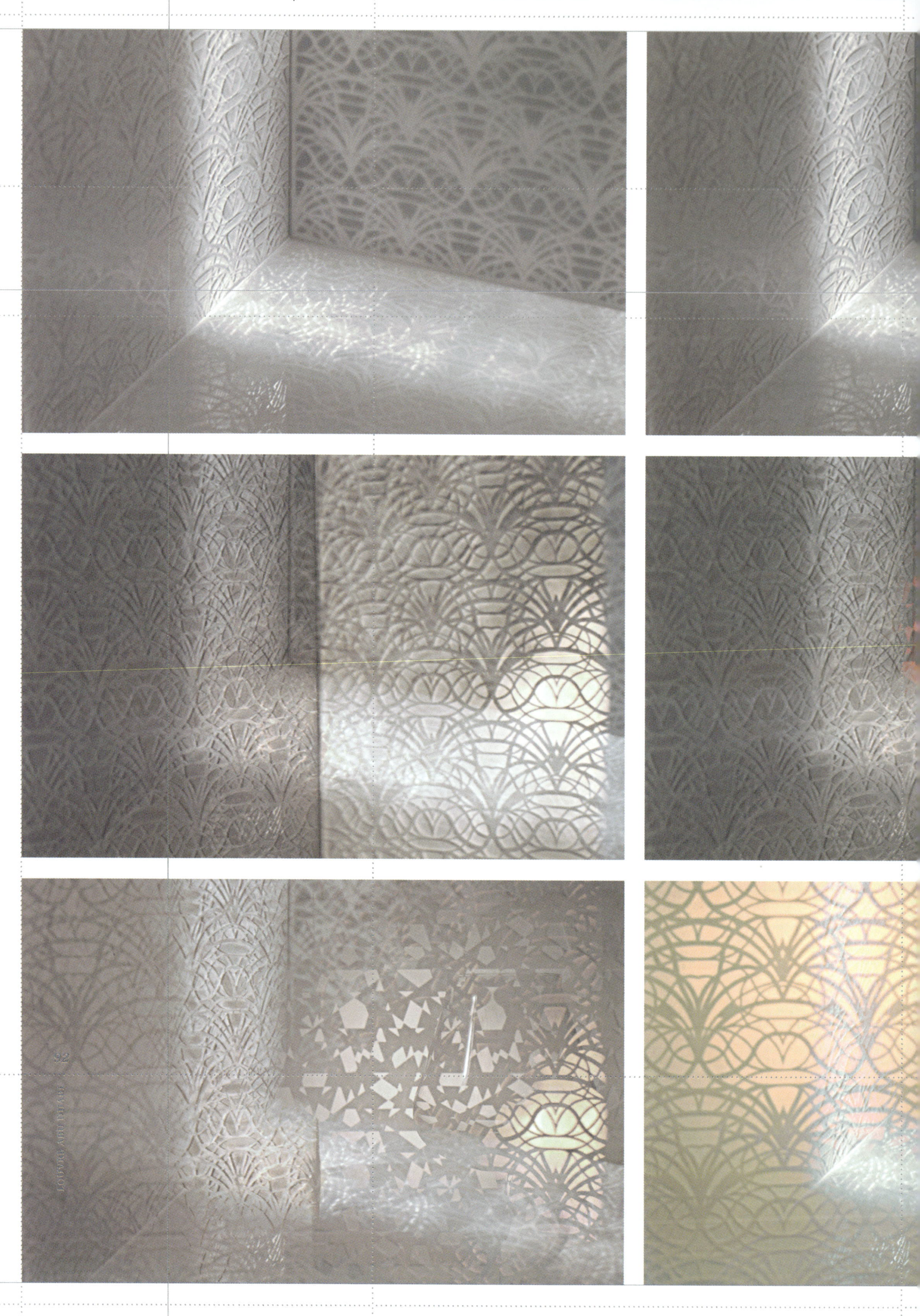

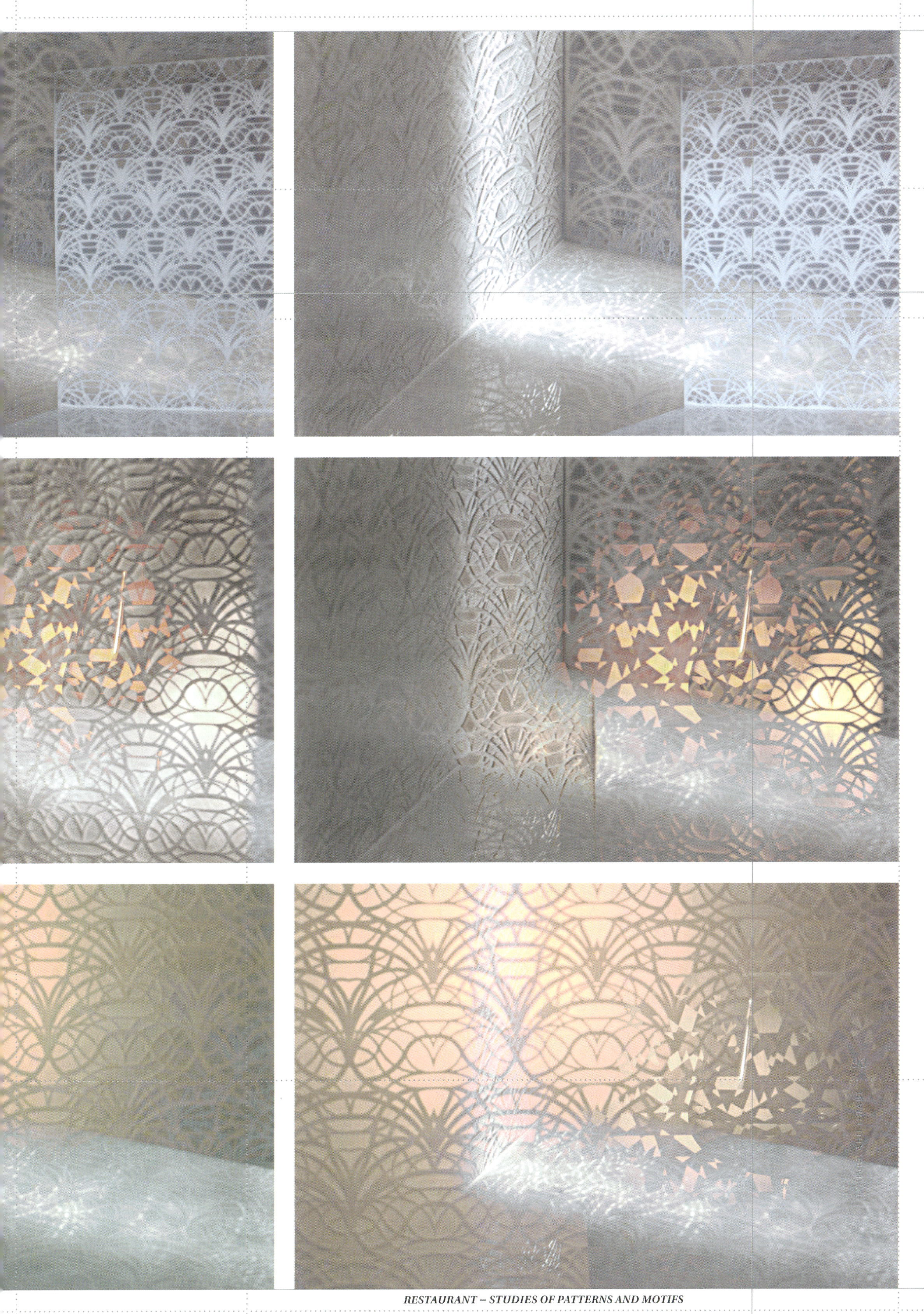

THE CAFÉ

Image, interference, mirage

The café has established itself in the museum-goer's ritual as a place to stop before, during or after a visit. Slightly isolated in its position at the end of the plaza, separated from the large temporary exhibition gallery by a broad expanse of water, on which it turns its back, the Louvre Abu Dhabi's café looks resolutely west towards the spectacle of the Khor Laffan, the opposite shore, the bustle of the Zayed harbour with its black and red cargo vessels, and the skyscrapers rising further away towards the city centre. It is a panoramic view that achieves its maximum splendour at sunset.

Designed for quick snacks and refreshments while exchanging impressions of the collections, it would be simple for the café to be no more than a banal copy of its counterparts all over the world (there are exceptions). Far from it. The place reminds us of Jean Nouvel's taste for images and spectacle. Seen from the Khor Laffan, it blends into the whiteness of the medina and affords only a glimpse of the odd silhouette moving behind its long glass frontage surmounted by a white lattice screen.

It is inside that the show takes place, as the urban landscape becomes duplicated in a shimmering, hazy, pixelated illusion tinted pink and blue, reproduced on the fabric of the upholstery of the furniture. While the stock image of the desert is that of dunes, a well or an oasis, the mirage encapsulates its disturbing, dream-like quality and mystery.

On the upper level of the café, we return to the tangible world and an unadorned view of the opposite bank of the Khor and the city. The bar offers an interval of sociability and cheerful relaxation. It is also the place offering the closest view of the interwoven motifs of the dome and its outer edge. The spectacle of reality.

CAPACITY OF 250 FOR TABLE SERVICE AND 100 FOR COUNTER SERVICE. TIERED LIKE A THEATRE WITH THREE LEVELS OF TERRACES.
SEATING: *INSIDE: "OXYMORE" SEATS, WITH ARMRESTS FOR THE CAFE AND WITHOUT FOR THE SELF-SERVICE AREA, BOTH UPHOLSTERED WITH A JACQUARD FABRIC DECORATED WITH AN IMAGE OF THE LANDSCAPE IN NUANCED COLOUR. "ELEMENTAIRE" SEATING AND BENCHES, TO SUPPLEMENT THE FIXED FURNITURE, WITH TALL BACKS AND FABRIC UPHOLSTERY, WHITE FOR THOSE FACING THE SEA AND COLOURED FOR THE OTHERS.*
OUTSIDE: WHITE "ELEMENTAIRE" ARMCHAIRS AND BENCHES WITH SLENDER BACKS, METAL FRAME, RATTAN WICKERWORK PANELS AND REMOVABLE CUSHIONS.
TABLES: *WITH TEAK TOPS TREATED TO WITHSTAND SUNLIGHT AND SALT WATER, FRAME OF BRUSHED STAINLESS STEEL AND BASE OF STAINLESS STEEL.* ***TERRACE BENEATH THE DOME:*** *"ELEMENTAIRE" RATTAN SEATING. LOW TABLE MADE OF MARINE PLYWOOD, GELCOAT FINISHING WHITE COUNTERTOP AND "MIA" STOOLS.*

FRESCO: ARTISTIC INTERVENTION BY MARIE MAILLARD

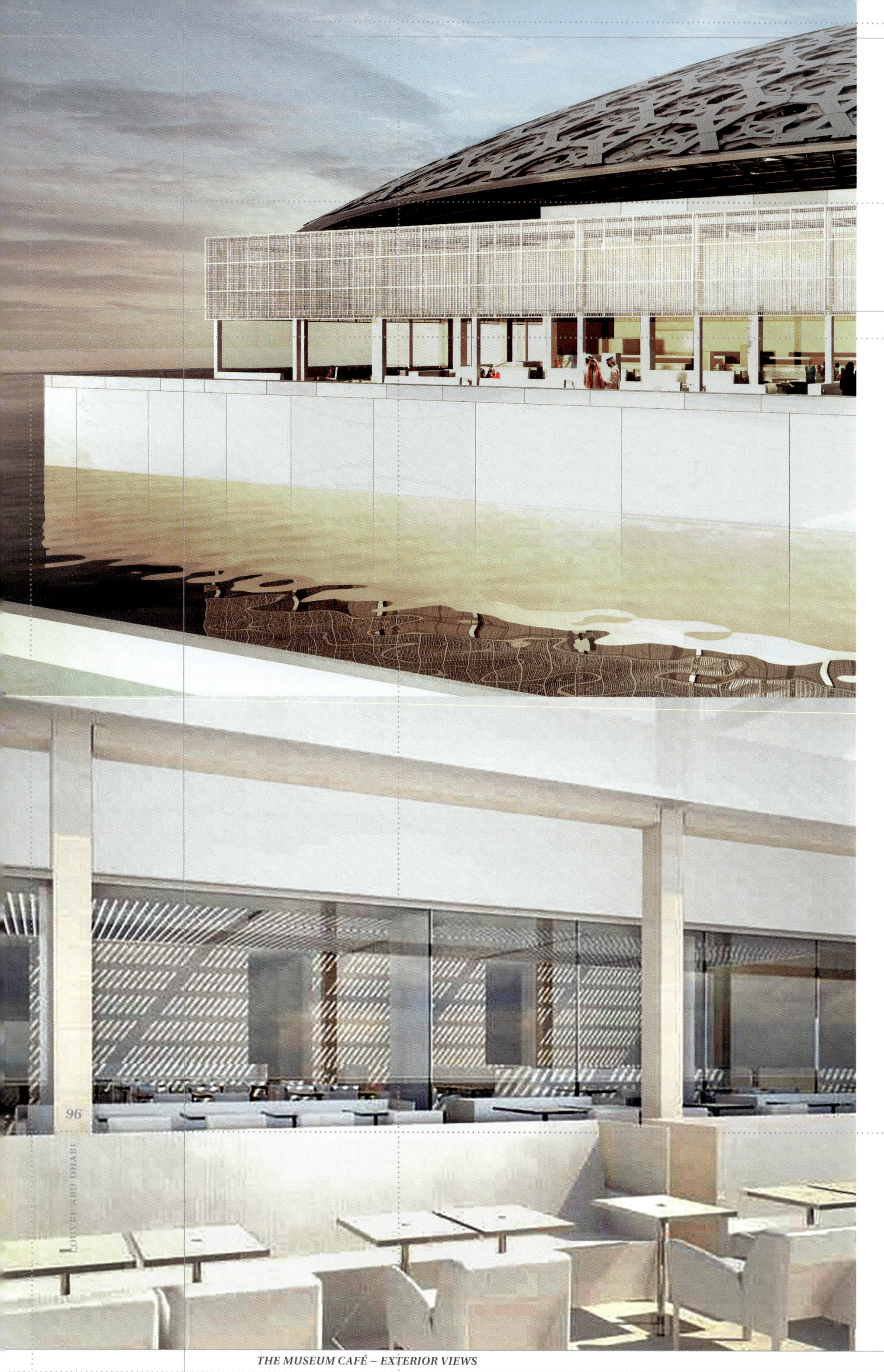

THE MUSEUM CAFÉ – EXTERIOR VIEWS

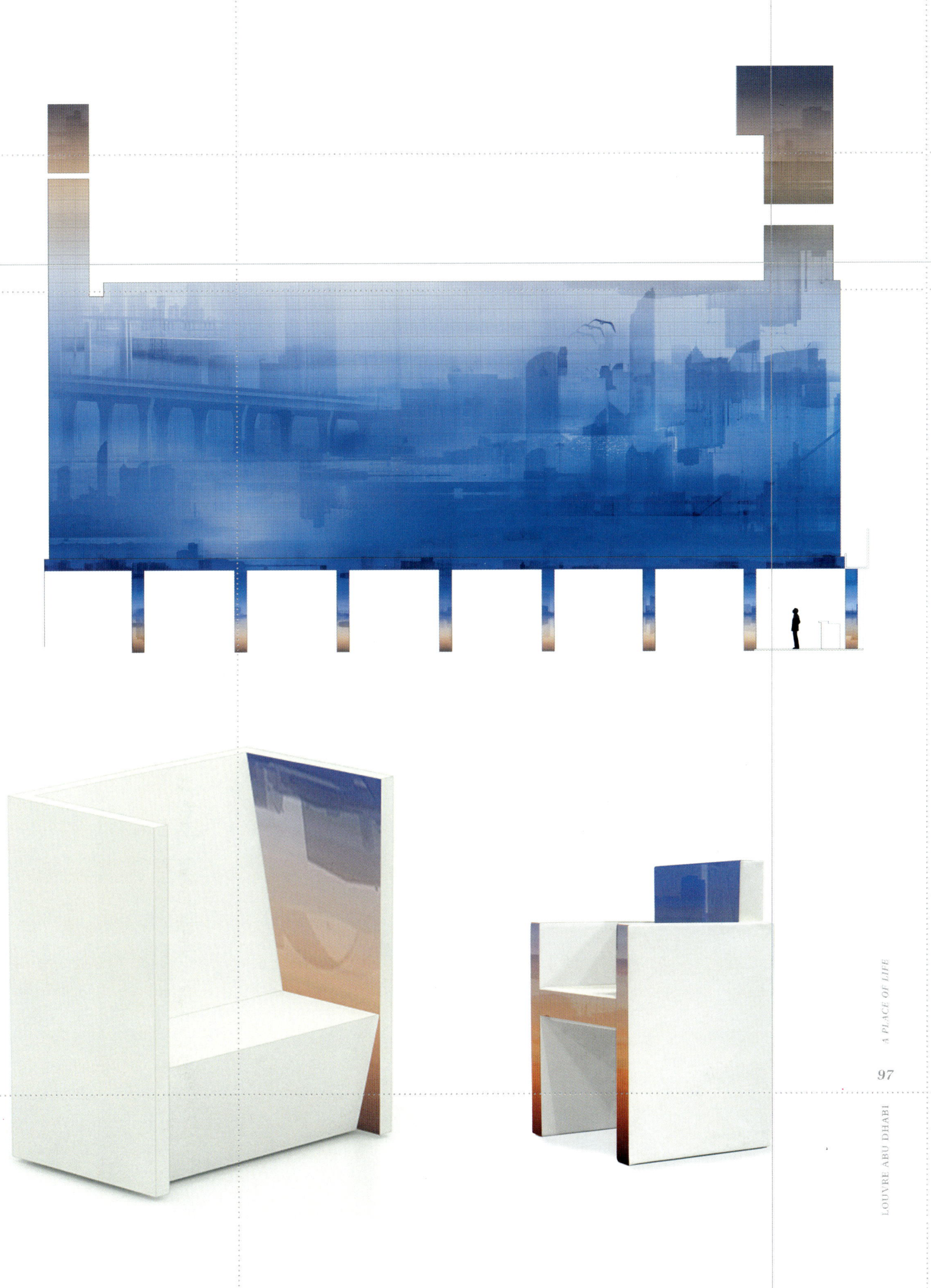

INTERNAL FRESCO (CEILING, WALLS AND FURNITURE) – ARTISTIC INTERVENTION BY MARIE MAILLARD

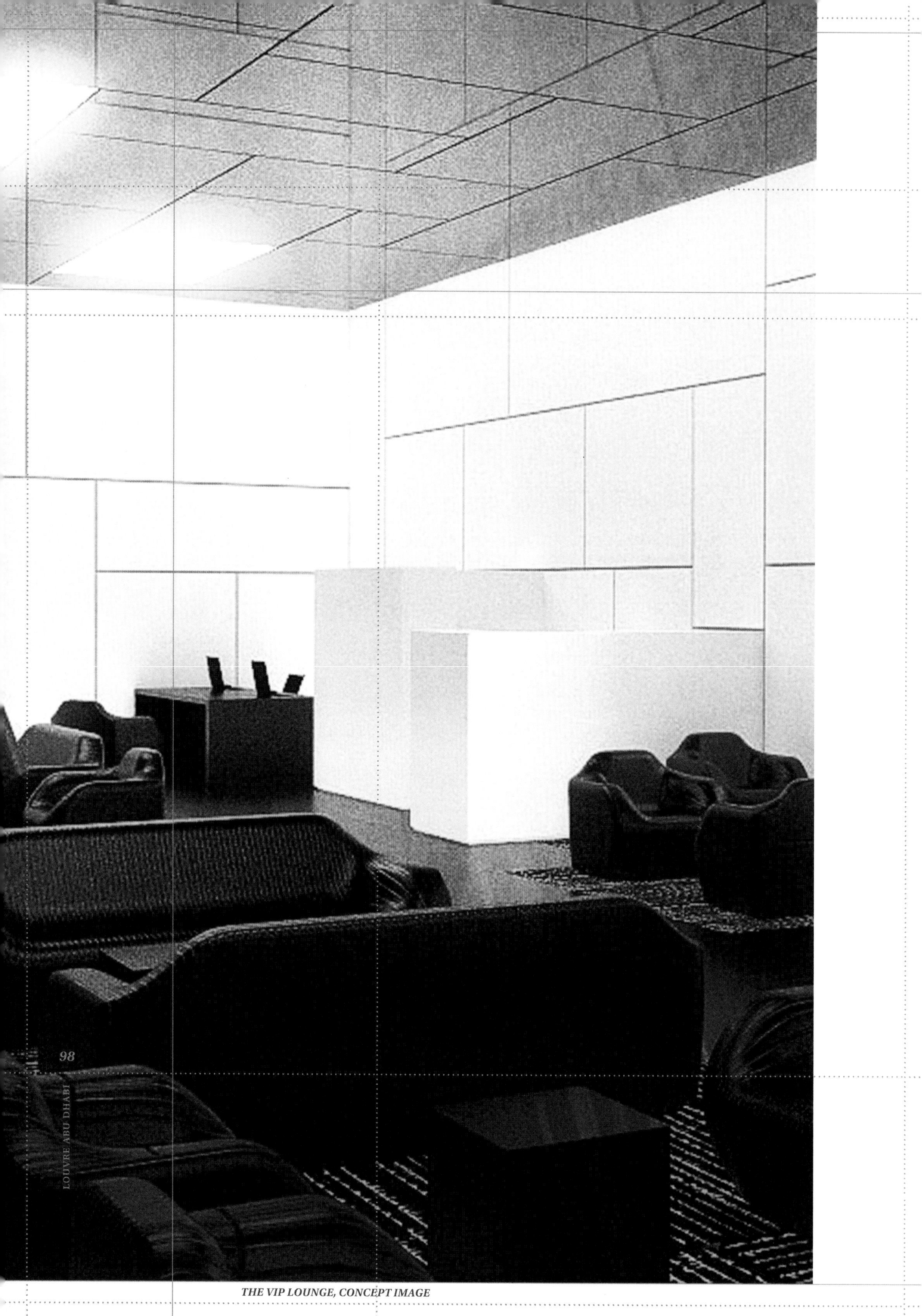

THE VIP LOUNGE, CONCEPT IMAGE

Laid out lengthwise above and alongside the temporary exhibition gallery, the VIP Majlis draws on the traditions both of the Arab world's small gatherings and of the Anglo-Saxon club. Members of local and cosmopolitan society from the worlds of politics, finance, trade, culture and the mass media gather here. It is a place of informal conversations and friendly meetings in a relaxed atmosphere for small groups bound by affinities. While the auditorium is a more appropriate venue for larger gatherings, those participating in the larger meetings and symposiums held there are always sure of an invitation to the Majlis during their stay.

They are welcomed by the comfort and luxury of a VIP lounge furnished with comfortable armchairs and sofas specially designed for the museum by Jean Nouvel. Shelves and bookcases line the walls, extrapolations of the cyclopean walls of the museum with their large white modules of fibre-reinforced concrete, the proportions of which are also reproduced in the Corian modules of furniture, cupboards, doorways and work surfaces.

FRIENDS OF LOUVRE ABU DHABI

The Friends of the Louvre Abu Dhabi is an association of individuals deeply involved in the life of the arts and museums, a learned assembly of perspicacious experts renowned for their knowledge and commitment to the world of art. They are also generous donators, patrons, collectors, intellectuals and art historians, capable of inspiring the museum with their vision and playing an active part in the acquisition of new works or the choice of living artists for commissioned works. The extension of their network of contacts to the other great international institutions enables them to facilitate exchanges and possible joint projects involving illustrious artists and curators. They hold the position of the counsellors and advisers at the Louvre Abu Dhabi, where they occupy a comfortable and discreetly luxurious space furnished with armchairs by Jean Nouvel, a huge table for meetings and a dedicated library.

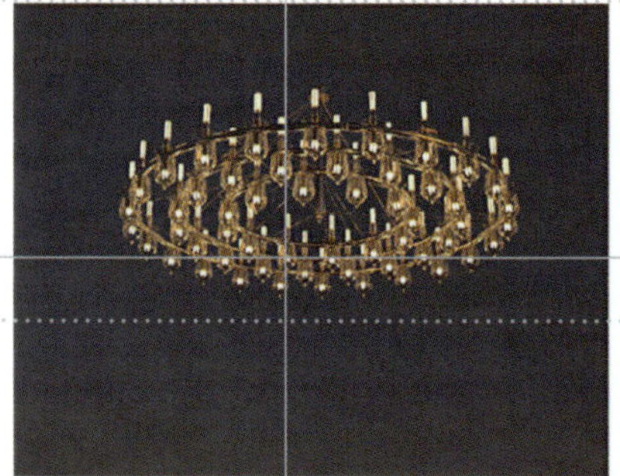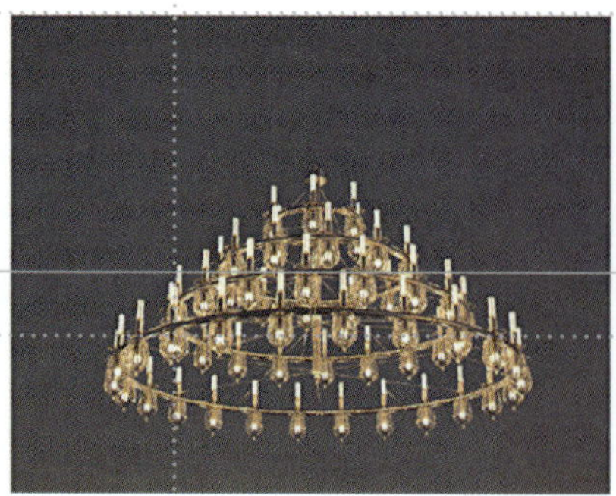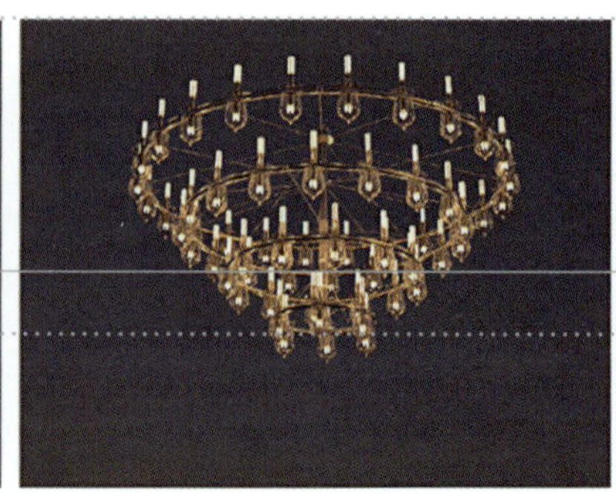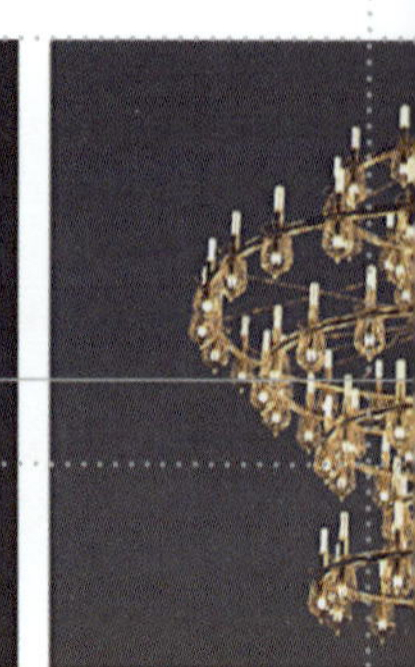

THE BOUTIQUE

The combined boutique and bookshop of the Louvre Abu Dhabi greets visitors before they enter the large hall leading to the exhibitions to offer them a foretaste of the museum and ensure that they will return at the end of their visit to make purchases through which their experience will live on in their memory. The museum's own publications, catalogues, works on art and civilisations are available in the bookshop, and reproductions of works, postcards, posters, stationery, gadgets and T-shirts in the boutique.

The fittings and fixtures of the combined boutique and bookshop continue upon the logic of the entrance area, with shelves, racks and stands in Corian, and technical systems in matte black in keeping with the starkness and sobriety of the area.

ELEMENTS OF DESIGN

Architecture does not stop at the front door. It is a sensitive and intellectual approach expressed in even the smallest details. The spirit of the Louvre Abu Dhabi is characterised by the light that dapples its white spaces, the precise scale of each building and component, and the pursuit of nobility, simplicity, purity, tension and calm. It rejects the picturesque plagiarism of historical themes, and the adoption of obsolete international formulas that claim to be professional but are no more than the result of a lack of imagination, effort and rigour.

Every element we propose for public spaces (security checkpoints, information desks, ticket desks, cloakrooms, storage, seating, our recommendations for the "VIP Lounge" and the auditorium) is designed specifically for this location and will act as yet another architectural mark of identity for the Louvre Abu Dhabi. This will also be the case for outdoor seating and signage, which might otherwise destroy the museum's precise and precious image. **JEAN NOUVEL**

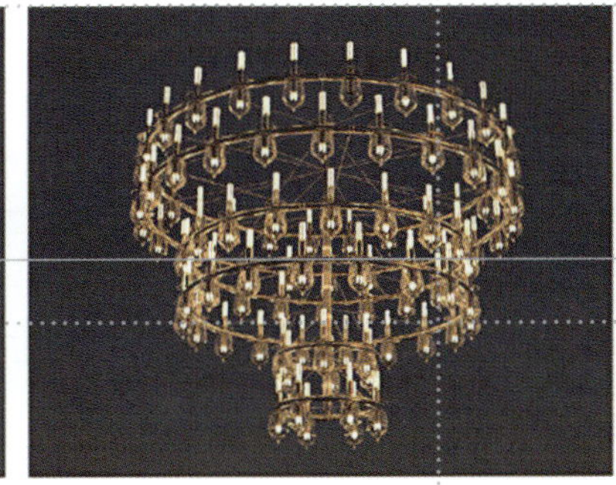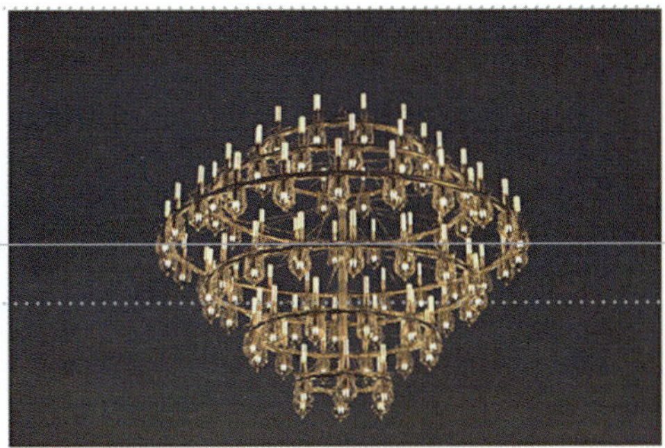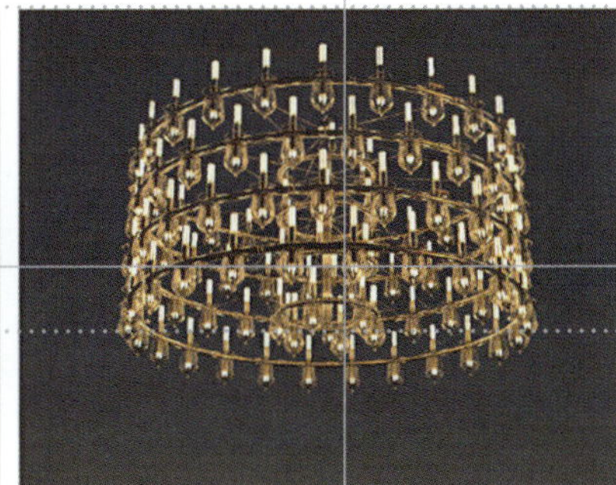

THE RESTAURANT'S SEVEN CHANDELIERS, MANUFACTURED BY MOBILIER NATIONAL IN PARIS

THE FURNITURE DESIGNED BY JEAN NOUVEL

Jean Nouvel, "an architect who does design", developed original models for the seating and tables for the Louvre Abu Dhabi, and a set of chandeliers for the restaurant.

THE SEATING

The seating establishes the lines of furniture designed for the Louvre Abu Dhabi. The first element is the sofa bench for public spaces, a solid form with taut curves. Each constituent profile has a thickness of a few centimetres, and these are assembled together to create a comfortable but austere sofa in black leather with ribbing every two or three centimetres. The skin is in fact a double skin (support material + foam + leather with structural stitching every three centimetres). Precisely positioned along the walls and distributed through the space, these long sofas accentuate the scale of the space and its lines of force. Ribbed leather is the material hallmark of the Louvre Abu Dhabi line, a graphic form of expression, an aesthetic of abstraction adaptable to countless situations. Armchairs of the utmost comfort display curves, arabesques deftly calibrated for different situations: low seating, club chairs, and so on.

A line of carpets with white calligraphy on a black background, closely related to the basic motif of the three-centimetre ribbing, completes the furniture range.

THE RESTAURANT TABLES

These are round tables whose diameter can be increased by the addition of a homothetic top and be extended by joining various units together. The Corian top is coated with epoxy resin.

THE RESTAURANT CHANDELIERS

The chandeliers consist of a series of rings of tubular metal 30 mm in diameter attached to a vertical tube by slender spokes of stainless steel. The rings are in four sizes – XL 173 cm; L 130 cm; M 88 cm; S 45 cm – and support the lights: below the ring, a LED bulb inside blown glass; above, a cylindrical LED bulb or a candle for exceptional events.

Seven configurations were defined:

Chandelier 1, on a single level: 1 XL + 1 L + 1 M

Chandelier 2, conical, pointed upwards: 1 XL + 1 L + 1 M + 1 S

Chandelier 3, conical, pointed downwards: 1 XL + 1 L + 1 M + 1 S

Chandelier 4, cone + cylinder: 1 XL + 1 L + 3 M + 2 S

Chandelier 5, 3 cylinders: 2 XL + 2 L + 2 S

Chandelier 6, 2 cones: 1 XL + 2 L + 2 M + 1 S

Chandelier 7, 2 cones: 4 XL + 4 S

The chandeliers are hung at three heights above the ground: position 0 at 1.95 m, position 1 at 3.4 m and position 2 at 5.1 m. The maintenance position is 1 metre above the ground.

THE SIGNAGE

The signage of the Louvre Abu Dhabi was conceived by Ateliers Jean Nouvel with the graphic designer Philippe Apeloig in four hierarchical levels: monumental signage, moulded directly in the ultra-high performance concrete panels of the walls to identify the principal areas of the museum; signage in luminous letters directing visitors in the spaces beneath the dome; directional signage including pictograms in colours related to the functions of the places indicated; museum signage in the galleries, including the artwork labels, explanatory labels, and entrance panels.

All the indications are given in three languages: Arabic, English and French. The font chosen for the Latin texts is Frutiger LT Pro, a sans serif typeface renowned for its legibility. The Arabic typeface was specially designed for the Louvre Abu Dhabi by the Lebanese typographer Kristyan Sarkis.

In designing the pictograms, Philippe Apeloig drew on the geometrical forms created in the building by the shafts of sunlight filtered through the dome.

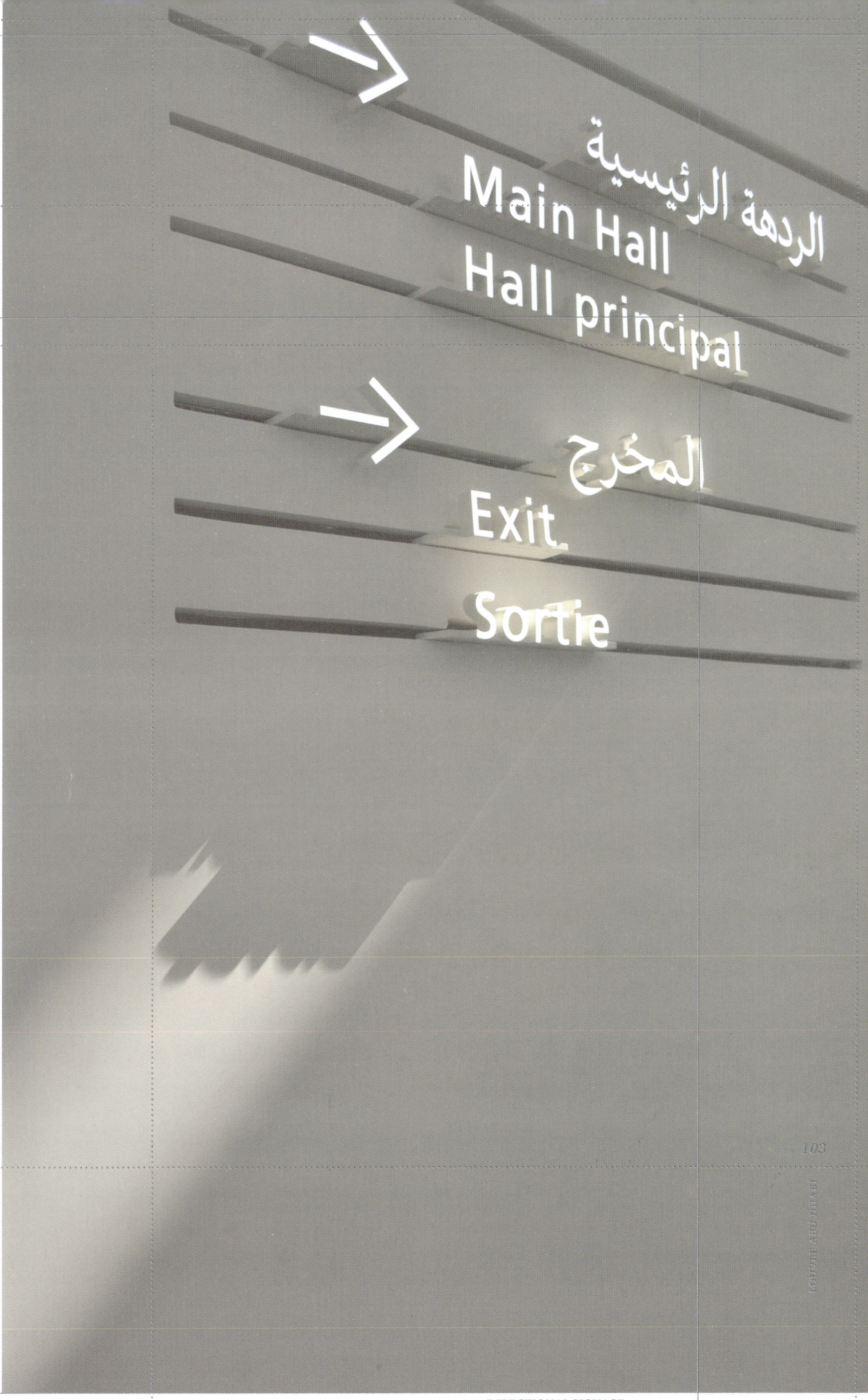

الردهة الرئيسية
Main Hall
Hall principal
المخرج
Exit
Sortie

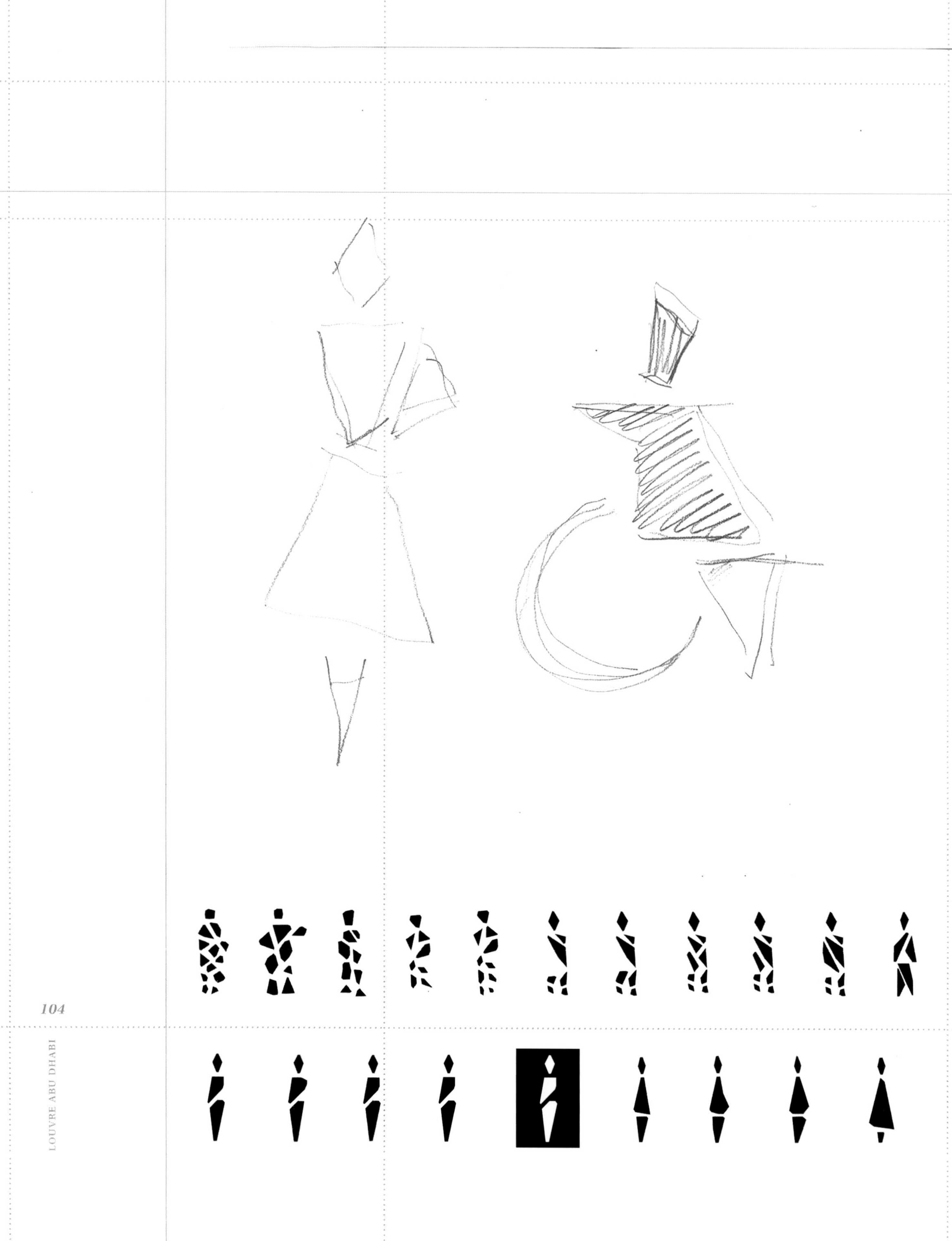

PICTOGRAM SKETCHES BY PHILIPPE APELOIG

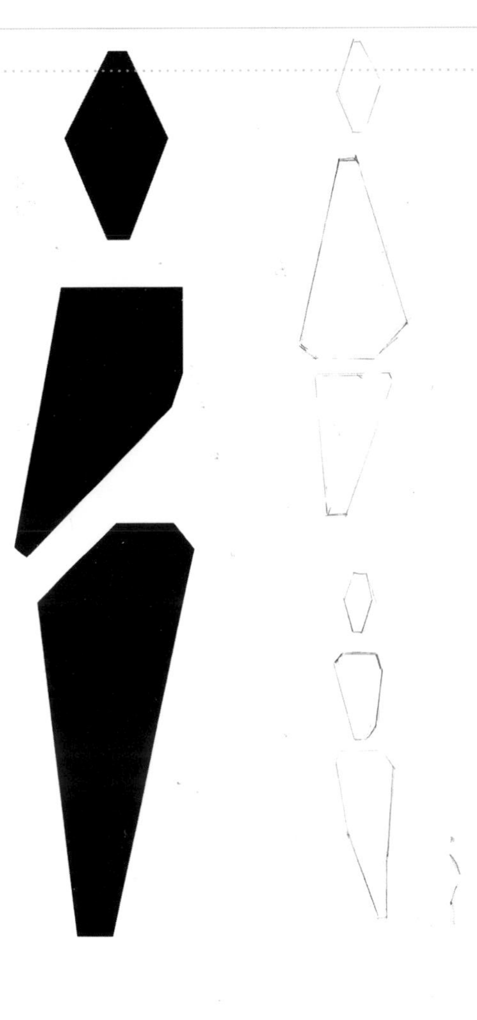

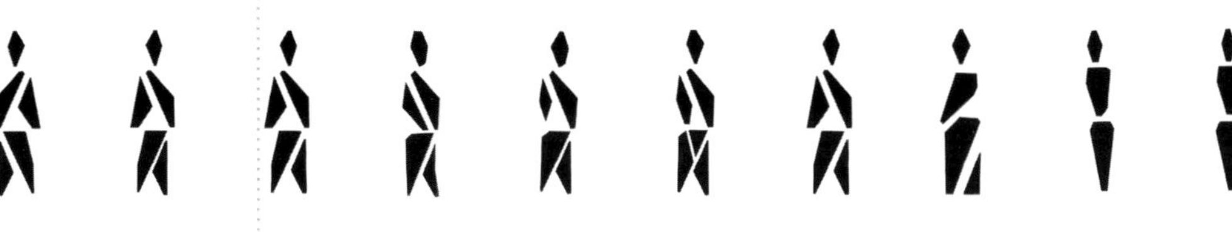

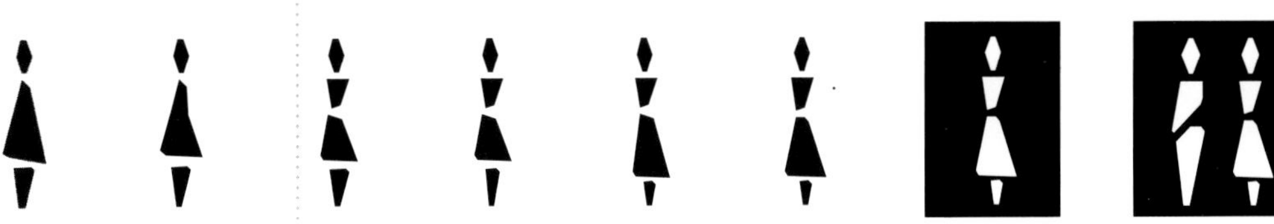

JEAN NOUVEL AND HIS TEAM ELABORATED THE SIGNAGE CONCEPT IN COLLABORATION WITH PHILIPPE APELOIG

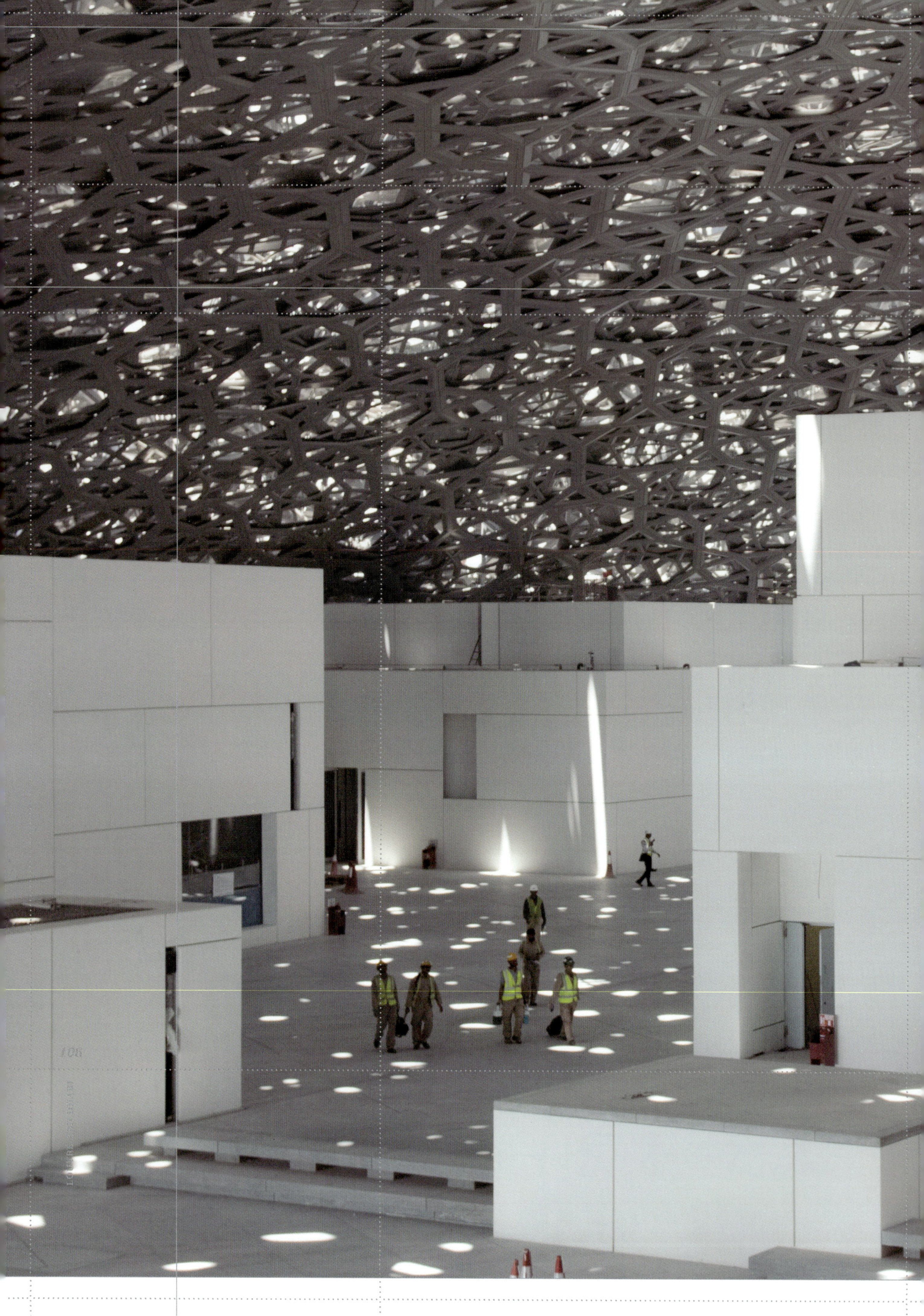

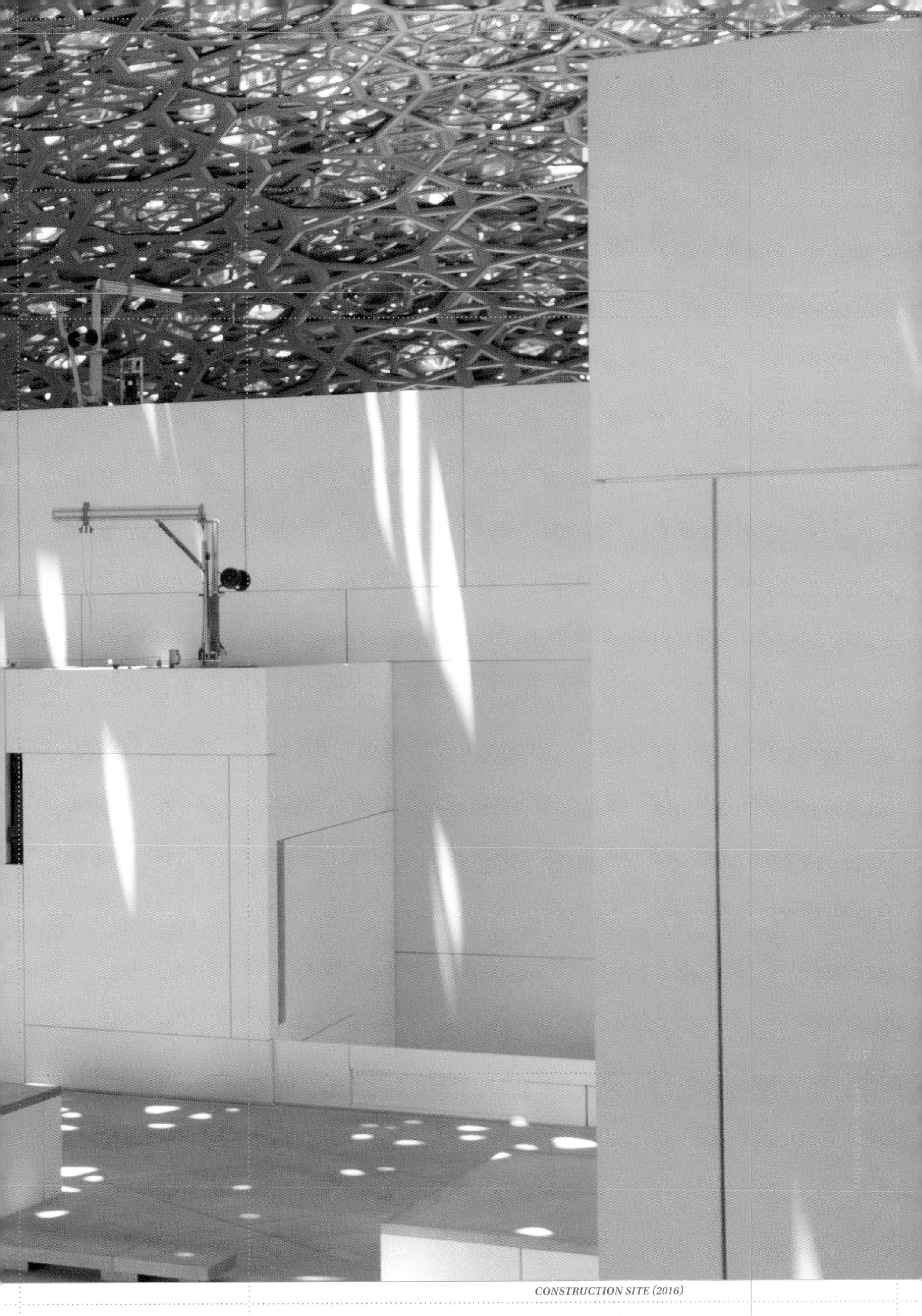

CONSTRUCTION SITE (2016)

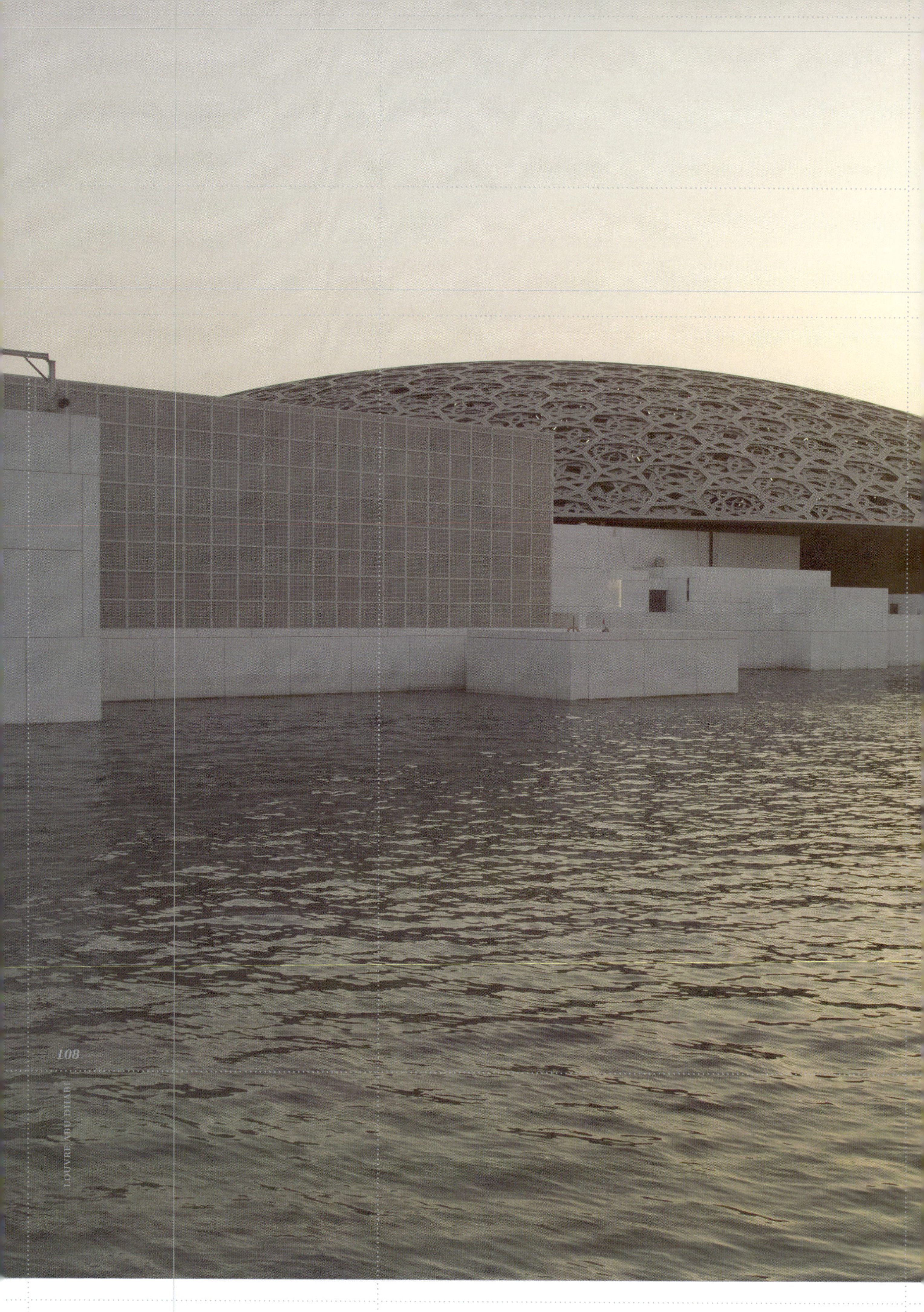

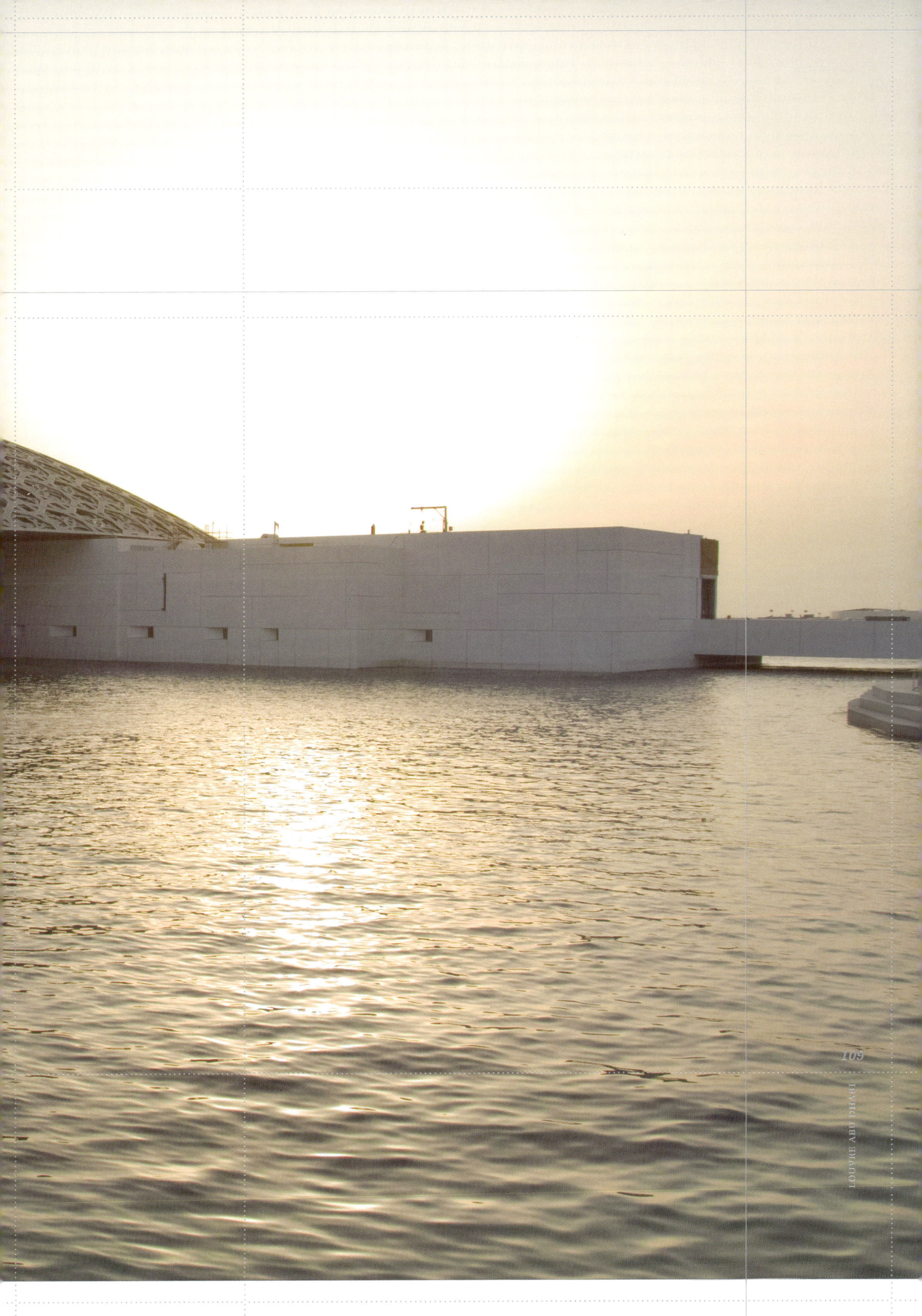

A FROZEN DREAM OF LIGHT

The ideas took shape and the dream took the risk of meeting unpredictable reality head-on and over a prolonged period.
A heavy-duty, protective museum has achieved a space in which objects and artworks testifying to different civilisations, past and present, are positioned, classified and resonate with each other. The building aims to conjure up the metaphysical depths glimpsed when such unimaginable and amazing encounters occur, speaking to us so eloquently of universal values... In these spaces, anyone wanting to invoke the universal finds allies... In the sky, the sea, the desert.

The Louvre Abu Dhabi rises from a sandy beach on the desert island of Saadiyat and, naturally, everything about it shows that it belongs to the cosmos, to the sea and the terrain. The thing that will hit visitors first, even if they're already familiar with images and drawings of the museum, is the actual reality and the shock that comes from realising "it's happened!" How many poetic ideas have enticed us for a moment when we see them on glossy paper or onscreen, never to be indelibly imprinted in our memories? The building is discovered and experienced slowly, by walking... The fact is that in this realm no photograph can really convey the emotions the reality produces: none is capable of capturing the scale – that is, the size of the space in relation to that of a human being – or the light, or the succession of discoveries, the thresholds, the perspectives and framed views, or the different times of day and their different emanations, or the rhythmic patterns and sequences crossed... So it's clear that this book won't be enough, that we really do need to walk through the Louvre Abu Dhabi ourselves to stock up on memories... And such a visit will need to take in the whole neighbourhood, too, and not just the building.

As part of a conversation between civilisations, the building is contextual, recalling two types of architecture: the first is the Arab village, white and geometric; the second is the dome, also white, and flagging the spiritual nature of the museum in terms of its sacred contents... Ambling along in the shade through the narrow walled passageways, we come to large and small squares where works of contemporary art have been conceived in harmony with the architecture: the engraved writings of Jenny Holzer, and the tree and ceramics of Giuseppe Penone... Under the dome, appearances contrast, the light raining down will always be characterised by variations in days and seasons... From the narrow alleys in the background, and from the squares, the ways the sea is framed remind us that the museum is part of the world, a feeling intensified by the presence of a remnant of marine archaeology, with its fine columns and its walls drowned by the sea... The framing of the port world, through the focus on the passing boats and on the long horizons where sky and sea meet, opens the museum to the imaginary worlds of seafaring and distant civilisations. It can also be visited by night. Sunset and sundown are part of the performance: evenings are more comfortable down by the seaside, where a gentle sea breeze routinely brings a delectable mildness... Visiting the collections goes beyond one more discovery of different sea and urban skylines: it's an incredible historical panorama of unlikely encounters between works created simultaneously in different places, or of artistic expressions coinciding at different periods in history... Memorable connections, invented for these unprecedented encounters, are made under precise and measured doses of light streaming through glass ceilings of variable geometries and intensities. The contextualisations – first and foremost, those of the era – have forced us to create something unique in the meeting of space and light... My ambition and my obsession have long led me to work that anticipates the life of buildings over time by programming a succession of calm moments in the course of their different phases, from birth to destruction... At the Louvre Abu Dhabi I've tried to induce a fleeting awareness of being in one of those places where, as the poet Paul Valéry said, *"Time scintillates and Dreaming is knowing"*.

JEAN NOUVEL

CONCLUSION-RECAPITULATION
IN THE FORM OF EVOCATION-ACCUMULATION
PRESENTED IN A DELIBERATELY RANDOM ORDER

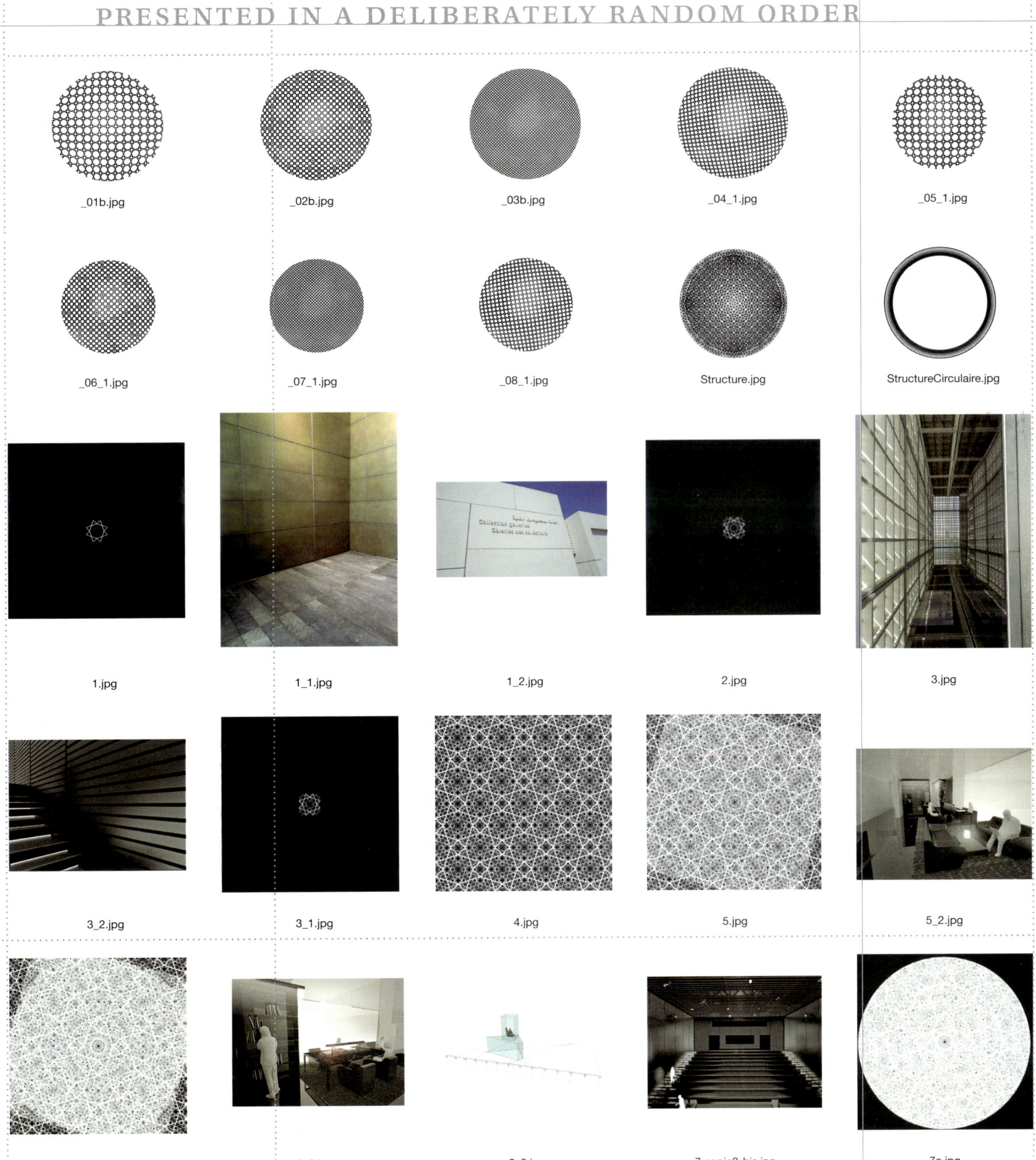

_01b.jpg
_02b.jpg
_03b.jpg
_04_1.jpg
_05_1.jpg
_06_1.jpg
_07_1.jpg
_08_1.jpg
Structure.jpg
StructureCirculaire.jpg
1.jpg
1_1.jpg
1_2.jpg
2.jpg
3.jpg
3_2.jpg
3_1.jpg
4.jpg
5.jpg
5_2.jpg
6a.jpg
6_2.jpg
6_3.jpg
7 copie3-bis.jpg
7a.jpg

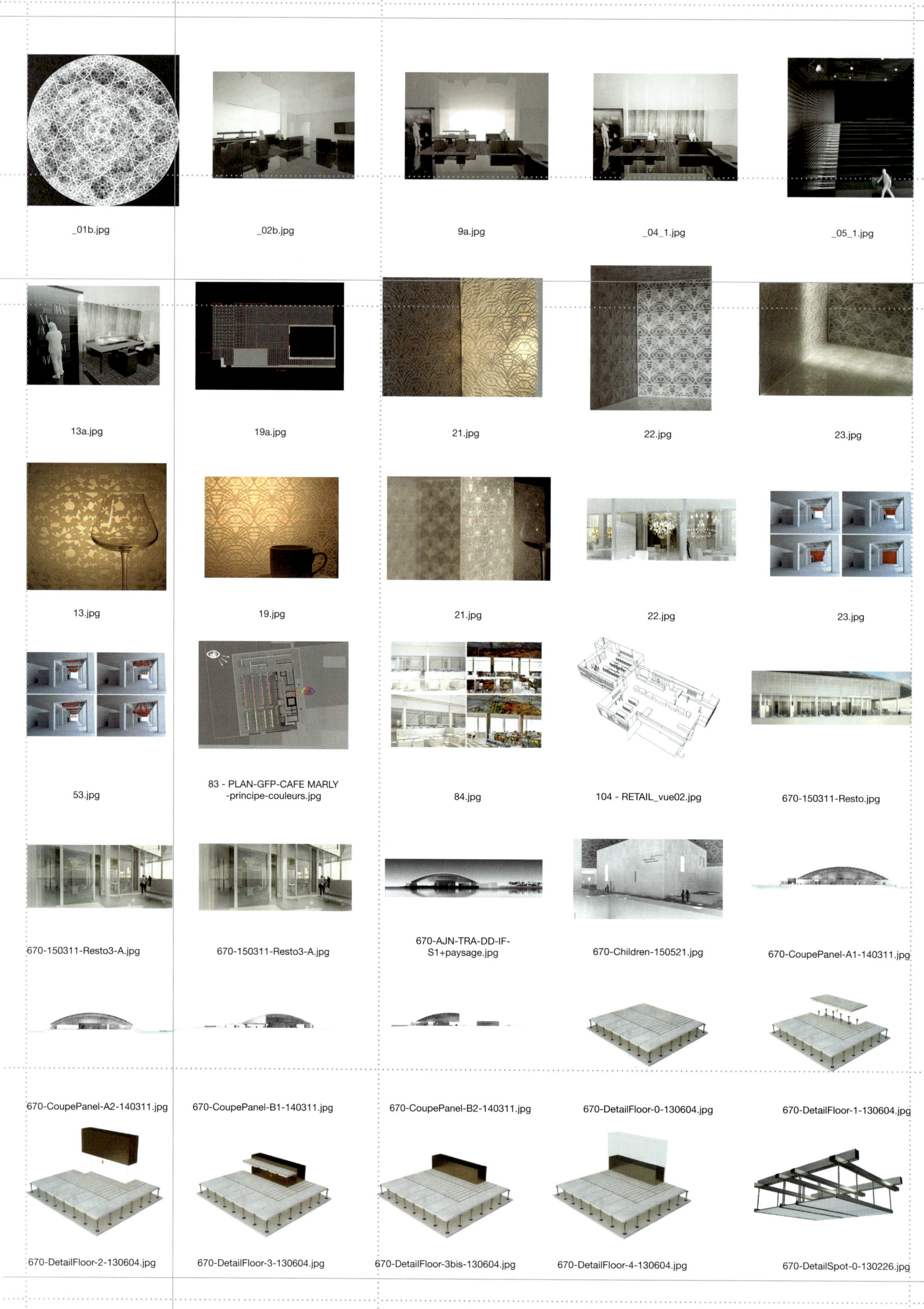

_01b.jpg

_02b.jpg

9a.jpg

_04_1.jpg

_05_1.jpg

13a.jpg

19a.jpg

21.jpg

22.jpg

23.jpg

13.jpg

19.jpg

21.jpg

22.jpg

23.jpg

53.jpg

83 - PLAN-GFP-CAFE MARLY -principe-couleurs.jpg

84.jpg

104 - RETAIL_vue02.jpg

670-150311-Resto.jpg

670-150311-Resto3-A.jpg

670-150311-Resto3-A.jpg

670-AJN-TRA-DD-IF-S1+paysage.jpg

670-Children-150521.jpg

670-CoupePanel-A1-140311.jpg

670-CoupePanel-A2-140311.jpg

670-CoupePanel-B1-140311.jpg

670-CoupePanel-B2-140311.jpg

670-DetailFloor-0-130604.jpg

670-DetailFloor-1-130604.jpg

670-DetailFloor-2-130604.jpg

670-DetailFloor-3-130604.jpg

670-DetailFloor-3bis-130604.jpg

670-DetailFloor-4-130604.jpg

670-DetailSpot-0-130226.jpg

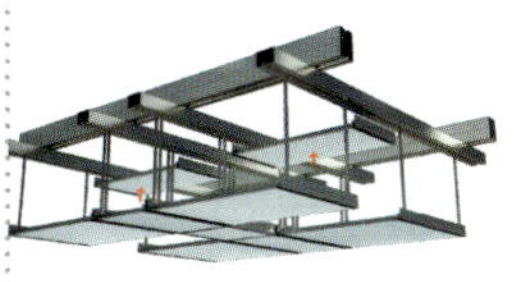

670-DetailSpot-1-130226.jpg

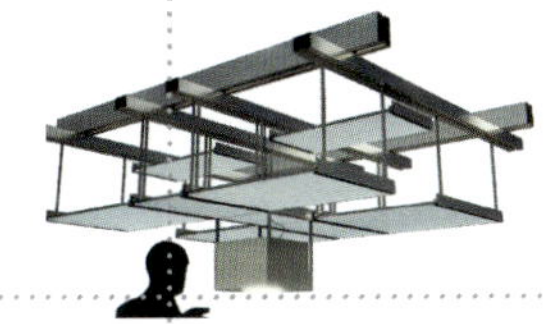

670-DetailSpot-2-130226.jpg

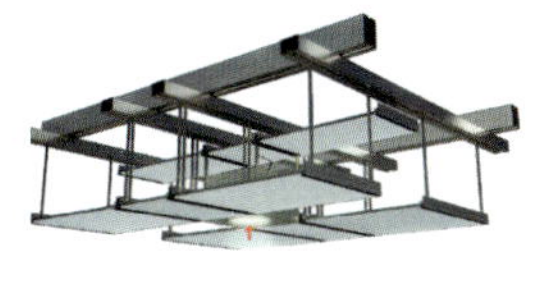

670-DetailSpot-3-130226.jpg

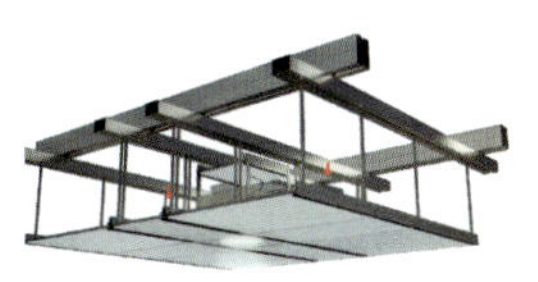

670-DetailSpot-4-130226.jpg

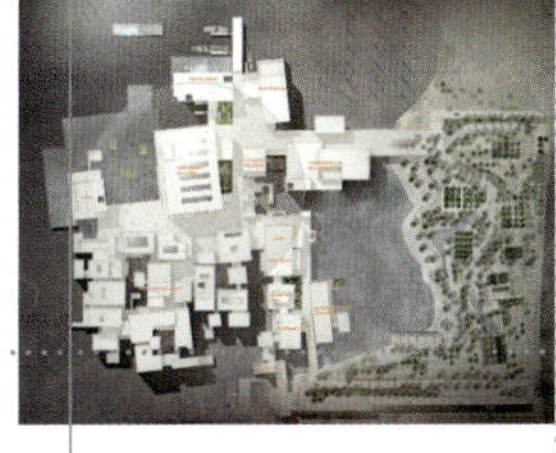

670-DomeTowerPlan-150608.jpg

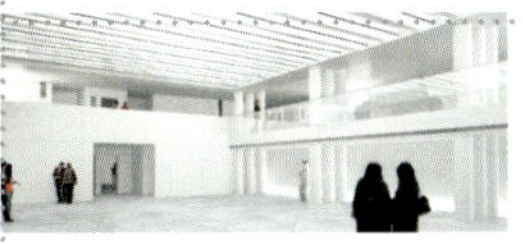

670-Forum-Vue1-150630.jpg

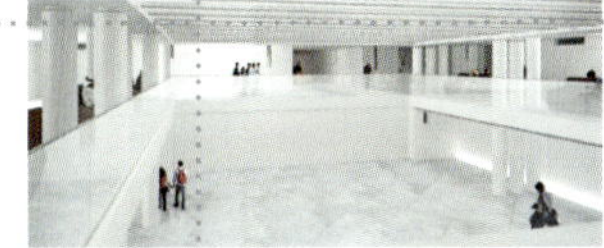

670-Forum-Vue2-150630.jpg

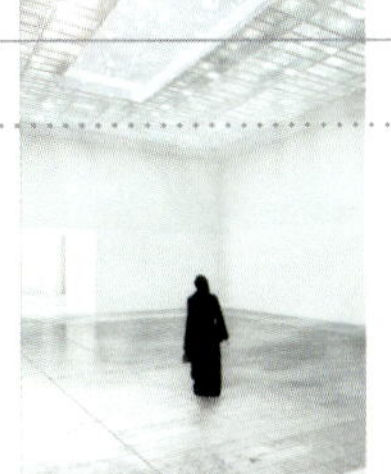

670-GV-130322.jpg

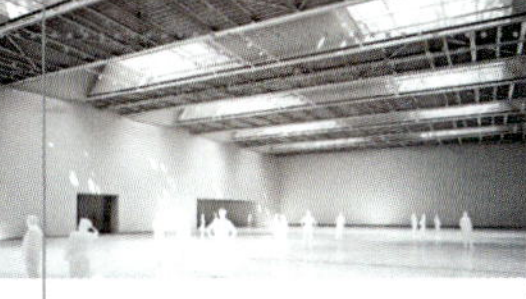

670-LAD_temp-natural_light-04.jpg

670-lad_temp-structure-2.jpg

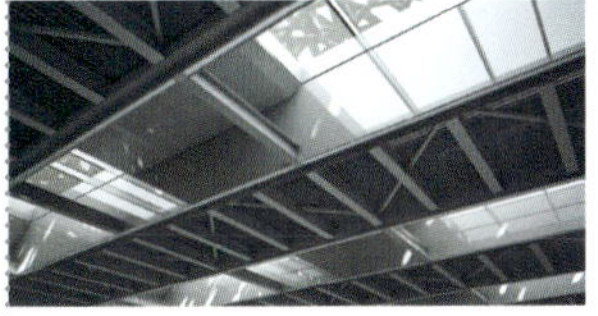

670-DetailSpot-1-130226.jpg

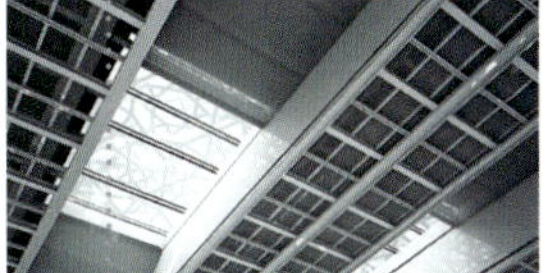

670-DetailSpot-2-130226.jpg

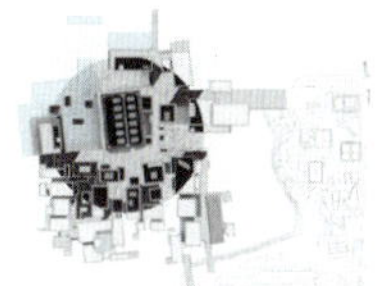

670-DetailSpot-3-130226.jpg

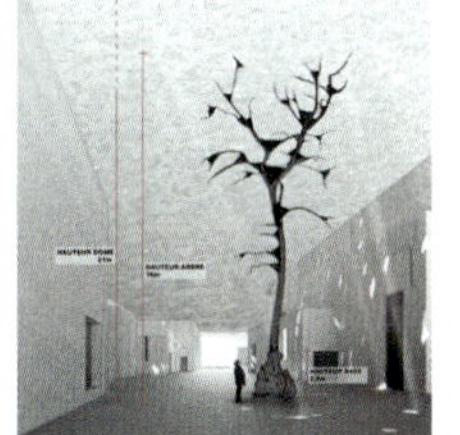

670-DetailSpot-4-130226.jpg

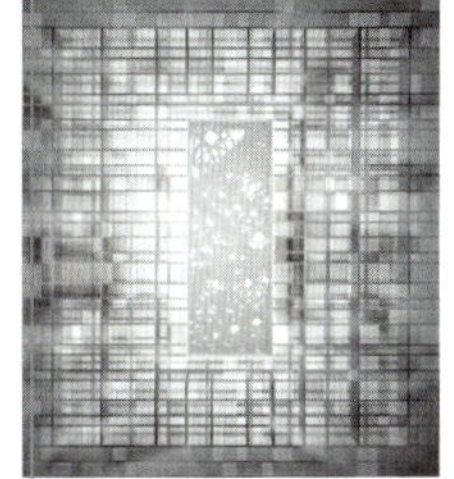

670-DomeTowerPlan-150608.jpg

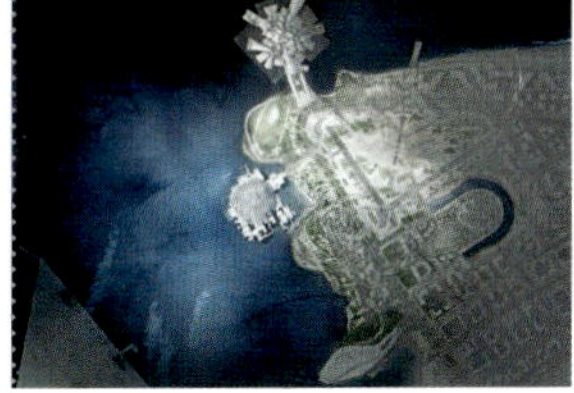

670-DetailSpot-1-130226.jpg

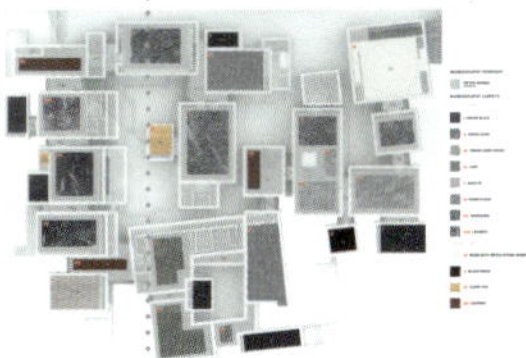

670-DetailSpot-2-130226.jpg

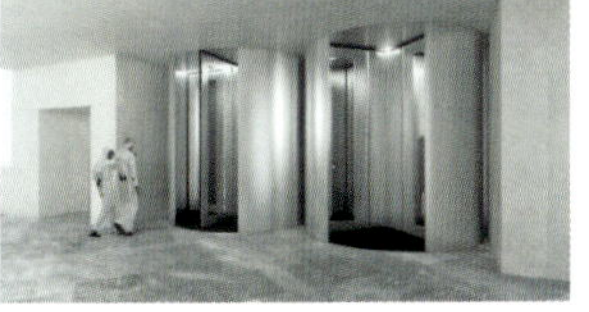

670-DetailSpot-3-130226.jpg

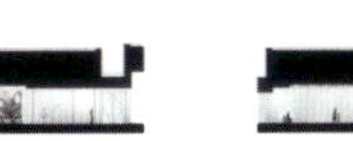

670-DetailSpot-4-130226.jpg

670-DomeTowerPlan-150608.jpg

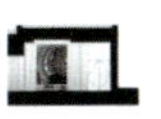

670-DetailSpot-1-130226.jpg

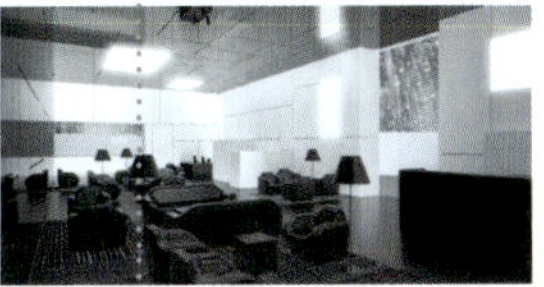

670-DetailSpot-2-130226.jpg

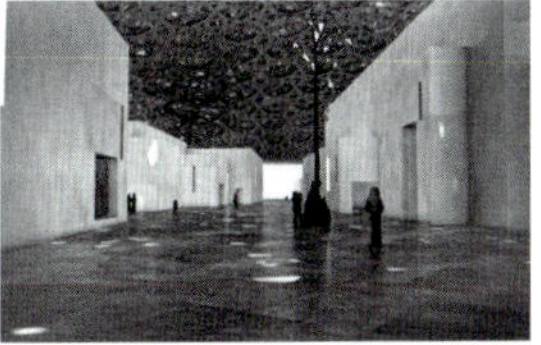

670-DetailSpot-3-130226.jpg

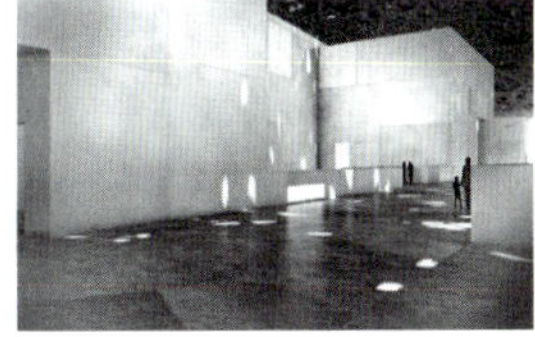

670-DetailSpot-4-130226.jpg

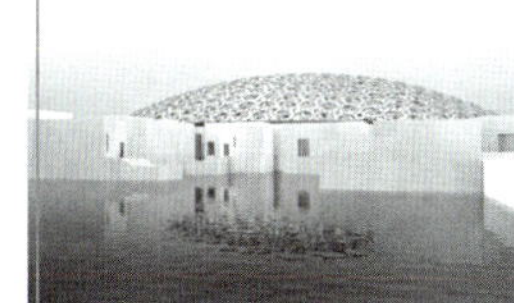

670-DomeTowerPlan-150608.jpg

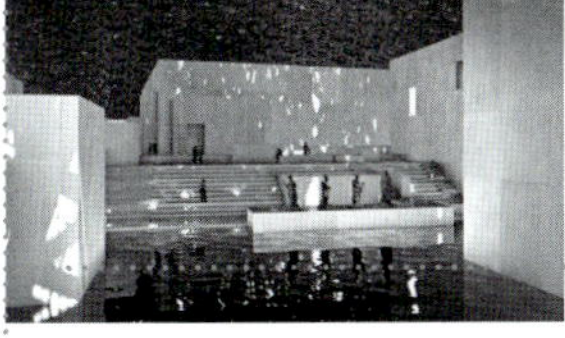

670-DetailSpot-1-130226.jpg

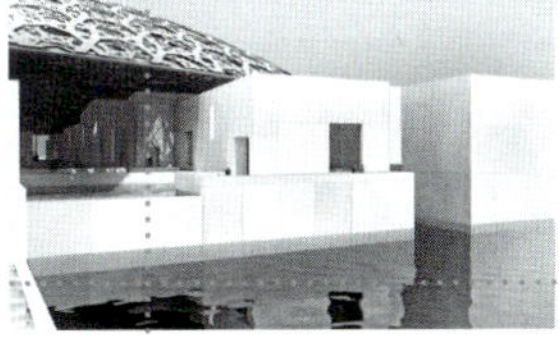

670-DetailSpot-2-130226.jpg

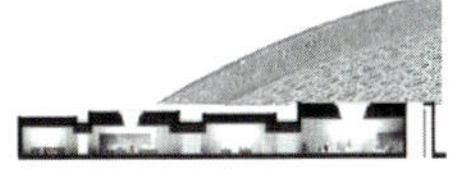

670-DetailSpot-3-130226.jpg

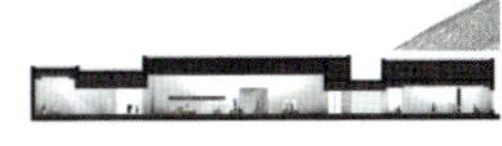

670-DetailSpot-4-130226.jpg

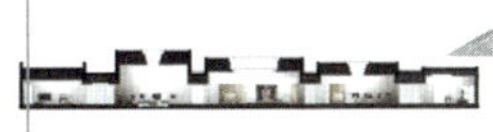

670-DomeTowerPlan-150608.jpg

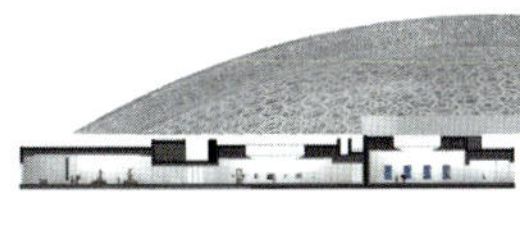

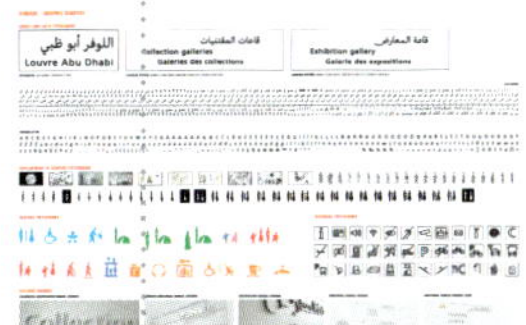

670-DetailSpot-1-130226.jpg

670-DetailSpot-2-130226.jpg

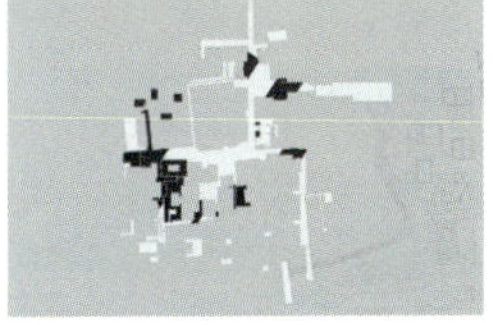

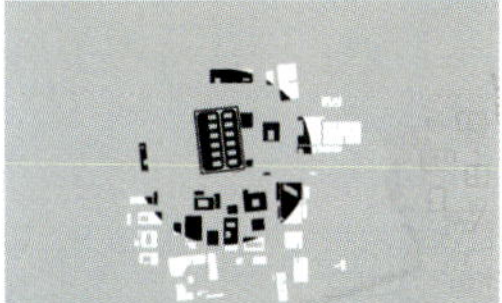

670-DetailSpot-3-130226.jpg

670-DetailSpot-4-130226.jpg

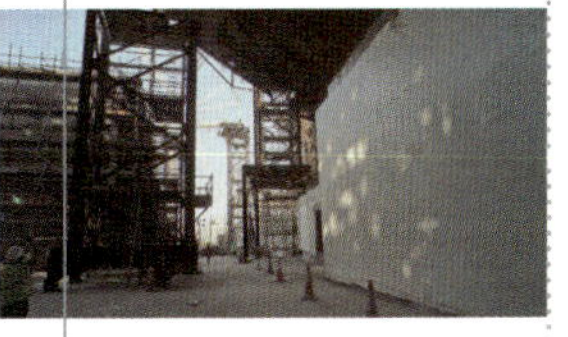

670-DomeTowerPlan-150608.jpg

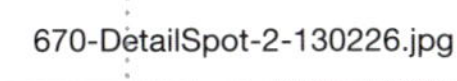

670-DetailSpot-1-130226.jpg

670-DetailSpot-2-130226.jpg

670-DetailSpot-3-130226.jpg

670-DetailSpot-4-130226.jpg

DSC03463-gris.jpg

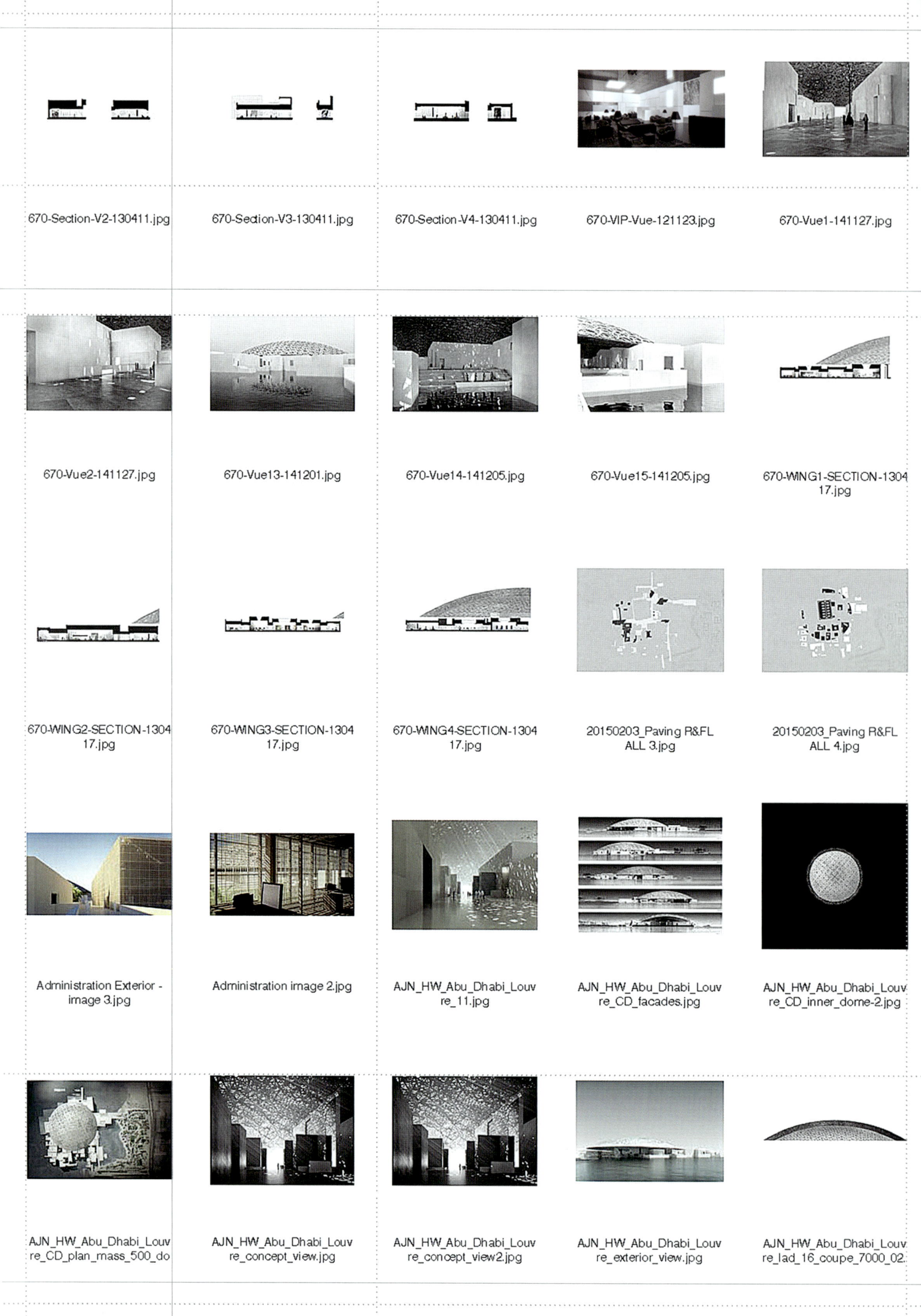

670-Section-V2-130411.jpg

670-Section-V3-130411.jpg

670-Section-V4-130411.jpg

670-VIP-Vue-121123.jpg

670-Vue1-141127.jpg

670-Vue2-141127.jpg

670-Vue13-141201.jpg

670-Vue14-141205.jpg

670-Vue15-141205.jpg

670-WING1-SECTION-1304
17.jpg

670-WING2-SECTION-1304
17.jpg

670-WING3-SECTION-1304
17.jpg

670-WING4-SECTION-1304
17.jpg

20150203_Paving R&FL
ALL 3.jpg

20150203_Paving R&FL
ALL 4.jpg

Administration Exterior -
image 3.jpg

Administration image 2.jpg

AJN_HW_Abu_Dhabi_Louv
re_11.jpg

AJN_HW_Abu_Dhabi_Louv
re_CD_facades.jpg

AJN_HW_Abu_Dhabi_Louv
re_CD_inner_dome-2.jpg

AJN_HW_Abu_Dhabi_Louv
re_CD_plan_mass_500_do

AJN_HW_Abu_Dhabi_Louv
re_concept_view.jpg

AJN_HW_Abu_Dhabi_Louv
re_concept_view2.jpg

AJN_HW_Abu_Dhabi_Louv
re_exterior_view.jpg

AJN_HW_Abu_Dhabi_Louv
re_lad_16_coupe_7000_02.

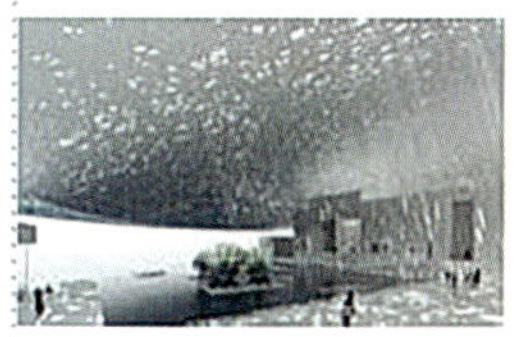

AJN_HW_Abu_dhabi_Louvr
e_View3.jpg

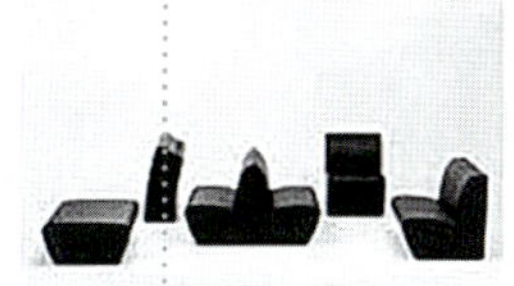

AJN_LAD Line
furniture_01.jpg

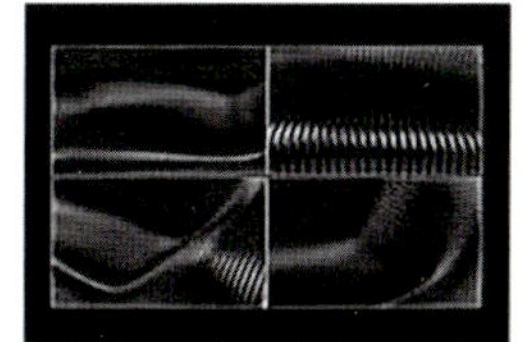

AJN_LAD Line
furniture_Close up.jpg

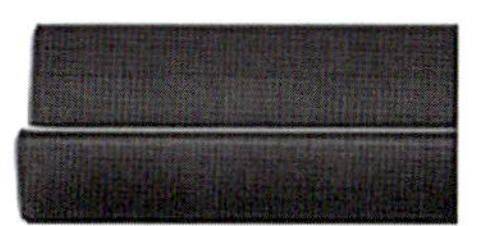

AJN_LAD Line
furniture_Double Seat close

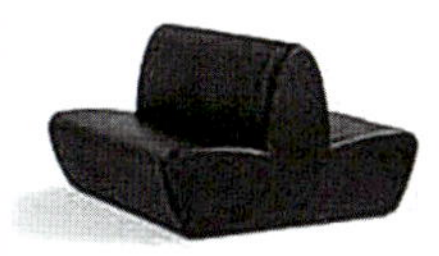

AJN_LAD Line
furniture_Double Seat-Two

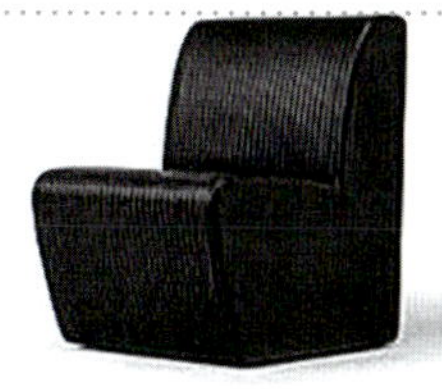

AJN_LAD Line
furniture_Single Seat-One

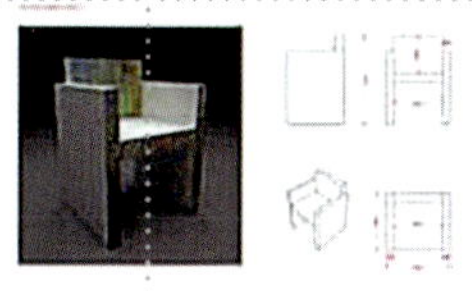

ARMCHAIR.jpg

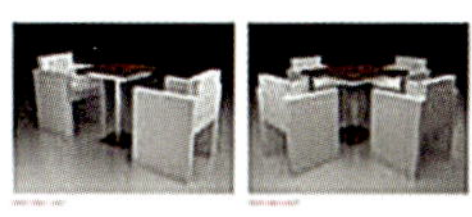

CAFE FURNITURE.jpg

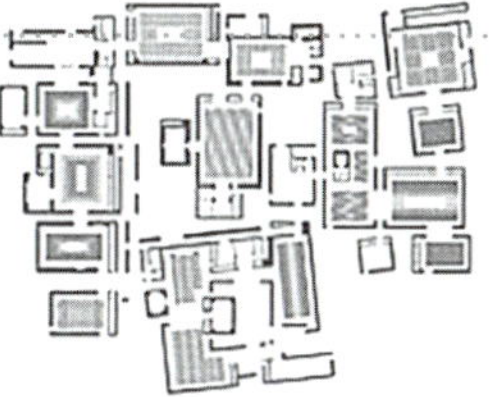

Ceiling.jpg

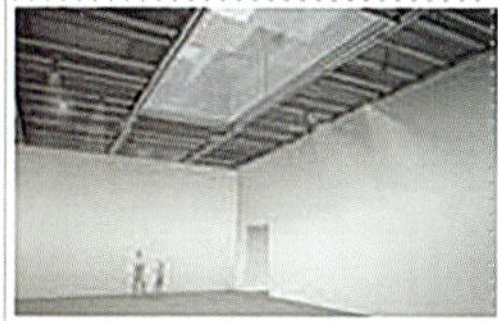

Childrens Museum 03 B.jpg

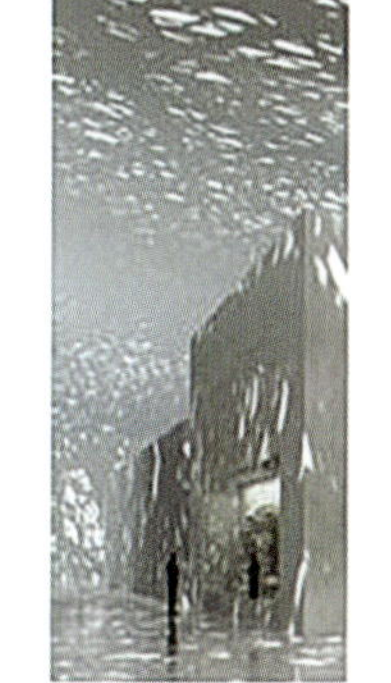

Courette matieres zoom.jpg

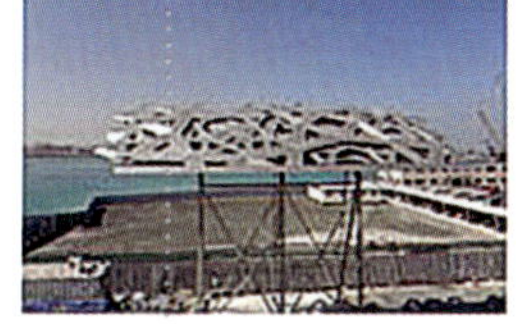

Dome Edge Mock Up.JPG

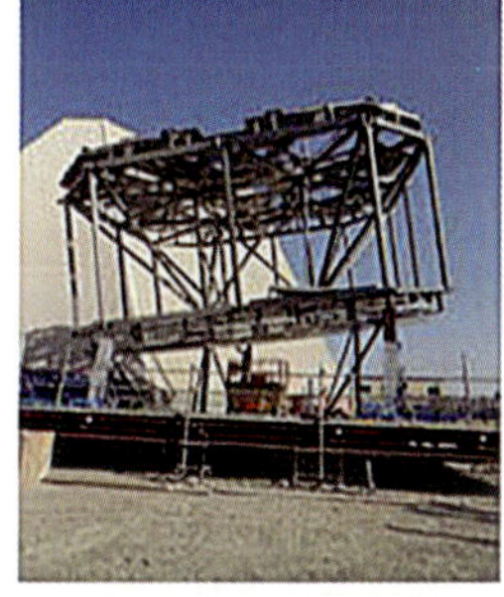

Dome Mock Up.JPG

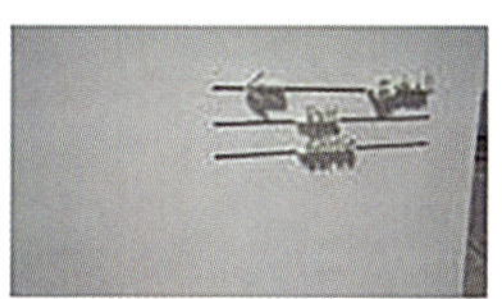

DSC03448.JPG

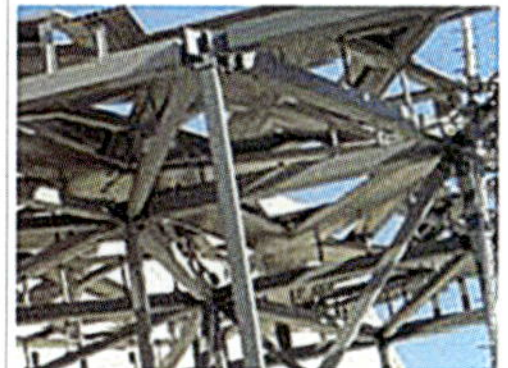

DSC04839.JPG

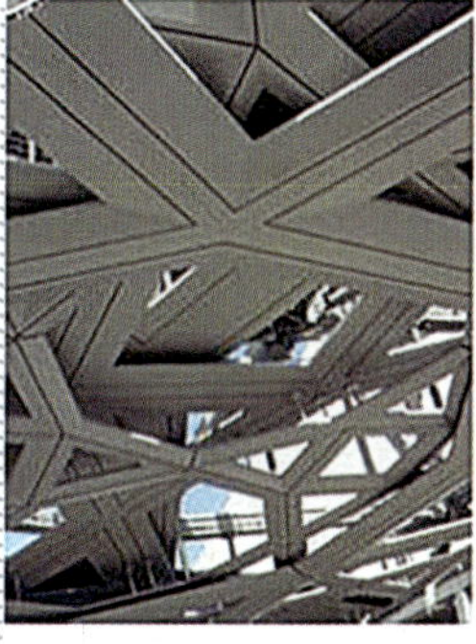

DSC04840.JPG

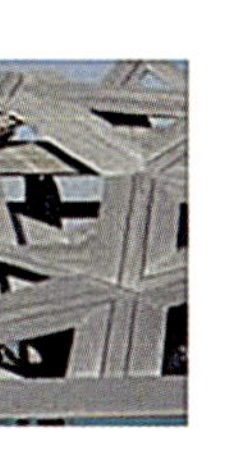

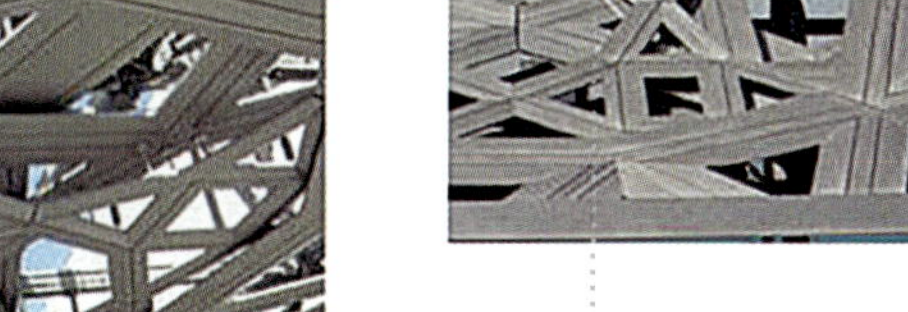

DSC04956.JPG

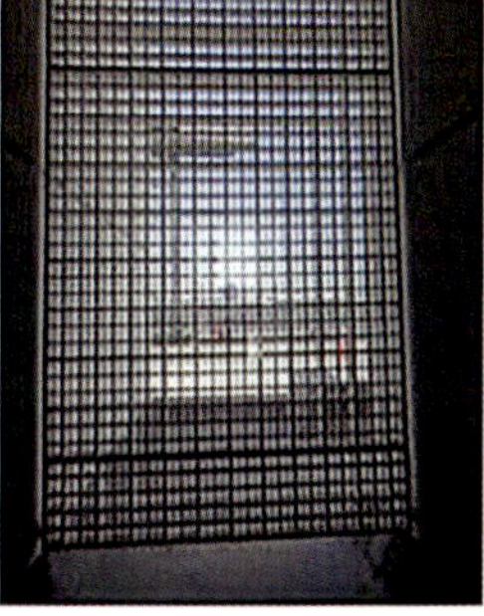

DSC04982.JPG

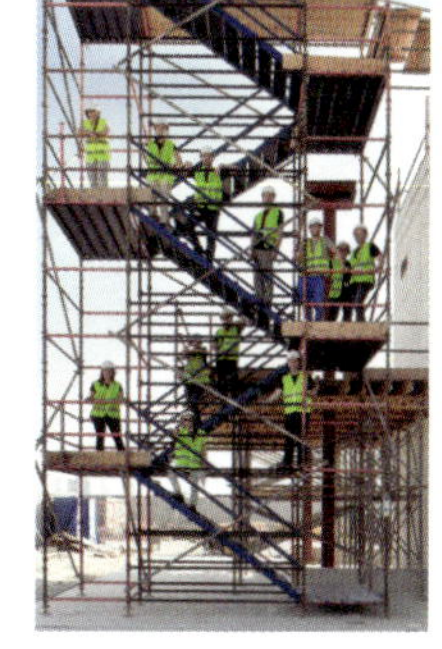

Team-AD_27062013.JPG

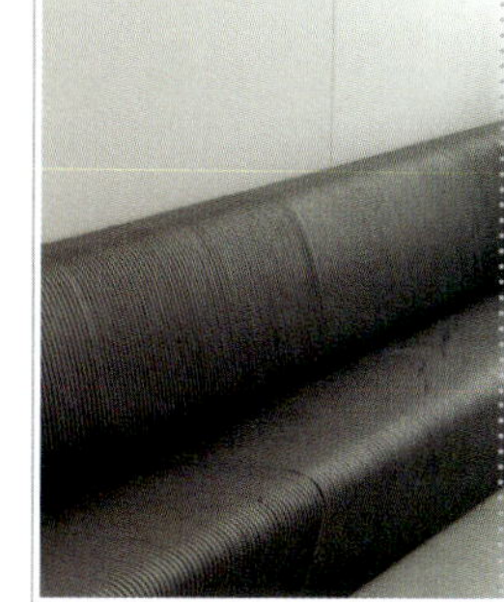

DSC_8579.jpg

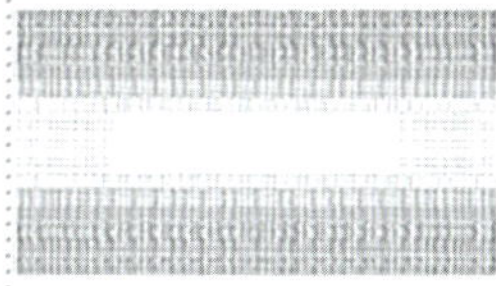

G2-2.jpg

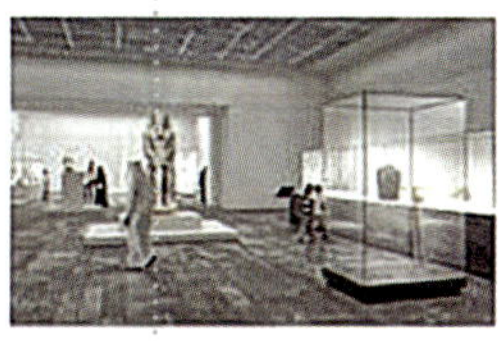

G02.jpg

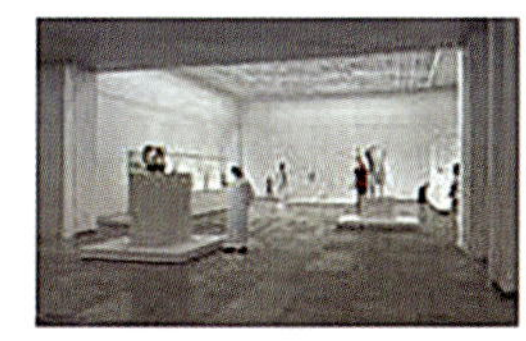

G05-1.jpg

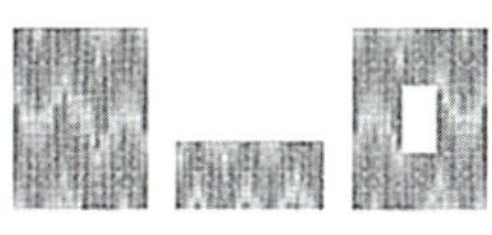

G5-2.png

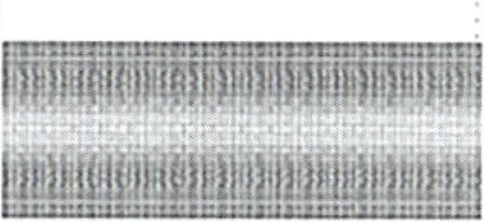

G6-2.jpg

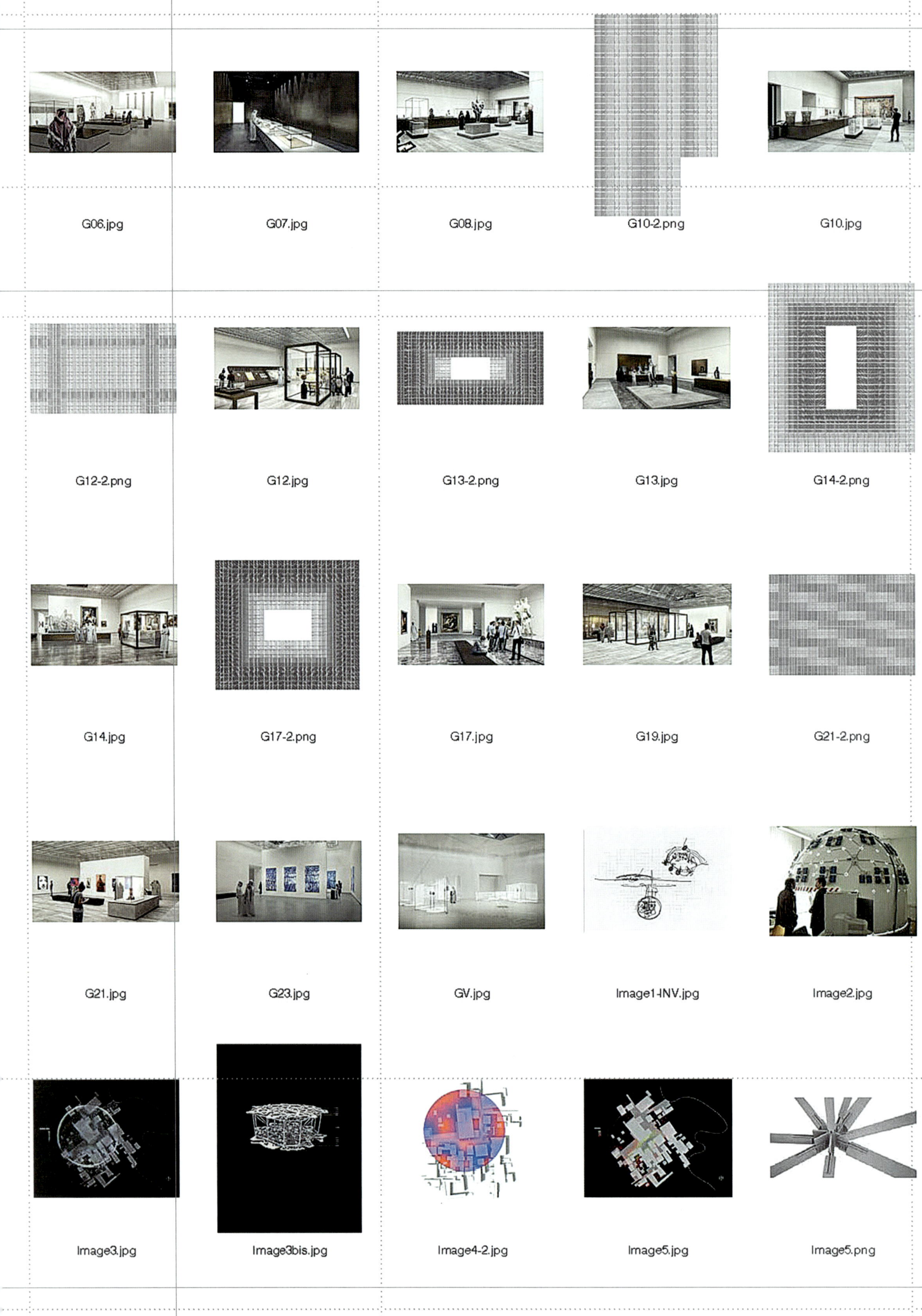

G06.jpg	G07.jpg	G08.jpg	G10-2.png	G10.jpg
G12-2.png	G12.jpg	G13-2.png	G13.jpg	G14-2.png
G14.jpg	G17-2.png	G17.jpg	G19.jpg	G21-2.png
G21.jpg	G23.jpg	GV.jpg	Image1-INV.jpg	Image2.jpg
Image3.jpg	Image3bis.jpg	Image4-2.jpg	Image5.jpg	Image5.png

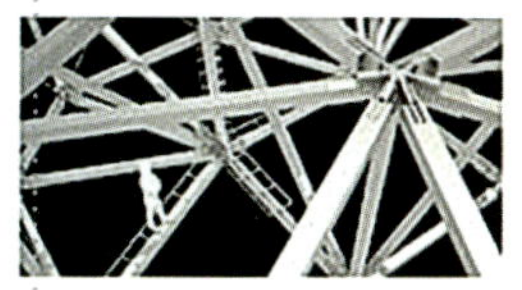

Image6.jpg

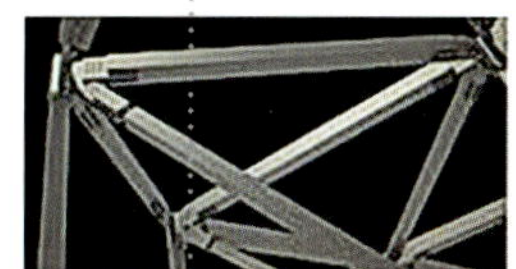

Image7.png

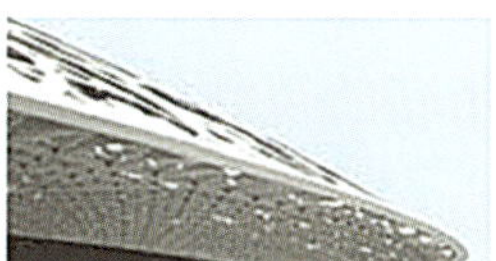

Image8.jpg

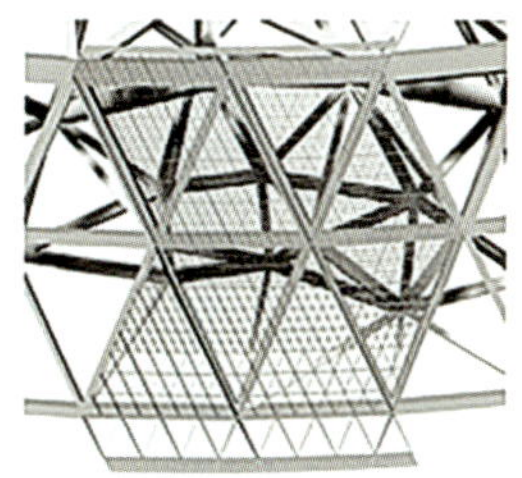

Image9.png

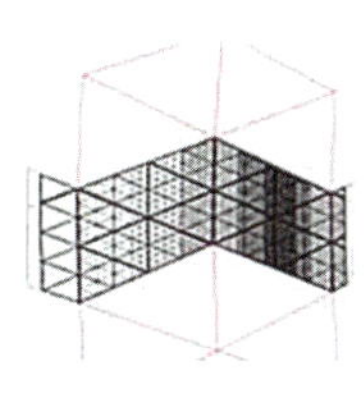

Image10.png

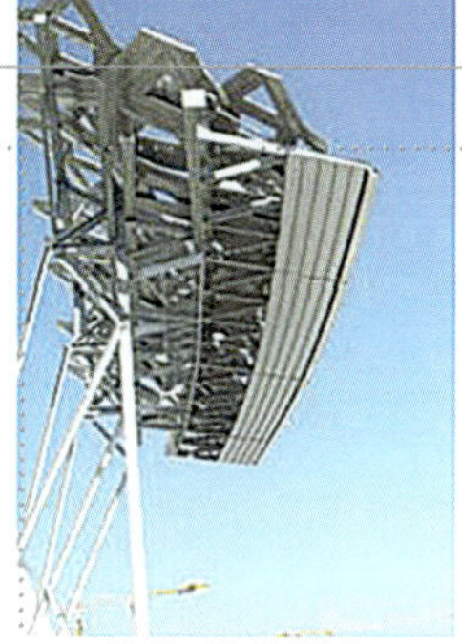
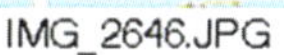

IMG_2646.JPG

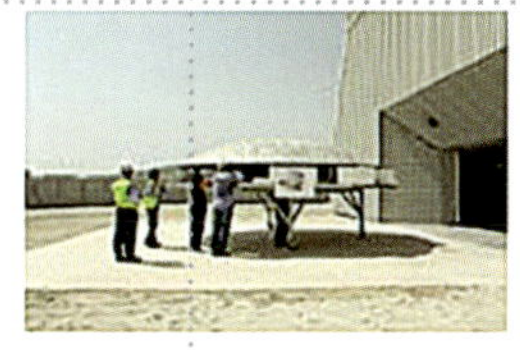

IMG_4969.JPG

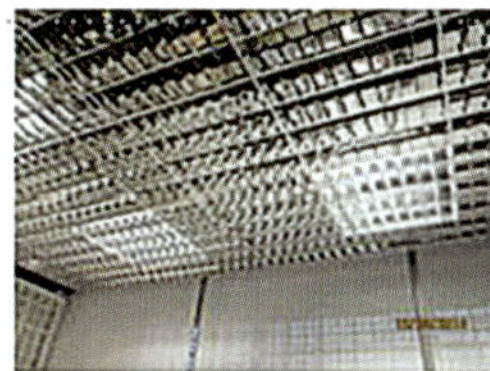

IMG_5907.JPG

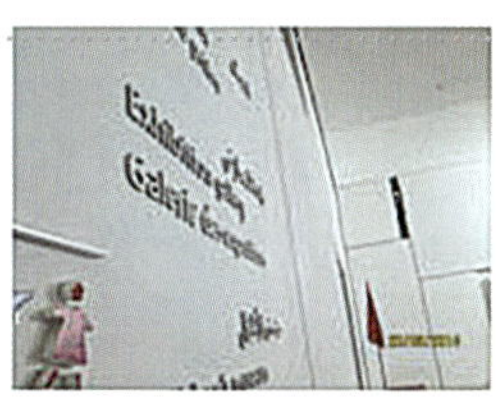

IMG_5951.JPG

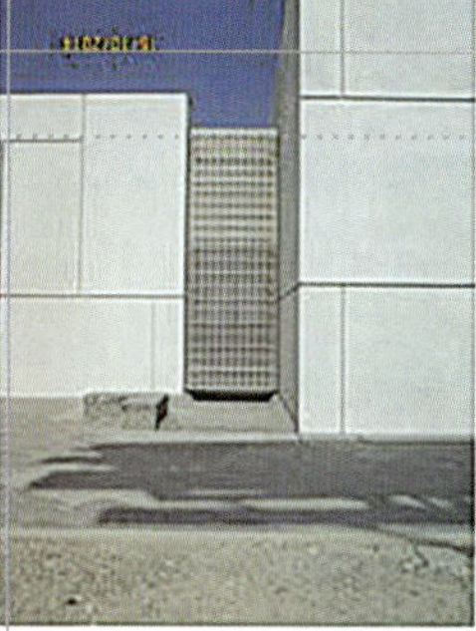

IMG_6451.JPG

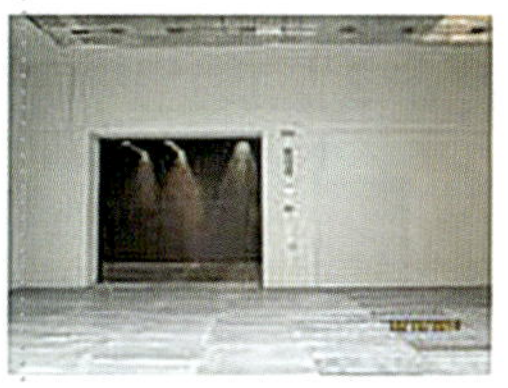

IMG_6461.JPG

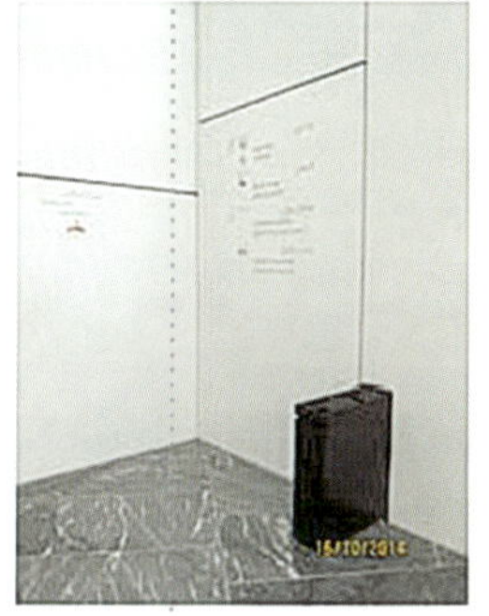

IMG_6462.JPG

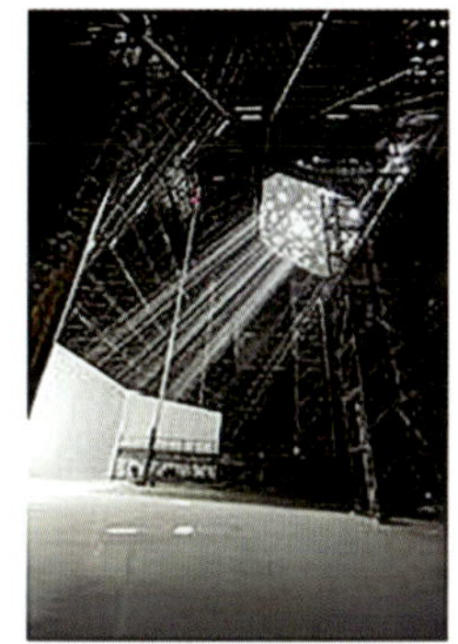

IMGP0226.JPG

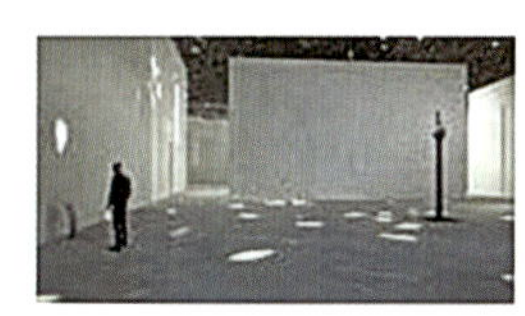

Label-1.jpg

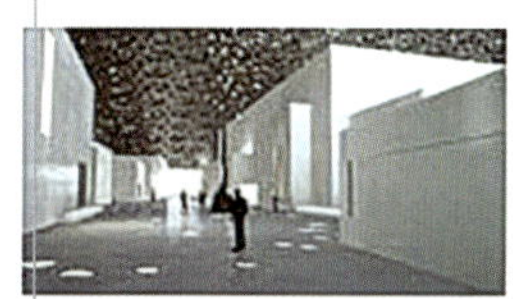

Label-2.jpg

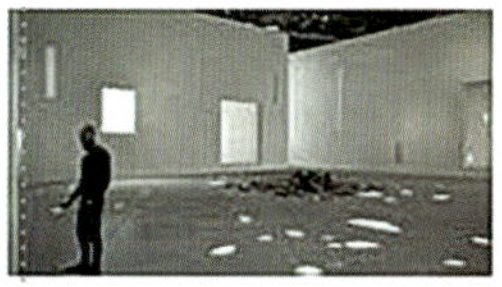

Label-3.jpg

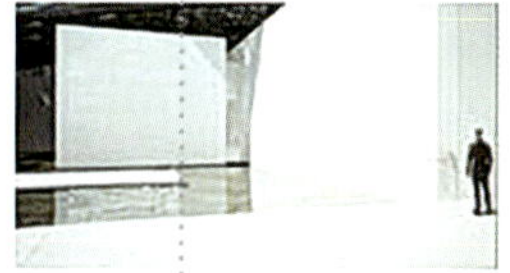

Label-4.jpg

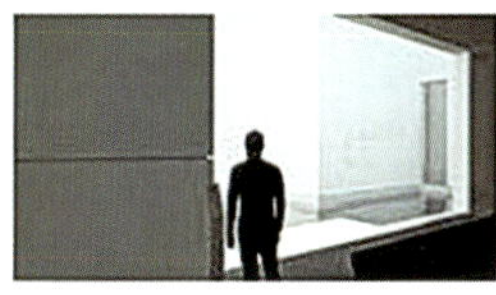

Label-5.jpg

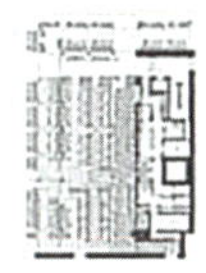

LAD-AJN-CD-GFP cafe.jpg

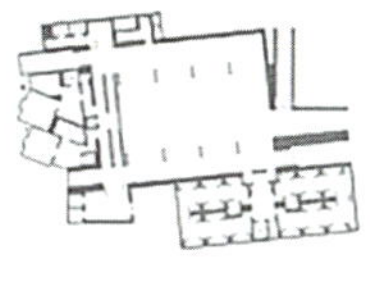

LAD-AJN-CD-LGF
FORUM.jpg

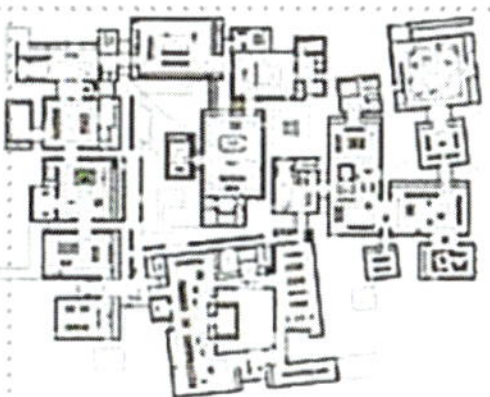

LAD-AJN-CD-M2.jpg

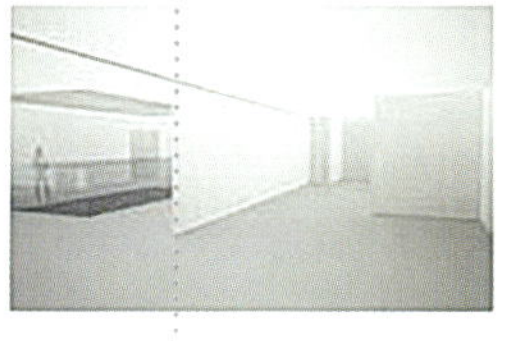

Level 01 0729 B2.jpg

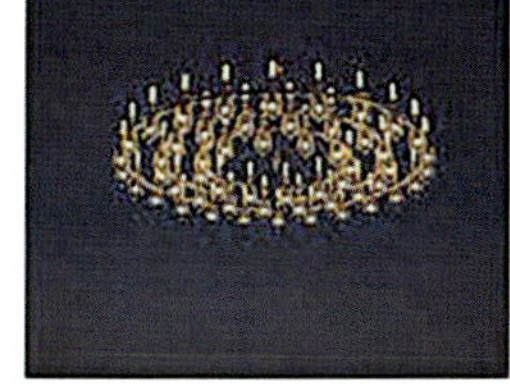

Lustre 01 JPG.jpg

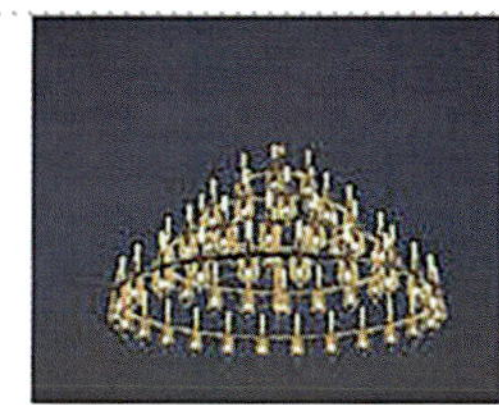

Lustre 02.jpg

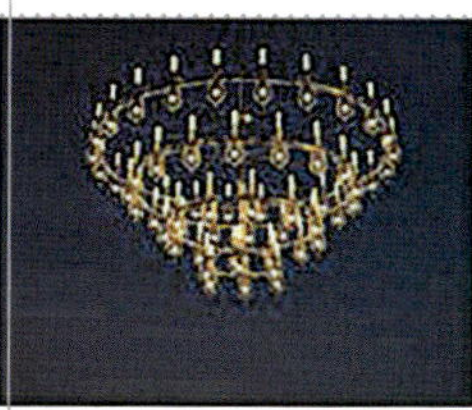

Lustre 03 JPEG.jpg

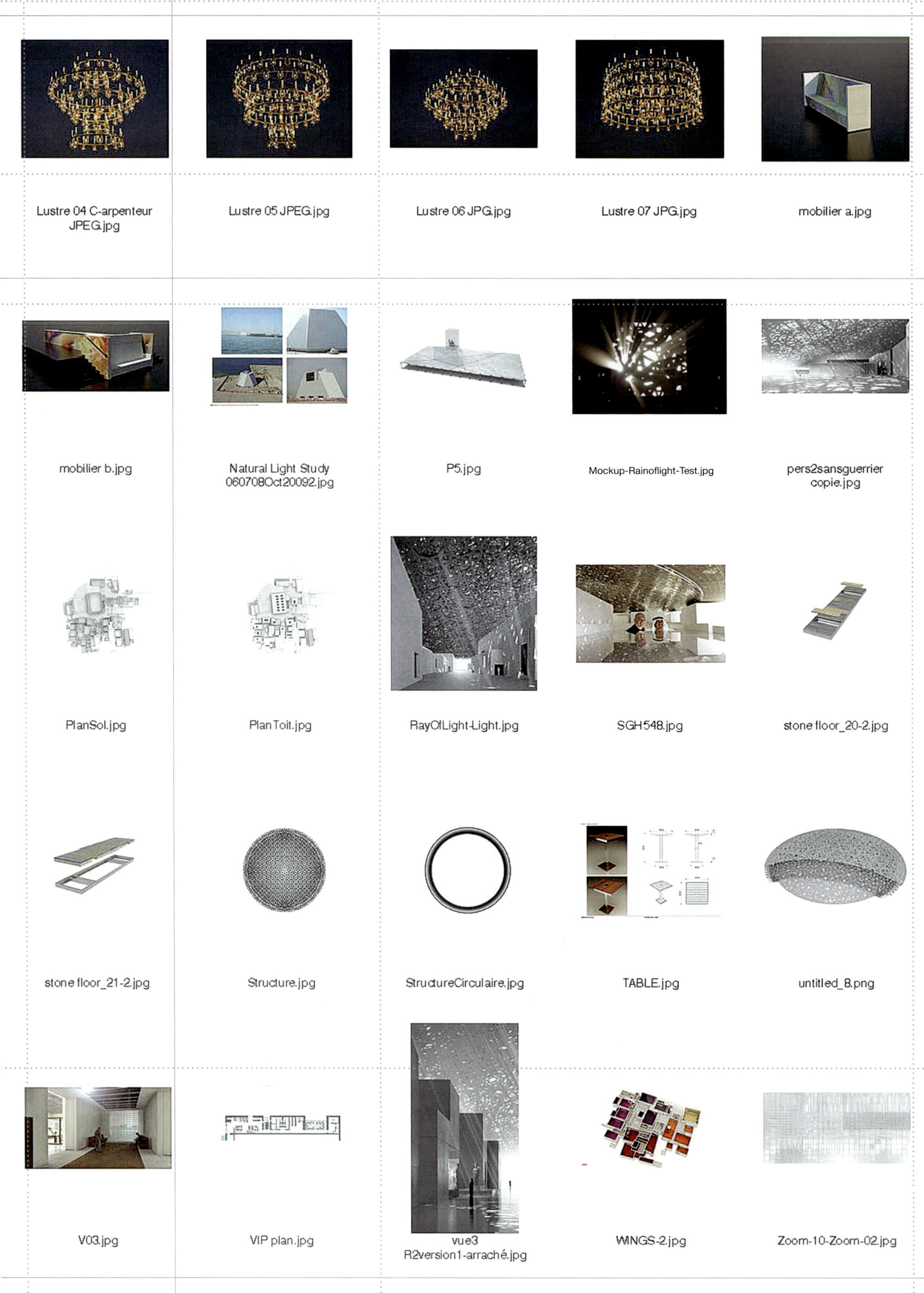

Lustre 04 C-arpenteur JPEG.jpg

Lustre 05 JPEG.jpg

Lustre 06 JPG.jpg

Lustre 07 JPG.jpg

mobilier a.jpg

mobilier b.jpg

Natural Light Study 060708Oct20092.jpg

P5.jpg

Mockup-Rainoflight-Test.jpg

pers2sansguerrier copie.jpg

PlanSol.jpg

PlanToit.jpg

RayOfLight-Light.jpg

SGH548.jpg

stone floor_20-2.jpg

stone floor_21-2.jpg

Structure.jpg

StructureCirculaire.jpg

TABLE.jpg

untitled_8.png

V03.jpg

VIP plan.jpg

vue3 R2version1-arraché.jpg

WINGS-2.jpg

Zoom-10-Zoom-02.jpg

Architect

JEAN NOUVEL (ATELIERS JEAN NOUVEL – PARIS, FRANCE)

Partner Architect

HALA WARDÉ (HW ARCHITECTURE – PARIS, FRANCE)

Artistic Commissions

JENNY HOLZER, GIUSEPPE PENONE

Architectural Design Team

Project Managers

ARCHITECTURE, INTERIOR DESIGN, MUSEOGRAPHY: **JEAN-FRANÇOIS BOURDET, ANNA UGOLINI**

CONSTRUCTION: **DAMIEN FARAUT, ATHINA FARAUT, KRIS GELDOF**

DEVELOPMENT PHASES: **STEFAN ZOPP**

DESIGN: **SABRINA LETOURNEUR, FRÉDERIC IMBERT**

Senior Architects

ROLANDO RODRIGUEZ-LEAL, MIREIA SALA FONT, ANNE TRABAND, MICHAL TREDER & NATALIA WRZASK

Architects

CONCEPT PHASE: **YOUSSEF TOHMÉ, RAPHAEL RENARD, REDA SLAOUI, QIANG ZOU**

DESIGN DEVELOPMENT PHASES: **ROULA AKIKI, ALESSANDRO BALDUCCI, CAMILLE DAUTY, MARK DAVIS, STACY EISENBERG, MARION FOUCAULT, STEVEN FUHRMAN, VIRGINIE HECKLE, STÉPHANIE MENEM, ABEL PATACHO, MIGUEL REYES, REDA SLAOUI, KATHRYN STUTTS, JORDI VINYALS, SÉBASTIEN YEOU**

CONSTRUCTION: **MARIAM ABUEBEID, SARA AL SAWI, KELLY ANASTASSIOU, DONNA ASHRAF, DANIELLA DE ALMEIDA, FAY EL MUTWALLI, STEVEN FUHRMAN, MARYAM HOSNY, ZAINA KHAYYAT, STÉPHANIE MENEM, YOUMNA NAJJAR, MIGUEL REYES**

Interior Design

FLORIANE ABELLO, LUCAS DUMON, ISABELLA GARBAGNATI, JIAYAO HUANG, TANGUY NGUYEN & FRANÇOIS ZAB

Computer Renderings

ARTEFACTORY (ERIC ANTON), JUGULTA LE CLERRE, CLÉMENT OUDIN, RAPHAEL RENARD

Graphic Design

HIROSHI MAEDA, RAFAELLE ISHKINAZI, LÉO GRUNSTEIN, CLOVIS VALLOIS

Artistic Intervention

MARIE MAILLARD

Engineers

CONCEPT DESIGN THROUGH TO CONSTRUCTION: **BUROHAPPOLD**

INITIAL CONCEPT DESIGN (2006): **ARUP**

Local Architects

PASCALL+WATSON, KEO INTERNATIONAL CONSULTANTS

Consultants

MUSEOGRAPHY: **RENAUD PIÉRARD**

GRAPHIC DESIGN & SIGNAGE: **PHILIPPE APELOIG, KRISTIAN SARKIS**

LIGHTING DESIGN: **8′18″ — GEORGES BERNE, RÉMY CIMADEVILLA, JULIEN CAQUINEAU, DAVID CHARETIER, LORIS TRETOUT**; CONCEPT PHASE: **YANN KERSALÉ**

SCENOGRAPHY, MULTIMEDIA: **DUCKS SCÉNO — MICHEL COVA, ALDO DE SOUZA, AMÉLIE CHASSERIAUX, KEVIN LARCADE**

LANDSCAPE: **MICHEL DESVIGNE, JEAN-CLAUDE HARDY, INGÉNIEURS & PAYSAGE**

EXTERNAL ARTWORKS: **JESSICA CALDI**

FURNITURE: **ERIC NESPOULOUS, JEAN NOUVEL DESIGN**

ACOUSTICS: **STUDIO DAP — FEDERICO CRUZ-BARNEY**

SEISMIC CONSULTANT: **SETEC — XAVIER DUCHATEL**

MICROCLIMATE (INITIAL CONCEPT): **TRANSSOLAR**

FAÇADES: **ANDREW SNALUNE**

COST CONSULTANT: **MDA CONSULTING — JOHN COLLINGE**

Models

JEAN-LOUIS COURTOIS, MICHEL GOUDIN

ACKNOWLEDGEMENTS

JEAN NOUVEL ARCHITECT

HALA WARDÉ PARTNER ARCHITECT

Department of Culture and Tourism – Abu Dhabi

MOHAMED KHALIFA AL MUBARAK CHAIRMAN

SAIF SAEED GHOBASH UNDERSECRETARY

SULTAN AL MUTAWA AL DHAHERI EXECUTIVE DIRECTOR OF TOURISM SECTOR

NAWAL R. AL HASSANI EXECUTIVE DIRECTOR OF STRATEGY AND PLANNING SECTOR

SAOOD ABDUL AZIZ AL HOSANI ACTING EXECUTIVE DIRECTOR OF SUPPORT SERVICES SECTOR

RITA AOUN-ABDO EXECUTIVE DIRECTOR OF CULTURE SECTOR

STEVE COPESTAKE ACTING EXECUTIVE DIRECTOR OF MARKETING AND COMMUNICATIONS SECTOR

MOHAMMAD AL FREHAT GENERAL COUNSEL

Louvre Abu Dhabi Management

MANUEL RABATÉ MUSEUM DIRECTOR

UGO BERTONI HEAD OF INTERNATIONAL AND INSTITUTIONAL AFFAIRS

EMMA CANTWELL ACTING DIRECTOR, MARKETING AND COMMUNICATIONS

FLORA CASTILLON VISITOR EXPERIENCE & EVENT MANAGEMENT DIRECTOR

VIRGINIA FIENGA MUSEOGRAPHY & COLLECTION MANAGEMENT MANAGER

WAIL KAYALI ACTING DIRECTOR, SUPPORT SERVICES

HEROS LEASK LEGAL COUNSEL

DOUGLAS MASUKU TECHNICAL OPERATIONS DIRECTOR

MARWA RUBAYEE AL MENHALI FINANCE AND PROCUREMENT MANAGER

CATHERINE MONLOUIS-FÉLICITÉ EDUCATION AND CULTURAL ENGAGEMENT DIRECTOR

DR. SOURAYA NOUJAIM SCIENTIFIC, CURATORIAL AND COLLECTIONS MANAGEMENT DIRECTOR

SHAIMA AL SUWAIDI ACTING HUMAN RESOURCES MANAGER

ARTISTIC DIRECTION: **JEAN NOUVEL**

HW architecture

29 rue du Louvre 75002 Paris *www.hw-architecture.fr*

PROJECT MANAGEMENT: **HALA WARDÉ**

GRAPHIC DESIGNERS: **RAFAELLE ISHKINAZI & JUGULTA LE CLERRE**

EDITORIAL COORDINATION: **JOANNA STAUCH**

ADMINISTRATION: **ALINE NAJM**

Louvre Abu Dhabi Publications

EDUCATION AND CULTURAL ENGAGEMENT DIRECTOR: **CATHERINE MONLOUIS-FÉLICITÉ**

PUBLICATIONS MANAGER: **LAURENT GERMEAU**

PROJECT MANAGER: **AMANDA NICOLE SMITH**

SENIOR VISUAL AND IMAGES OFFICER: **CÉLINE MILLINDER**

PUBLICATIONS SENIOR EDITOR: **MOHAMED ZAGGAR**

Éditions Skira

14 rue Serpente 75006 Paris *www.skira.net*

HEAD OF THE PUBLISHING DEPARTMENT: **NATHALIE PRAT-COUADAU**

ART DIRECTOR: **MARCELLO FRANCONE**

EDITORIAL COORDINATION: **MARÍA LAURA RIBADENEIRA, EMMA CAVAZZINI, SERENA PARINI**

EDITORIAL ASSISTANT: **LOUIS MOISAN**

COPYEDITING: **TIMOTHY STROUD**

TRANSLATIONS: **PAUL METCALFE FOR SCRIPTUM, ROME**

Agence France-Muséums

SCIENTIFIC DIRECTOR: **JEAN-FRANÇOIS CHARNIER**

EDITORIAL COORDINATION: **ELISABETH DE FARCY & GENEVIÈVE DE LA BRETESCHE**

ISBN 978-2-37074-081-6

Printed and bound in Abu Dhabi: January 2019

First edition

Distributed in USA, Canada, Central & South America by ARTBOOK | D.A.P. 75,

Broad Street Suite 630, New York, NY 10004, USA.

Distributed elsewhere in the world by Thames and Hudson Ltd., 181A High Holborn, London WC1V 7QX,

United Kingdom.